# This Is My
# Black Kiss-Story

ANTHONY X

authorHOUSE®

AuthorHouse™
1663 Liberty Drive
Bloomington, IN 47403
www.authorhouse.com
Phone: 1 (800) 839-8640

Published by AuthorHouse  11/07/2016

ISBN: 978-1-5246-4943-2 (sc)
ISBN: 978-1-5246-4942-5 (e)

Print information available on the last page.

# CONTENTS

## ANOTHER KISS FAN IS BORN

In 1974, on a cold January day in Anchorage, Alaska, a Kiss fan would be born into the world. In addition, the following month, Kiss would release their debut album.

## *NO NIGGERS ALLOWED!*

One late afternoon when I was just a little boy, I went with two neighborhood boys, who were both white, to the house of another boy who lived in our neighborhood. His mother answered the door. She was a pretty woman who had a warm demeanor and smile. She said hello to the two other boys, took the presents from them, and told them to come inside. She then looked at me; still smiling, she said, "You can't come in." My smile instantly went away. One of the other boys I came with said, "Why can't Anthony come in?" She looked at him, and still smiling, again said, "Because he's a nigger, and niggers can't come inside my house." As she closed the door, she told me to go home.

My little feelings were hurt. Nevertheless, I didn't go home. Instead, I stood outside of the house looking into the window with puppy dog eyes. I could see all of the other kids inside running around and playing games like hide and seek and tag, popping balloons, and drinking punch. I saw the cake and all of the neatly wrapped presents on the table. I'm sure the kids inside were wondering who the little kid with the afro was staring in through the window. Again, I was heartbroken. I wanted more than anything to be inside having fun and playing games with the other kids. Instead, I was outside in the cold and snow, being an observer with teary eyes.

Then there was a moment of hope. Through the window, I saw the woman come back toward the door. I was ready for whatever she was going to say. When she opened the door, she told me to get off her porch and to go home, then slammed the door. I was rejected again. Still, I didn't go home and continued to watch all of the other kids through the window having fun without me.

About an hour had gone by and at that point, my little feet were numb from the cold. I stood outside the door waiting for any sign of hope that the woman would change her mind and let me come inside and be a part of the fun. Then the door opened. It was the woman. She had a plate in her hand that had a piece of cake and some ice cream on it. She handed it to me and said, "You can have this, but you'll have to eat it outside." I looked up at her smiling, I was so happy. It turned out that I was right, she was a nice lady. I was also very grateful that she would do that for me. Still smiling at her, in my squeaky voice, I said, "Thank you," and sat on the cold, snowy porch eating my cake and ice cream. Even though my bottom and the back of my legs were wet and cold from sitting in the snow, it didn't matter. The nice lady gave me cake and ice cream, and I enjoyed every bite of it.

After I finished eating, I stood up and stared through the window again. The kids inside were playing duck, duck, goose. I really wanted more than anything to come inside and play and knew in my little heart that eventually the nice lady would let me come in. Even though I wasn't playing the game, I smiled and laughed along with the other kids from outside the window.

Finally, after about an hour and a half had gone by, the nice lady saw me still standing on the porch through the window. We made eye contact. I could see her making her way to the front door, which gave me hope. I stood up straight and prepared myself to be let in. I even smiled. I was going to finally be let in to play with the other kids, be a part of the festival, and get warm. When the nice lady finally reached the door, everything became silent. It didn't open. I waited with anticipation to see her smile when she opened the door. Instead of opening the door, she turned the porch light off. As I stood there in the dark and cold, it finally hit me, I'm a nigger! To her, that's all I was. My face was different, my skin color was different, and my hair was different. Everybody else inside the home was white, and because I didn't look like them, I wasn't allowed to be around them. I got the point. With tears running down my little cheeks and so cold that I could barely feel my fingertips, I slowly walked home through the cold snowy night.

When I got home, I didn't tell my parents what had happened. I walked straight to my bedroom and did what I always did to make myself feel better, play my Kiss records. I pulled out the Gene Simmons solo album, put the needle on, and lay on my back in bed. I let my mind wander while Gene was singing about a girl who was "Radioactive."

Growing up, that's what Kiss could do for me. Make me forget about the world and all of its problems and evils. What it meant to escape in the world of Kiss was that there was no such thing as hate, racism, fighting, black, or white. It was just Kiss. Four of the most awesome guys in the entire world who had the coolest makeup and outfits I had ever seen. For me, to escape in the world of Kiss was magic, mystery, wonder, and awe. I could just stare at a Kiss album cover or a picture of them in a magazine and forget the world around me. I could listen to a Kiss album and forget anything that was bothering me. Growing up in a hate-filled world, Kiss was my happy place, my escape, my life.

# FIRST TIME KISSED

In 1978, on a warm Alaskan night, my sister's friend was staying the night with us. She brought over a bunch of records. Later in the evening, when my mom took them to the store to buy ice cream, I went into my sister's room to look at her friend's records. While flipping through them, I came across an album that totally grabbed my attention. It was called *Alive!* by Kiss. There were four weirdoes on the front wearing makeup and outrageous outfits. Never in all of my four and some change years on the earth had I seen anything or anybody that looked like this. I was mesmerized. I couldn't stop staring at it. I didn't know who they were, what they sounded like, or if they were even real people. *They're obviously not real people*, I thought.

After staring at it obsessively for a while, I decided to take the album and hide it under my mattress. No one ever found out that I took it. Every day, I would take it out and stare at it, still not aware of what it was or what it sounded like. Nevertheless, I would just stare. Then when I was done, I would just calmly put it back under the mattress. About a month or so later, I approached my mom, handed her the record, and asked her to play it for me. She didn't ask me where I got the album. She just put it on the turntable for me and left the room.

First, a man's voice appeared, introducing the band. Then a guitar started playing, and then a loud explosion and a voice began to sing, and that was all she wrote. From that very moment, I was instantly transformed into a die-hard Kiss fanatic/nut.

At four years old, I had no real concept of rock music. I didn't know what he was saying in his lyrics; I didn't know what playing bass, rhythm, lead guitar, or drums was. I didn't know their personal names, how long they'd been a band, where they came from, or if they had super powers. All I knew at that moment in my life was that the cover was intriguing and the sound off the record was loud and in my face. From that moment on, I never looked back. I would be forever known as "That guy who likes Kiss."

# ALASKAN RAISED

When most people think of Alaska, they think of snow, hunting, fishing, and the outdoors. I don't even tell people I'm from Alaska anymore, because the first thing they always want to ask me is, "Is it true that it stays dark for twenty-four hours a day for six months out of the year and twenty-four hours of daylight for the rest of the year?" I wish people would stop asking me this question. In all of my thirty-six years of living there, I have never personally experienced twenty-four hours of darkness or daylight. Not saying it doesn't exist or is a rumor/myth. However, I've never seen it. I was raised in the city of Anchorage, the biggest city in Alaska. It's a city like any other city in the United States. I compare it to Seattle. Sometimes it's funny, because when I tell people in the States I'm from Alaska, they look at me like I'm from a third-world country or not even American. Like the first time I spoke to my cousins in California. One of them asked me if I knew what rap music and McDonald's were. As if living in Alaska meant that we were twenty-five or forty years behind the times or something.

I remember one time at a grocery store here in Vegas, a brotha asked me, "Do they have any of us up there in Alaska?"

"What do you mean?" I asked him.

"I mean black people," he said.

His question was odd. Do people really think Alaska is that disconnected? However, I guess we all have stereotypes and preconceived notions about places we've never been to. Hell, I was surprised to find out that it snowed in Arizona.

Most people who visit are surprised to find out that the Alaskan summers can be boiling hot, and sometimes, if you don't have air conditioning, you can melt in your car while waiting for the red light to change. The downside to living in Anchorage is the murder and crime rate is through the roof. In the '60s and '70s gambling and prostitution were heavy in Anchorage, but in the early/mid '80s when crack came on the scene, the whole city changed and people were walking around my neighborhood like *The Walking Dead*. Crack zombies were everywhere. Then by the late '80s early '90s, the murders began and haven't stopped since. Nevertheless, when meth hit the scene, meth labs began popping up all over Alaska, and there is a major market for meth there. Now, to my knowledge, it's dominating the drug market in Alaska. What was once a nice city to raise a family in has turned into another drug-infested city in America.

# DRUGS HELPED PAY FOR MY KISS OBSESSION

If you remember Cher's character as the mom in the 1985 movie *Mask*, that was my mom back in the day, same attitude and everything. As a kid, walking into the kitchen to see drugs and money on the table was normal for me. She would also let me smell her bags of weed because as a kid, I loved the smell of weed. Even to this day, when I smell it or walk into an apartment building and smell that someone is smoking it in his or her apartment, I love it. To me, her letting me smell her bags of weed was like her letting me lick the chocolate off the spoon after she mixed cake batter. As early as the age of five, I was also a carrier for my mom. It was my first job. When my mom's supplier would bring her "packages" over for the week, she would cut and divide it up. Then whatever customers she had in the neighborhood, it was my job to deliver to them. She would take my backpack and put drugs that were concealed at the bottom. Then she would put clothes on top of them and send me out the door. For every delivery I made, I got a dollar. I would save up my money and buy new Kiss records or magazines with Kiss on the cover. Especially *16 Magazine*. I loved being a runner for my mom because it meant I would be paid for it, and that meant more Kiss stuff for me. I will never forget one day after making my rounds, I had made enough to buy myself the Kiss lunch box. I was the happiest kid in the world when I purchased it. I carried that lunch box everywhere I went, even when school wasn't in session. I would carry snacks and action figures inside of it so I'd have something to eat and play with when I did things like run errands with my dad. However, being exposed to the drug life was also a blessing for me. Because I was always around it so much, I was never curious about it or had any desire to do it. I grew up and saw the effect drugs had on people, so I stayed away from drugs, drinking, and smoking. My only addiction and vice, while growing up and still today, is Pepsi. I'm drinking one now. Nevertheless, just because I wasn't a user didn't mean that, as a teenager, I would avoid selling drugs and stealing cars. Some lessons in life I had to learn the hard way. And getting locked up and watching close friends being murdered was a wakeup call for me.

My father was a hustler; a big black man who could be very intimidating when he walked into a room. He wore a lot of gold rings and pimp hats. He even smoked cigars and a pipe. To me, my dad was Super Fly, Black Caesar, and the black Superman. My dad was also supportive of my Kiss obsession. He spent a lot of money on Kiss for me over the years. One day when I was five, we were driving and my dad looked at me and said, "What do you want to be when you grow up?" I responded, "I want to be in Kiss!" Now, most parents, especially black parents, would say that was stupid or tell me to be realistic. However, my father looked at me, smiled, and said, "I tell you what, if you work hard enough, you can be in Kiss."

# SERIOUSLY, A BLACK KISS FAN?

While growing up, being a Kiss fan was one thing. As a Kiss fan back in those days, you always had to defend yourself and the band. You were looked at as weird, stupid, and dumb for liking Kiss. You heard repeatedly that "Kiss sucked!" However, imagine having to go through all of that hatred, negativity, and disgust for being a Kiss fan and on top of that, you were black, grew up in a black neighborhood, and for the most part went to black schools. If being a Kiss fan already made you weird and an outcast, then being a black Kiss fan meant that you were from another planet. Jendell maybe? In this day and age, it's more acceptable to be a black Kiss fan or a fan of other types of music in general. After all, who would have thought that so many white teens would be listening to rap years after rock was so dominant. Things have changed a lot since 1978. However, back then, for the most part, it was still a different world.

My dad's music of choice was R&B, funk, and jazz. My three older sisters, Lorraine, Michelle, and Denise, and older brother, Andrew, were into rap that was starting to come out, R&B, and funk. In other words, black music/black culture. Then there was my older brother, Mark, who also appears on the cover of this book, leaning up against the car, wearing the funky bell bottoms. That's me doing my best Gene impression from the *Hotter Than Hell* album cover. Did you notice the devil horns on my right hand? Mark and I were the youngest and had the same mom. My other brother and sisters were from my dad's first marriage. I was always closest to Mark because not only were we closest in age, but it turned out, while growing up, he would be just as obsessed with Kiss as I was. Kiss was our immediate bond. I will say this, my father and other brother and sisters never ridiculed or talked down to us because we liked Kiss. In fact, they were very supportive. If they heard something that had to do with Kiss, like Kiss news or updates, they would always tell us about it. Even though Kiss wasn't my dad's kind of music, my dad loved Peter's drum solo on "100,000 Years" from *Alive!*, and would tell us to play it for his friends when they would come over to hang out to chill or drink. My dad would say, "That white boy's pretty good on the drums!"

On the other hand, if my dad got a little drunk, he would get us out of bed and have us perform Kiss songs for him and his friends. My dad would come into our room and say, "Y'all come out here into the living room and do that Kiss thing you do!" We loved it because it meant we would have an audience to perform our Kiss songs in front of. My sister Denise would be on drums, Mark would be Gene, and I was always Paul. Nevertheless, in front of all of my dad's friends who didn't like rock music we would be jammin' to "Room Service." They'd be drunk, laughing and carrying on, encouraging us to keep playing. I remember one time while we were doing this, Mark ran to the kitchen, put red Kool-Aid in his mouth, and came back out and took a swig of beer. All of my dad's friends were laughing hysterically while Mark tried to spit blood out of his mouth. By the way, to this day, Mark can make the best Gene faces I've ever seen. He can do '77–'79 Gene the best, without effort.

Still, as much fun as we were having being Kiss fans, we still had to take some stones that were being thrown at us. Don't get me wrong, we weren't punks by any means. We were all street fighters, all my brothers and sisters. But just because I could fight, that didn't mean I wanted to constantly be getting into fights or arguments over Kiss all of the time. However, while growing up, other kids or teens would always approach me and say, "Is it true that you like Kiss? Are you that kid that likes Kiss? Are you really a Kiss fan?" And so on. They would always ask it like they were asking me "Is it true that you eat bugs?" or "Is it true that you still wet the bed?" Like it was a malfunction or there was something wrong with you if you were a Kiss fan. I remember around the age of seven, while walking down the street, two sistas (black females) were standing across the street from me. I could hear them whispering to each other and heard them saying, "Ask him. No you ask him." Finally, they approached me and one of them said,

"Is it true that you like Kiss?" I nodded and said "Yeah," then they both started screaming loudly, "See, I told you so! I don't believe it!" They got really excited because I admitted to liking Kiss and they thought that I was weird because of it, but I thought it was even weirder that they and other people were so fascinated by the idea that I liked Kiss. Why was it such a big deal to people that I was a Kiss fan and black? I didn't get the joke. Now, as of today, Kiss is still around and still going strong, I did get the last laugh!

# SCHOOL HOUSE KISS

At school, I was known as "the kid who likes Kiss." Probably because while at school, it was all I talked about. I drew Kiss pictures all over my notebooks. I always brought my Kiss albums and merchandise to school just to show it off and brag that I had something the other kids didn't even want. In addition, every week, for show and tell, the other kids would get mad when it was my turn because they knew that I was going to show something about Kiss. A new magazine poster, album, new Kiss T-shirt, and so on. Once, I brought the *People* magazine issue with Kiss on the cover with Eric Carr. I asked my teacher to read the article in front of the class, and she did. The whole article. One time when I had nothing new of Kiss to show in front of the class, I told the class I was going to sing "Firehouse" for them. So there I was at seven years old, singing "Firehouse" in front of my class. I was actually doing all of the guitar and drum sounds. I'm laughing to myself as I'm writing this. All of the kids in the class and the teacher were just looking at me like "What the fuck?" I didn't care how stupid I looked to them because to me, Kiss was the greatest thing in the world, and I wanted everybody else to know it, meaning everybody at my school. I would also get in trouble because when I would turn in my work, all of my S's were written with the Kiss lightning bolts. Whenever I would get in trouble in class, my teacher would call my mom. One time they came up with a plan to take away my entire Kiss collection for a month if I didn't start acting right in class. Sure, the thought of losing my Kiss records and magazines scared me, but I still acted up in class—I was just slicker about it.

When I ran into old friends in person or they would hit me up online after not seeing them in twenty or thirty years, one of the first things they would say to me was, "I always remember how much you liked Kiss back in the day," not realizing that I was still a big Kiss fan. As I'm writing this, I'm going on my thirty-eighth year as a Kiss fan. That's a long time to be a fan of anything. One friend who contacted me after so many years said, "Wow, you're still a Kiss fan? But that was so long ago, when they were popular." As if my love for the band was based on them being the flavor of the month. I will never forget at the age of twelve, the first time I brought my best friend Jimmy over to my house, two months into our friendship. Jimmy was a nonstop clown. He was like Richard Pryor and Chris Tucker wrapped into one. He walked into my bedroom and was floored when he saw all of the Kiss posters that covered my walls and ceiling. He looked at me bug-eyed and said, "This is your bedroom; you like Kiss?" "Yeah," I responded without hesitation. After staring at the walls for a few more minutes, he held his head down, put his arm on my shoulder, and said, "Anthony, it doesn't matter, you still my nigga, but we gonna get you some professional help." By the time I was done laughing, I knew we were going to be best friends. And we were, for sixteen years; we were like brothers until he passed away from a car accident in 2002. RIP Jimmy.

# WHY I WROTE THIS BOOK

As two grown men, no matter what we're talking about, my big brother Mark, who again, appears on the cover with me, leaning against the car, and I always have a way of bringing the subject back to Kiss. We could be talking about a Bruce Lee movie and before you know it, we're talking about the *Hot in the Shade* tour. Again, the conversation always comes back to Kiss. So many times I've said to him, "You know we're the only two black people on earth who sit around talking about Kiss all the time?" So one day a few years back, I said, "Since we're always talking about Kiss and what we like and don't like, we should start a YouTube Kiss show where we talk and discuss all things Kiss past and present." We both agreed that it was a good idea and we would. The plan was for me to drive to Arizona from Vegas once a month and record five or six shows, then air them weekly. I began writing a bunch of notes and ideas for the show. I wrote about albums, tours, merchandise, opinions on this and that, and so on. Then three guys came around and put a stop to our plans.

One day while online, I came across this show called *Three Sides of the Coin*. They talked about all things Kiss. I began to watch it. I didn't know if this show was going to be a continuous thing or just a few shows and then they would quit or what. Therefore, both Mark and I followed the show to see where they were going with it. After a while, not only did we realize that the hosts were cool, smart, very knowledgeable about the band, and connected to the band to some degree, but at the end of the day, it was just a good show. We both agreed that we probably weren't going to be able to top or compete with what they were doing. "They've already got a pretty good lock on this," I said. So we decided to scrap the idea of our show. A year later, I began going through some of my notes that I had written down to actually throw them away. But when I began reading them, I actually liked what I had written. I thought as a Kiss fan, these are my personal thoughts about my favorite band. I really didn't want to throw them away but what was I supposed to do with them, and that's when it came to me—write a book! And so I did.

# MY THOUGHTS, MY OPINIONS ONLY

Remember, I love all things Kiss. Even if there's something I don't like, an album, song, merchandise, or whatever, I can always find a way to appreciate it on some level or another. These are just my thoughts and opinions. The idea of this book is to have fun sharing some of my experiences, thoughts, opinions, and ideas with other Kiss fans around the world. Some things you'll agree with and other things, you'll think I'm crazy because it doesn't mesh with your opinions or perspective. Nevertheless, that is one of the things that makes being a Kiss fan great; every fan has their own opinion on how they look, hear, and see the band over their forty plus years of existence. Some Kiss fans like to see if other Kiss fans agree with them on some things, and others like to argue and challenge each other when they disagree. Can't we all just get along? In the end, this book is just all about having fun!

"Kiss My Black Ass," is just my way of saying "I win!" For all of the years I was put down or looked at as being weird or strange for being a Kiss fan (and a black Kiss fan at that), my band is still here and is still very successful. It's for all the years of hearing "Kiss sucks!" and how other people were always telling me that their band from the '70s and '80s were supposed to be so great and so much better than Kiss but now aren't even around anymore or are playing small clubs and state fairs while Kiss has become even stronger, bigger, and moved on to legendary status! Again, I win! "Kiss My Black Ass!"

I'll tell you straight up, I'm not a rock fan. Meaning I didn't grow up buying rock albums, I didn't go to rock concerts. If you were to ask me right now to name one song from Iron Maiden, I couldn't do it. If you were to ask me to name one member of Judas Priest, I couldn't do it. Because I don't know. My knowledge of rock came from watching groups on MTV like Poison, Def Leppard, Mötley Crüe, Bon Jovi, and the other hair bands. I know of those songs and groups because that's what I saw on TV. Also working in kitchens or jobs where my bosses liked to play the classic rock stations. And yes, there were other rock groups and songs I liked when they were on the radio or when their videos came on, but I was never a follower of those groups or music.

For me growing up, it was all about rap, hip-hop, and the latest R&B. I've been rapping and writing rhymes for twenty-eight years. And as an adult, my choice of music is classic R&B. Groups like Ohio Players, Bar-Kays, Fatback, Brothers Johnsons, Slave, and Cameo. So how does a kid who wasn't drawn to rock music and grows up to become a rapper end up becoming the world's biggest Kiss fan? Because it's Kiss! That's how. Because Kiss isn't just a rock band but a power, a movement, and bottom line, my heroes!

I know an old woman who's not a fan of the game of basketball but has a Michael Jordan shrine in her house. She said it best: "I'm not a big fan of the game of basketball, and I don't even care to watch it. But I love Michael Jordan and love watching him play!" I guess that best describes my feelings for Kiss.

# Chapter 1

## KISS' DEBUT ALBUM

I think the first time I got this album was about the age of eight or nine. I don't remember how or where I got it.

This is an album that I've listened to all the way through maybe six times in my whole life. Even as a kid, I had a hard time getting through it, and I worshipped everything with Kiss' voices on it. To me, it's just so poorly produced and engineered, and the fact that some of the songs, like "Firehouse" and "Cold Gin," are slow and drag along just adds to it being one of my least favorite Kiss albums. Every time I hear those two songs on that album, it always makes me wonder whose idea it was to play them so slow and at that tempo. It's as if the producers finished the songs then purposely slowed the tape down before putting them on the master because they thought it would sound better that way. How could the producers and even Kiss think that recording these songs at that tempo was a good idea? Especially since a lot of Wicked Lester's music was so up-tempo, with funky grooves. To this day, I have always wondered what conversations and thoughts the band were having in the studio while recording this album. When I was younger, I always imagined the band recording this album in a dark studio with very dim lighting. The music just always sounded dark to me. Maybe I thought that because the album cover was so dark.

It's hard for me to get into the music because it's just one of those albums I always have to critique while listening to it. I would think to myself *Why do the rhythm and lead guitars sound the way they do? Why do the drums sound like those cheap drum sets you would find in an old Sears catalogue?* This first Kiss album just sounds like a bad garage band. I don't know their musical production history, but Kenny Kerner and Richie Wise should have lost their jobs and association with the label after turning in this record. It's funny because I have a lot of R&B music that came out in '74, and those songs' productions, arrangements, and instrumentations sound so professional, up-tempo, and fresh. Sometimes I'm amazed when I think that *Kiss* and *Hotter Than Hell* were released the same year these particular R&B albums were because quality wise, there's no comparison. Yes, I understand that they're two different types of music, but the point I'm making is that the guitars and drums on these R&B albums sounds like guitars and drums!

As a kid, I could stomach the album a little bit more, but as the years go by, it's not an album I care to play, even for nostalgic reasons. I'll play it maybe once a year. It's just too bad that the producers couldn't get the songs to sound closer to the demos. More up-tempo and feel.

## THE SONGS

### STRUTTER

Sometimes I can get into this version of "Strutter." But I've always loved that '76 live version that's on *Kiss Exposed*. I have that version saved to my favorites on my computer.

### NOTHIN' TO LOSE

As a kid, I didn't know that it was Peter on the chorus of "Nothin' to Lose." I used to imagine it was some overweight white comedian with a great sense of humor. It's one of my favorite songs on the album. I even like the honky tonk vibe to it. Love the piano.

### FIREHOUSE

To contradict myself and even though I don't like the way that it drags so slowly, because of Peter's slow kickin' it drumming style and Gene's funky bass, "Firehouse" is probably my favorite song on the album.

## COLD GIN

I hate it when the local classic rock radio stations play this version of "Cold Gin." It sounds like throw up put to a bad beat. It's long, slow, and drags something awful. I always wondered why Gene sang it in the tone of voice he did, like he just had throat surgery.

## LET ME KNOW

I love this song! Back in the day, I probably played this song the most from this album. It seems like a song that doesn't belong on the album. It also sounds like a cover. But at the same time, it has such a good feel to it. I would always wait for Paul's part to come on, and then it was time to get serious!

## KISSING TIME

A fan online once said that the intro of "Kissing Time" sounds like music from a '70s game show. I think he's right. My favorite thing about this song is the way Peter is hitting the ride cymbal. I love the feel of this song. Its up-tempo and my favorite to sing along to from this album.

## DEUCE

I have always thought the studio version of "Deuce" is just horrible, as is the rhythm guitar, and I wonder how it even got on the album. I think it's the worst version of this song that exists.

## LOVE THEME

When I was younger, I used to love this song a lot, probably because it appealed to my R&B side. Now that I'm older, I usually just skip past it.

## 100,000 YEARS

Even though I complain about the way the rhythm and lead guitars sound on the album, I actually like what I consider to be a generic guitar sound on the studio version of this song. I think it's Ace's best solo on this album. I enjoy listening to it. I also play the demo version from the box set a lot. I like Paul's rap on the demo.

## BLACK DIAMOND

I never liked the intro acoustic guitar. It sounds too plinky. Don't care much for this version. The slow, dark ending of this version would make me think of the wastelands on the back of the *Destroyer* album.

## ALBUM COVER

When I was a kid, I used to look at the album cover and two things would always come to mind. I would wonder, "Why does Paul's face look so fat? And that silver scarf around Gene's neck looks like something that my mom would wear or have in her closet." As an adult, I don't think the album cover is good at all, but as a kid, it had so many mystiques to me. I would stare at Gene and wonder why he was the way he was. I used to believe that he was posing with his mouth open because he was really in some kind of pain. Ace looked to me like he really possessed some kind of cosmic power, as if he could read the stars and planets, especially the way he was looking up. In addition, I would look at Ace and be bothered that he was wearing the star earring instead of Paul. That actually bothered me when I was a kid. My big brother Mark once said to me that Ace would put salt and pepper his hair and that's the reason why his hair looks like that on the album cover. Of course, I believed everything my big brother said, so I would actually visualize Ace putting salt and pepper in his hair and thinking how cool and different he was for doing that.

Now when I look at the outtake photos from that album cover shoot, I believe there were many other pictures that actually looked better, more edgy, and had more of a metal look to them. Especially the photos with the red lighting. There's one picture where Paul is looking sharply at the camera, really sinister and edgy. I think they should have cut and pasted that picture of him on the cover instead of the one that ended up there, where he looks fat and with a funny haircut. There's a picture of Peter from that photo shoot where his eyes are looking to the right. I feel that picture of him would have been a better choice. Ace and Gene are fine to me, but at the same time, there were a few choice ones of Gene from that photo shoot as well.

I hated the way the logo looked on the album. The crystals/diamonds/ fake glass or whatever you want to call them just looked ugly to me and brought no edge to the name or logo at all. Moreover, the way the credits looped in the back made the album look even more ridiculous, confused, and hard to read.

FAVORITE SONG: "Firehouse"
FAVORITE RHYTHM GUITAR: "Firehouse"
FAVORITE LEAD GUITAR: "Kissing Time"
FAVORITE BASS: "Let Me Know"
FAVORITE DRUM: "Kissing Time"
THROWAWAY: "Deuce"

## Chapter 2

# *HOTTER THAN HELL*

I'm not gonna stress on the obvious and make a big issue about how the high-pitched recording makes this album sound awful. All Kiss fans know this, and it's been the topic of many discussions from Kiss fans worldwide for years. Moving on.

This is another album I don't play that much and have probably listened to all the way through in one sitting maybe ten or twelve times. Other than that, I usually just play my go-to songs.

As a kid, I don't remember how or where I possessed this album. I just remember owning it for the first time in 1981. Again, they used the same whack ass producers from the first album; why, I don't know. I do think out of the first three sister albums, *HTH* is the best. Not my favorite, but song for song, the best.

THE SONGS

GOT TO CHOOSE

I have always thought this version is just horrible. Like "Cold Gin" on the first album, "Got to Choose" is slow and dragging. It sounds like the instruments are melting and smearing over each other. In addition, Gene's voice on the track is annoying to listen to; it's as if he's getting an electric shock whenever he sings his part.

## PARASITE

When I was a kid, I used to imagine that an angry woman was singing the chorus on "Parasite." Seriously, I would visualize that she was white with black hair, and for some reason, she was friends with Kiss and they had her sing on this song. Also, with Ace's name on the credits, as a kid, I used to think that Ace sang "Parasite" and I would wonder, *Why does Ace sound like that?*

With Ace delivering strong written lyrics and rhythm guitar to "Parasite" and "Strange Ways," you would think that would have been a revelation for them to push for Ace to write more and come up with more unique guitar melodies for future songs. Who knows, maybe they did and Ace was holding back, or maybe they didn't push him hard enough. Alternatively, maybe they didn't want to give him too much creative responsibility and keep more control of the music and him. Who knows, I'm just speculating at this point. But if I were in the band and had some control, I would have definitely sat Ace down and told him to create as many unique rhythm guitar parts as he could and start building some good hard rock songs around them. "Parasite" has the most unique rhythm guitar track on the whole album.

## GOIN' BLIND

I think it's the second best song on the album! I remember Mark playing it all the time. The lead guitar playing on the chorus and solo are what gives this song so much feel.

## HOTTER THAN HELL

Again, why is the title track off the album so damned slow and dragging? Still, I like it a lot, especially the outro music. "Kill the power!"

## LET ME GO, ROCK 'N' ROLL

This version of "Let Me Go, Rock 'n' Roll" has always sounded like a silly ass song to me, from the opening line of Gene saying "Rock 'n' Roll!" until the last guitar lick. I also think Peter's drums on this song sound weirder than they've ever sounded on any Kiss song. However, without a doubt, it's the funniest song on the album, and I always smile a little when I hear the *HTH* version of this song. I love the demo version that was on the box set and how it's extended, it just jams.

## ALL THE WAY

I loved this song as a kid and played it all the time, still love it today. I love the rhythm guitar and lead solo.

## WATCHIN' YOU

Honestly, I probably purposely played this version of "Watchin' You" maybe five times. I just never liked this version. There's a demo version of "Watchin' You" on YouTube that sounds great, without the high-pitched sound.

## MAINLINE

This song just feels good whenever I hear it. I think if the label would have released this as a single, and if radio would have given this song a chance, it could have been a big single for the band. No one could have sung this better than Peter. The guitar solo is perfect for this song. I love the outro music.

## COMIN' HOME

Even though "All the Way" is my favorite song on the album, growing up, I played "Comin' Home" more than any other song from this album. You cannot help but sing along to it. It's a true classic Kiss song for me. Again, I love the outro music.

## STRANGE WAYS

Why is there only one "Strange Ways?" Why couldn't the other songs from the first three albums have the balls, backbone, attitude, and lead guitar solos of "Strange Ways?" Kiss has never recorded another song like it, and that's too bad. From the moment they finished recording this song in the studio, it was an instant classic! "We're going to pass the production and writing over to Ace Frehley, 'Strange Ways'!"

## ALBUM COVER

As a kid, it looked cool as hell to me. There was a lot of stuff going on with that cover and the back. On the front, I was always obsessed with the way Peter looked. He just looked really cool to me. And I used to think that his suit was some kind of black metal with studs. I would also think, *What's wrong with Paul's arm?* It always looked deformed to me, the way it wrapped around Peter's leg, like his shoulder was out of its socket.

The pictures on the back also had a lot of mystique to me when I was a kid. I would wonder, *Where is all of this happening, this world where Kiss is doing all of this crazy, weird stuff? I would give anything in the world to see this reality with my own eyes.* I used to think that the woman in the picture with Peter was Beth (Lydia). And she was just being naked and sexual for Peter on that particular day. Nevertheless, I have also seen a photo of Peter sitting in a chair from that same photo shoot, with a woman on him and her ass is exposed. She definitely looks like Lydia. In fact, I would say that it was Lydia. Maybe it's her and I'm just late. I used to think the woman in Paul's picture was a mannequin. I don't know why, but looking at Ace's facial expression, I thought he looked like he was in trouble or on restriction and he was sad because of it. I was a kid, OK? And I thought the upper body outfit Gene had on looked cool as hell, and I would wonder why he never wore that in concert.

That cartoon face on the back with each Kiss member's makeup on in the middle always had a significant meaning to me. I didn't own the record at this time of the story but knew of its existence. I remember around the age of six, my brother Mark had a magazine with Kiss in it. They were posing with *Circus Magazine* publisher and editor-in-chief Gerald Rothberg, and like the cartoon face on the back of *HTH*, he was wearing each member's face makeup. Therefore, my brother, being the storyteller he was, told me that this guy in the picture was Kiss' fifth member, and he only played with them sometimes in concert and he also sang on certain songs. He also told me some of the songs that I thought were Gene's songs were really the fifth Kiss member singing them, not Gene. I believed every word my brother told me, and for a few years after that, I was always trying to find out as much as I could about this fifth Kiss member. I was obsessed. When I would talk to other Kiss fans, which were few and far between where I was from, about the fifth Kiss member, they didn't have a clue as to what the hell I was talking about. And some told me it wasn't true. I didn't believe them because, after all, it came out of Mark's mouth, so it must be biblical. He wouldn't tell me which songs this fifth member sang on, so I would listen to Gene's songs and obsess on which ones could be Gene's or the fifth member. I thought "Let Me Go, Rock 'n' Roll" was one of them. It took a few years before I started to realize that maybe Mark wasn't telling the truth.

I remember taking the album to school and asking Chinese and Japanese students to tell me what the foreign writing on the artwork said and meant. They would just look at me as if I was stupid, not for asking them to interpret the words for me, but for being a black kid walking around the school with a Kiss record in his hand. I didn't care. I would do just about anything to talk or brag about Kiss at school to the other students—I'm talking anybody who would listen, or pretend to.

As an adult, I think because of the light colors and the artwork, the album cover is weak and a little too all over the place for me. I think they should have kept the picture of Kiss but come up with something a little heavier/ edgier to go with the title *Hotter Than Hell*. Something to make the band look a little more kick-ass to rock audiences who hadn't discovered the band at that point. I've seen many of the black and white pictures from the photo shoot that would have made good pictures for the cover. I guess it doesn't matter; because of the recording, *HTH* has turned out to be an album only a Kiss fan could appreciate. My opinion.

FAVORITE SONG: "All the Way"
FAVORITE RHYTHM GUITAR: "All the Way"

FAVORITE LEAD GUITAR: "Strange Ways"
FAVORITE BASS: "Going Blind"
FAVORITE DRUMS: "Comin' Home"
THROWAWAY: "Let Me Go, Rock 'n' Roll"
MESSING UP THE LYRICS:
"Hotter than Hell," second verse: "She showed me how, where, and when."
"Mainline," "Like an oven, it's soul food."

## Chapter 3

# DRESSED TO KILL

I remember when I was six years old and getting ready to leave the house with my mom and Aunt Gloria. My mom was in a really good mood, so I asked her if we could stop at the store and if she could buy me a Kiss record. She said yes. From the time we got in the car and drove around town to run their errands, all I could think about was that I was getting a new Kiss record. I remember feeling the excitement.

It wouldn't be until almost eight o'clock that night before we would finally make it to Long's Drugstore, where my new Kiss record would be waiting for me. I remember running into the store and toward the record department. Back in those days, you didn't have to dig or search for a Kiss record, they just jumped off the shelves at you. My mother, who was in a hurry, took charge of the situation, flipped through a few Kiss records, and pulled out *Dressed to Kill,* saying, "Here, take this one." It was as if she handed me tickets to Disney World, because I was the happiest kid in the world holding onto that record.

During the car ride home, I sat in the back seat staring at my new Kiss record in amazement. I mostly stared at the back and wondered why they were all in white. Oohhh, how I couldn't wait to get home and play it.

When I got home, the first thing I did was show Mark. He was just as excited as I was. Instantly, we asked our mother to put it on the record player. As she was putting it on, Mark said to me, "Anthony, I'll sing all of Gene's and Ace's songs, and you sing Paul's and Peter's songs." Of course, Ace doesn't have any songs on the album. "OK" I said with a big, silly smile. At this point, the only songs we knew off *Dressed to Kill* were the songs that were on *Alive!* because we had *Alive!* first. We didn't know "Room Service," "Ladies in Waiting," "Anything for My Baby," and so on. So what does Mark do? Like the ball hog he was, he sings every song that came on, and the songs he didn't know, he mumbled along to. I would yell out, "Mark, stop singing, it's my turn to sing!" and he would say, "OK, you can sing the next song." Nevertheless, when that next song would come on, again, he would sing it. Finally, I had enough and went to tell my mother in tears that Mark wouldn't let me sing any of the Kiss songs. Since we couldn't figure out how to share, my mom got mad and took the record away from us. A couple of days later, in the afternoon, she gave it back to me, and I finally got to listen to it all by myself without Mark pestering me. And that was how I was introduced to *Dressed to Kill*.

## THE SONGS

*Dressed to Kill* has always been an album that I can listen to from beginning to end. Out of the first three sister albums, it's always been my favorite. It's simple, up-tempo, poppy, happy and to the point. They're not songs you have to read into or figure out their meaning. I'm not saying that I don't like deeper songs, I'm just saying that for me, this record is perfect for what it is. Definitely an album that makes you want to sing along to it. Never has there been a Kiss album where Paul is singing with so much funk and soul in his voice, tone, and delivery. Ace's lead guitar work really shines and stands out on this album to me, much more so than on *Kiss* and *HTH*. His leads on "Room Service," "Two Timer," "Ladies in Waiting," "Getaway," and "Love Her All I Can" have so much feel to his playing. There is not another Kiss album where he sounds not so much as good as on *DTK*, but with that unique sound and vibe. It also sounds like Neil pushed Peter's drumming even more on this album than the other producers did on the first two or even before Bob Ezrin did on *Destroyer*. Peter's big band swing style of drumming really shines on this album. Lenny Kravitz said it's his favorite Kiss record of all time.

## ROOM SERVICE

Growing up, this was my favorite song on the album. I love Peter's drumming on it. To me, it's still an underrated Kiss song. I think it can easily be added to classic rock stations.

## TWO TIMER

As a kid, when I would listen to "Two Timer," I actually thought this was supposed to be a funny song and Gene was trying to be funny in his delivery, especially on the first verse. Of course, as I got older, I realized that it was just the way he was singing that made him sound funny to me. I love how Ace's solo sounds really thick on this song.

## LADIES IN WAITING

I like the way Gene sings this, like he's pushing and straining his voice. Again, another unique Ace solo.

## GETAWAY

I remember as a kid, I actually thought this song was about rejecting God. I thought Peter was saying "God, get away!" And I thought in the chorus he was trying to make a decision on what he was going to do, stay and follow God or leave and start a new life somewhere else. I tried to read between the lines on just about everything Kiss said or did. I think this is a much-underrated Peter song. As a kid, I would usually skip past this song, but now, as an adult, when I play this album, it's a must play for me.

## ROCK BOTTOM

The acoustic guitar intro was always a beautiful piece of music to me. I remember no matter what I was doing, I would always stop when it came on and just listen to it. It was hypnotic in a good way. When I got my first turntable with added cassette stereo, I looped it over and over so I could just listen and enjoy it. "Rock Bottom" always seemed like a throwaway song to me, but a good throwaway.

## C'MON AND LOVE ME

I liked "C'mon and Love Me" because Paul said he was a Capricorn like me. To this day, I still love the rhythm and background acoustic guitars on this song.

## ANYTHING FOR MY BABY

Loved it as a kid and played it all the time. I like Peter's drumming on the chorus. I also like the rhythm guitar. It's always fun to imitate Paul's voice on this song.

## SHE

To me, "She" always had an R&B feel to it. I don't know why. Maybe it's because of the funky rhythm guitar or the drums and bass on the breakdown. As a kid, this version had a lot of mystery to me. It was one of those songs that added to the idea Gene was so mysterious and deep. Something about this song always made me pay attention to it when it was playing. The song didn't make sense to me, but at the same time, it was genius because after all, Gene sings it, right? In 1990, while in the studio, I tried to get my producer to sample the rhythm guitar for a gangsta rap song I was making. I had all of the lyrics written, song title, and chorus ready. In the end, he couldn't sample it because he said it keeps looping on the offbeat. So I never got the song recorded. I was so disappointed because in my head, it was going to sound tight!

## LOVE HER ALL I CAN

Peter's drumming shines on this song. I've always liked cowbells on rock songs and love the way Peter is kickin' it on this song. Ace's solo is tight! The beginning of his solo used to remind me of country/rodeo/bull riding music. I wonder how it would sound being played on a banjo?

## ROCK AND ROLL ALL NITE

I remember the first time I heard the *DTK* version of "Rock and Roll All Nite," the chorus sounded so weird to me. I honestly thought it was a church choir singing on the chorus. I actually went up to my mom and said, "Mom, there are church people singing on my Kiss record." So for a long time, I wouldn't listen to this version. However, after a while, Peter's kickin' it bass drum started growing on me, and then I started liking it. Now, not only do I love it, but I actually like it better than the *Alive!* version. And to think it only took thirty-five plus years for this version to grow on me.

## ALBUM COVER

I think the cover is tight for this record, and it matches the sound, feel, and vibe of the songs perfectly. I remember being obsessed with Gene's high waters on the cover. I used to think because he had a silly grin on his face that he was purposely trying to be funny by wearing high waters and what I used to see as slippers. I would also visualize that Gene was wearing the suit on the album cover when he sang the chorus to "Anything for My Baby." Of course, Ace looked the coolest. And I think his makeup probably looked better than it ever had up to that point. Paul's jaw always looked big to me in that photo. Like it was broken and the swelling hadn't gone down yet.

I think the back of the album should have been an outtake picture instead of the same picture of the band in white. The outtake photos where Kiss is standing on the street corner, the guy is laughing, and the little boy is looking into the camera, to me, would have been a good photo for the back of the album. If they could have gotten them to sign release forms. Or even the photo where they're standing next to the subway and reading the newspapers. Or walking in and out of the phone booth.

FAVORITE SONG: "Getaway"
FAVORITE RHYTHM GUITAR: "C'mon and Love Me"
FAVORITE LEAD GUITAR: "Getaway"
FAVORITE BASS: "Anything for My Baby"
FAVORITE DRUMS: "Room Service"

THROWAWAY: "Rock Bottom"

MESSING UP THE LYRICS:

"Room Service," first verse: "Not a rock and roll soft drink."

"Anything for My Baby," chorus: "Title, Ace Frehley steal, repeat title, I would wrong on Neil."

"Ladies in Waiting," first verse intro: "Been to *The Muppets*."

## Chapter 4

## *ALIVE!*

I guess depending on which article, interview, story, book, band member, manager, or producer you read or listen to, everyone has a different story about exactly how *Alive!* was recorded, how much of it was live and how much of it was done in the studio. I believe Peter said that his drums and Paul's raps are the only things on the album that were live but the rest was studio work. I personally have a hard time believing him because he has a tendency to try to make himself look good and authentic, drawing sympathy to himself by putting others down. Still, I have never heard an original member talk in detail about the recording of *Alive!* Not saying they haven't, I've just never heard them.

To me, that episode on VH1 about *Alive!* still didn't give much insight, just drops of seeds about what might or might not have been authentic on the album. I guess how I feel about it is whether it was all the way live or half of it was live or if Peter was right in what he said about the recording, I really don't care. To me, it's a great album and was executed properly. It doesn't change the way I hear or appreciate the music. *Alive!* will always be *Alive!* to me, and some secrets deserve to be buried in the backyard and forgotten about. Then again, if Eddie Kramer or Paul ever came forth and told detail by detail about the recording of that album, I'd be at attention. However, there are so many things from our childhoods that are very special to us, and we don't stop liking or loving them just because we find out there was a wink involved. It was my first Kiss record and better than any toy I have ever gotten as a child. And I don't care how it was recorded or who really played what instrument on what song. I don't care how it all came to be; I'm just glad that it is.

Not only have I heard *Alive!* more than any other Kiss record but I've also bought it more times than any other Kiss record, on album, cassette, and CD. I stole my first *Alive!*, but the memory I have of the first time I bought it always stands out for me. For most kids in Anchorage in the late '70s and early '80s, their favorite places to go were Chuck E. Cheese, the arcade, roller-skating, or the lake. My favorite place to go was a used record store in midtown called Robert Joe's. They always had the best used Kiss records and posters. And whenever I had enough money saved up, Robert Joe's was the only place in the world where I wanted to spend every penny of it. One day, I went there without any money just to see what they had in the Kiss section. I saw a used but in good condition *Alive!* album. Yes, I already owned *Alive!*, but mine was scratched up and had a lot of wear and tear on it. But something else about this *Alive!* album caught my attention. Something was sticking out of it. A paper. I picked up the record, pulled the paper out of it, and saw something that blew me away. The eight-page poster booklet that came with the album. I had never seen it before. I stared at the booklet in amazement. Four big pictures of each member and small pictures of the craziest live shots of Kiss I had ever seen at that point. I just stood in that same spot for an hour looking at what I thought was the most awesome thing in the world. Then when I flipped through the Kiss records, I again saw an album that I had never seen before. It had the same picture as the first Kiss album, but this one also had fire on the cover. It was *The Originals*. It, too, had a booklet with pictures. There were pictures of Kiss with the Cadillac High staff, though at that time, I didn't know it was the Cadillac High staff, I just thought it was the most bizarre obscure pictures of Kiss with people in business suits that I had ever seen. Those Cadillac pictures were blowing my mind right there in the store. To me, this was better than finding a bag full of money.

Once I stopped shaking—yes, I was shaking—I came back to the reality that I didn't have any money. But I knew that my mission in life was to buy these two albums. I hid the two records in the best place I could think of, in the very back of the other Kiss records. Duh—no one would ever find them there. Then I went up to the cashier and told him I would be right back and please don't sell the two Kiss records that I'd stashed away. I made absolutely no sense to him at all. I jumped on my bike, rode home as fast as I could, and thought about one person, my dad, Big Black! The richest man I knew. He could easily give me the money I needed to purchase these two pieces of gold. I quickly went home and threw myself at my dad's mercy. My life depended on buying these two records, not just for the music but also for the magical booklets that were inside of them. Those booklets were mine and no other kid deserved to possess them. Other kids, even if they liked Kiss, didn't understand the true glory of Kiss the way that I did.

My dad saw the passion that was in my eyes. He told me if I cleaned out his truck, he would give me the money. I agreed. I was so anxious and nervous that someone else would buy them out from under me that I did a fast, shitty job on cleaning his truck. When I was done, I went to get the money from my dad. However, before I could approach him, my mom intercepted me and said, "You're dirty, get in the tub." I responded, "But, Mom, I have to get to Robert Joe's before they close, I have to buy something. They're going to close." "Get your black ass in the tub now!" she yelled. I just sat in the tub, heartbroken, and cried. My dad, seeing my sadness, said that he would take me to Robert Joe's the next day when I got out of school.

The next day after school, I got off the bus and ran straight home. I ran in the house and up to my dad, and he kept his word. When we finally pulled up to Robert Joe's, I jumped out of the truck before my dad even came to a complete stop. He got on my ass about that. I ran to the Kiss section, and the first thing I saw was the *Alive!* album in the front. Someone had found my hiding place! But that was OK because now I had the album. "Precioooouuss!" I double checked for the booklet inside, and it was still there. "Yes!" Then I quickly searched for *The Originals* record, but couldn't find it. I searched a second, third, fourth, and fifth time, but still no *Originals*. It was gone. I ran to the cashier and described the album to him, but he just gave me a weird look. I decided to give up. That amazing *Originals* record with the awesome booklet and pictures inside wasn't going to be mine after all. It just wasn't meant to be. But I still had the *Alive!* record with its cool booklet. I was happy and grateful about that.

When I showed my dad the *Alive!* album, he took it out of my hands and said, "You already have this. Don't they have any other Kiss records?" I looked at my dad with a serious need in my eyes. "But, Dad, I have to have *this* album. It's got the coolest pictures of Kiss on the inside." My dad looked down at me, and then he smiled. He knew Kiss was my whole world, and to make me happy, he bought me the *Alive!* album. I couldn't describe the hypnotic hold this band called Kiss had on me. But I ate, slept, and lived it.

## THE SONGS

I have listened to *Alive!* more than any other Kiss album, especially when I was a kid. Now, as an adult, I don't listen to it that much anymore. It's not usually in my top five Kiss picks. But back then, I played sides one and four the most. I didn't know if it was because I liked those sides better or if it was just out of habit. But I do remember as a kid, when I listened to it from beginning to end in one sitting, I would feel like I accomplished something and deserved a reward or bragging rights. Of course no one cared. When I do listen to it today, it's usually when I want to get my "Watchin' You" or "Got to Choose" fix.

I don't think any Kiss record shows off Ace's raw meat and potatoes lead guitar playing ability like *Alive!* does. It has so much feel. His playing, to me, is definitely the musical highlight on this album. In most cases, the drums are the backbone of a song or songs, but to me, Ace's solos in so many ways carry this album. From the lead power chords of "Deuce" to ending the record with the long lead guitar jam session of "Let Me Go, Rock 'n' Roll," Ace is the real highlight on this album.

## DEUCE

To me, this is the best version of this song ever recorded. Ace's solos—nuff said! One day, I commented to Mark about the guy who did the intro before "Deuce" and said he sounded funny. Mark told me that it was Gene who did the intro. So for a few years after that, I believed it was Gene and thought it was so weird that he talked like that. After all, Gene's voice was so animated on his solo album that I had no real reason to doubt Mark. Of course, as I got older, I realized it wasn't Gene. But even I was surprised to learn, as an adult, that it was actually J.R. Smalling. Now when I listen to it, I can totally tell it's a brotha's voice.

## STRUTTER

This is a good version. For me, the best part of this song is Ace's solos.

## GOT TO CHOOSE

It's funny, because since I was a kid, I would usually skip past "Got to Choose" to "Hotter than Hell." But since the acoustic version appeared on the box set, I've developed a new love and appreciation for it. Now it's my favorite song on *Alive!* The bass line is just funky as hell, and it's probably the funkiest lead guitar solo I've ever heard Ace play. I also love the way Peter is hitting the cowbell during the solo. I love this song!

## HOTTER THAN HELL

As a kid, I played "Hotter than Hell" so much. I loved the way Peter was kicking the foot pedal and hitting the hi-hat. I also love the outro music going into "Firehouse."

## FIREHOUSE

Like the studio version, it's really funky! Sometimes, for no reason at all, when I'm out in public, I'll yell out, "Firehouse, whew, all yeah!"

## NOTHIN' TO LOSE

I love this version. Another song I played a lot off this album growing up. There's just something about that opening guitar with that cowbell that would get me excited when it came on. And the entire break and solo is tight! I love Peter's drumming and his vocals on this version.

## C'MON AND LOVE ME

I don't know if the song was mixed louder than the others were or if it's the guitars that were mixed loud, but this song always seemed loud when it came on. Paul's vocals also seem low in the mix. My favorite parts are Gene's vocals and Ace's leads.

## PARASITE

You know how sometimes classic rock stations rotate a particular band's live versions of their songs? This version of "Parasite" is a song that they need to add to their rotation. Can you imagine how cool that would be? This song has one of the most unique rhythm guitar licks in the history of Kiss music. And it has never shone more than on this album. You take that mixed with Peter's drumming and it's an amazing live song. Again, because Ace's name was on "Parasite," as a kid, I thought he sang it and I would wonder, *Why is Ace trying to sound like Gene?*

## SHE

I never thought too much of the *Alive!* version of "She" until I saw the way Peter was jammin' and how fast he was playing it live on *Kiss Konfidential.* I never realized that he was hitting the ride cymbal and all of those tom-toms the way he was until I saw that video. Now I listen to "She" totally differently on *Alive!* I can hear and key in on Peter's drumming and what he's playing even more, which has made me love the *Alive!* version. As a kid, whenever the instrumental would come on after "She," I would always play Peter's solo over and over again. I loved the way he was hitting the cymbal and the snare drum at the same time.

## WATCHIN' YOU

I think this is the best song on the album. You don't have to agree, but to me, "Watchin' You" is just the shit! Again, it's another live Kiss song with one of the most unique rhythm guitar melodies in the history of the band's existence and at the same time, so underrated. Especially before the lead solo, when the drums stop and the rhythm guitar keeps playing,

I love that part! The way Peter's hitting the cowbell, forget about it, it's the shit! Again, classic rock stations need to rotate this version. As a kid, when this song would start, I would listen to the rhythm guitar and stare at Paul's guitar on the *Alive!* cover, imagining he was using that particular guitar to play that part.

## 100,000 YEARS

This is one of those Ace solos I am always doing with my mouth when I'm out in public. I love that solo. As a kid, I used to think Peter was playing that drum solo really fast, and it sounded great on *Alive!* until years later, when I got a bootleg copy of the *DTK* tour. Watching Peter actually playing it on video, not only was it slow, but it didn't sound all that great to me. It was pretty basic and simple. But I still like to listen to it on *Alive!*

As a kid, during Paul's rap, I thought he said, "I got a question for the white people over here." I used to think, *That's rude and messed up that Paul would say that to the white people in the audience.*

## BLACK DIAMOND

I've never really been a big fan of this song. But this is the only version I do like. Then again, I actually also like the version from the '84 MTV concert.

## ROCK BOTTOM

During the chorus, I used to think it was Ace saying "Rock Bottom." Yes, I know a lot of you Kiss fans were smarter than that when you were younger, but it was what I thought. I love this version. I like the way Peter's hitting the hi-hat and how Gene's bass is loud in the mix. I also like how Ace's solo is simple but cool. Again, I love this version.

## COLD GIN

To me, this version is a hundred times better than the album version. It comes to life on *Alive!* The classic rock station where I'm from, The Fox, plays it all the time. I love the solo that Ace does at the end of the song. Another solo I always do with my mouth.

## ROCK AND ROLL ALL NITE

Even though I like the *DTK* version better, I still think this is the best version of this song. I love Peter's kickin' it bass drum. Growing up, I usually skipped past it to listen to "Let Me Go, Rock 'n' Roll."

## LET ME GO, ROCK 'N' ROLL

The rhythm guitar and Ace's solos—nuff said! Oh yeah, what the hell is Gene saying in the middle of the song/drum break? "C'mon fasu"?

## ALBUM COVER

I have never heard anybody make the comment I'm about to make, and I know that I was only one year old when *Alive!* was released and have no business or marketing fact of the record to back me up, but I think part of the reason *Alive!* was initially a runaway success was because of the album cover. It was their first time on an album cover where they really looked dangerous, mysterious, bigger than life, exciting, and a force to be reckoned with. Paul said that when it came to *Creatures of the Night,* audiences were listening with their eyes. Of course, he meant that in a bad way. I think when it came to *Alive!,* audiences were listening with their eyes but in a good way. How can you see that album cover and not want to hear it or know more about what this thing called Kiss is? Especially back in '75, when controversy in musical acts hadn't even scratched the surface yet. Then you see an album cover like *Alive!* with four guys who capture your imagination with that still shot. I mean, the way Gene looks on that cover alone is enough to make you say "What the fuck?" I once got into a fight with a neighborhood kid because he was making fun of the way Gene looked on the cover. I took it personally. I know if I were a teenager in '75 and had never heard of Kiss or their music, I would have bought that album based on the album cover alone.

As a kid, I would look at the audience on the back and be so jealous of them because they were at a Kiss concert and I wasn't. I wished it could have been me that was there. Remember the rumor that Kiss was in the audience without their makeup? I would spend hours trying to figure out which person in the audience might possibly be Gene or Peter, etc. I also remember thinking for years that those two guys on the back holding up the banner were girls. In '84, I was at a grocery store looking at a rock magazine with Kiss in it. Kiss was taking a picture next to those two guys during the *Animalize* tour. That's when I found out that they weren't girls. I yelled out "Those two are guys?" really loud in the store.

To me, the inside of the album jacket is too boring. Those letters from each member and the first three records are dull. I always thought all of the live shots from the eight-page booklet—and yes I know some of them weren't live shots, but from the photo shoot—but I thought those photos should have been what you saw when you opened up the jacket, with the flames going up on each side. And that live picture in the booklet from the *Hotter Than Hell* tour that's in red with the confetti coming down. I always thought that should have been the picture for the back of the album instead of the bored looking audience waiting for something to happen.

I couldn't tell you why, but whenever "Great Expectations" was playing, I would always stare at that big picture of Gene from the booklet where he's making a fist and holding his bass. I also thought that the blurred drum set behind him was a carousel from a carnival.

What used to bother me about Ace's big picture from the booklet was that his wrist strap on his right hand was undone. I've been OCD my whole life.

FAVORITE SONG: "Got to Choose"
FAVORITE RHYTHM GUITAR: "Watchin' You"
FAVORITE LEAD GUITAR: "100,000 Years"
FAVORITE BASS: "Rock Bottom"
FAVORITE DRUMS: "Hotter Than Hell"

THROWAWAY: I don't think that there is one throwaway on *Alive!* But if I had to pick one, even though I love it for so many reasons, I would have to pick "Rock Bottom." It seems more like an album filler to me. Speaking of which, I would love to hear the versions of the other songs that didn't make the record.

MESSING UP THE LYRICS:

"Intro"/J.R. Smalling: "The hottest man of my man, Kiss!"

"Firehouse," "Chill you, but your head feet locomotion."

"Cold Gin"/Paul's rap: "Like to drink the killer!"

"Cold Gin," second verse: "And get another coat, around the corner I could leave your soul, and she said snuff is a all I need, to get me back oh my feet don't care."

# Chapter 5

# DESTROYER

Stacey was a kid who lived in the building next to us in the late '70s. He was a couple of years older than me. He looked and acted just like Kelso from *That '70s Show*. Same goofy smile and personality. I remember the first time I went to his apartment with Mark. When we entered his bedroom, I was instantly bug-eyed by what I saw. He had a wall full of Kiss posters. It was the greatest thing I had ever seen at that point in my life. Someone's walls that were covered in Kiss faces. He was the luckiest kid, no he was the luckiest person in the whole wide world to have this great honor right there in his bedroom. All the latest Kiss toys and merchandise were scattered on the floor, just waiting to be stepped on. The Ace Frehley doll was just lying there missing one arm, poor thing. He had the Kiss radio. He had the Kiss Marvel comic book with a 7-Up can on top of it. And just a bunch of stuff that would sell for a good profit today on eBay for memorabilia dealers. Oh, how I was so jealous of him, the spoiled, ungrateful kid.

I would always try to be his friend just so I could go into his apartment and look at the cool Kiss posters in his bedroom. Sometimes we'd go in there and play action figures or watch a TV show. Either way, where the Kiss posters and merchandise were is where I wanted to be. For a kid who had a lot of Kiss stuff, he always seemed so "whatever" about it. Like it was no big deal. That was strange to me. How can you be surrounded in all this Kiss glory and act like it's no big deal? There were two types of Kiss fans back in those days, fair-weather fans and fans who were obsessed. I was an obsessed fan. Back then, I would actually start shaking when I saw something cool that was about Kiss. Or in some cases, I'd hyperventilate. But Stacey just seemed like a fair-weather fan. A fan who was just jumping on the bandwagon and would eventually grow out of it once their popularity died down. Whether they were popular or not, I had no plans of outgrowing Kiss anytime soon.

I'll never forget one afternoon while we were out riding our bikes, Stacey rode into the woods and said he had to take a crap. About ten minutes later, he called my name and said he had nothing to wipe with. He asked me if I would go home and get him some toilet paper. I said no because it was too far for me to ride for toilet paper. He told me that if I got him some toilet paper, I could have one of his Kiss posters. He knew what button to push, and that's all I needed to hear. I hauled ass home, grabbed the toilet paper, and got back as fast as I could. Afterward, he said he wanted to keep riding bikes, but I insisted we go back to his place so I could get my Kiss poster. At that moment, that's all I cared about. He kept his word. I picked out a three-page pullout from a *16 Magazine*, with Kiss wearing their *Destroyer* outfits.

One day, I was outside, in the parking lot of my building. Stacey and his mom pulled up in their car. He jumps out holding a bag and says "Anthony look what I got." He pulled an album out of the bag. It was a Kiss record I had never seen before. It was *Destroyer*! That was the most awesome album cover I had ever seen in my life. It was so intriguing. Even seeing the *Alive!* album cover the first time didn't do for me what the *Destroyer* album cover did. Kiss was in this powerful cartoon picture, standing on uneven boulders and looking like the masters of rock. It was beautiful. Once again, it reminded my young mind why Kiss was the main focus of my life.

We went upstairs to his apartment and played the record. I'll never forget it. It was the first time I heard the intro to "Detroit Rock City." I was mesmerized and that was just the intro. When "Detroit Rock City" started playing, I instantly knew this song sounded different from any other Kiss song I had heard before. I immediately fell in love with Peter's drumming on that song. We got halfway through "King of the Night Time World" when his mom yelled out to him to turn the record off and it was time for me to go home. Stacey told his mom that we were listening to the record and to leave us alone. I was shocked! I couldn't believe he'd spoken to his mom that way. "Leave us alone?" I braced myself and waited for his mom to kick the door in and start swinging. After all, that's what parents did when their kids disrespected them or talked back, right? At least that's how it was in black households. But all she did was say "No." Again, Stacey said, "Mom, leave us alone," then he looked at me and said, "She's such a bitch!" I was floored, confused, and shocked. It was the first time I had ever heard a kid talk to his mom or any parent in that way. Still, she never came into the room to correct him. Back then, my experience was that around their parents, black kids didn't throw tantrums, whine, or be disrespectful. And we definitely didn't tell our parents no! If we did that, it meant an immediate ass beating with the belt, switch, or whatever was lying around. Or you got the shit slapped out of you. In fact, in my neighborhood, even if you weren't their kid, other black parents would beat your ass if they caught you being disrespectful or doing something you weren't supposed to be doing. It was just the times. Back then, most black kids had a healthy fear of their parents. But Stacey talked to his mom like he was in charge!

For the next few weeks, I begged my parents to buy me the *Destroyer* album, and they both kept telling me maybe tomorrow, but tomorrow never came. They had other things on their minds and just because I needed my *Destroyer* fix like a junkie needs a heroin injection, my Kiss obsession wasn't exactly top priority to them at that moment.

Over the next few weeks, I did my best to get back into Stacey's apartment so I could finish listening to the album. But I always came at the wrong time; he was just leaving with his mother, they were about to have dinner, he's got the flu, etc. One day, while I was outside playing with my toys, Stacey walked up to me and began admiring my plastic cars, boats, and action figures. He liked one toy boat I had in particular. In fact, he was smitten by it. He picked it up and said, "Can I have this boat?" Of course my response was no, but he kept begging me for it, and after a while, he spits out, "I'll give you another Kiss poster for it!" Again, he knew at that time that I would sell or trade my soul for anything to do with Kiss, including a cheap plastic boat. I don't know where the words came from or what made me be so bold, but I responded with, "I want your *Destroyer* record!" He countered, "Give me two of your action figures and the boat, and I'll give you the record." My eyes lit up something awful. He was going to do it. And so easily, without protest or hesitation. Like I said, fair-weather fan. What he didn't know was that I would have given him all of my toys for that record.

I could already feel that record in my hands and see myself staring at the cover for hours. I had to have it at that moment. "Let's go get it" I said. We went upstairs to his apartment and into his bedroom, where we made the exchange. While Stacey held the boat in his hand, I held that *Destroyer* record up in the air like it was gold. I was now the happiest kid in the whole world. I couldn't imagine any kid smiling more than I was at that very moment. Then we were interrupted by his mom, who was yelling from the kitchen. "Stacey, what are you two doing?" "We're just trading some stuff, Mom." He should have never said those words because it was the beginning of the end. "What are you two trading?" she asked, "Anthony gave me his boat for my Kiss record!" She yelled, "Oh no, you're not, you're not trading anything, do you understand me?" "Yes we are, Mom. Leave us alone!"

Instantly, my joy was shifted to disappointment and uncertainty. His mother was throwing a major monkey wrench into my plans of possessing the *Destroyer* album. Why were the planets aligning against me? Stacey disregarded his mother, and told me not to worry about her and that we would still trade. That made me feel a little bit better, temporarily. Then he said something that was dumb as hell: "Just take the record and walk out the front door. She won't say nothing to you." Was he kidding me? His mom just yelled at us not to trade anything and now he just expects me to just walk out the front door with his new *Destroyer* album? "No, you hold the record and walk out with me," I said. "My mom doesn't care; she's not gonna do nothing," he responded. At this point, Stacey walked into the bathroom and began filling the tub with water. He was that anxious to play with the boat. I couldn't threaten to take my boat back because I didn't want it back. I just wanted to be at home in my bedroom with my new Kiss record. I pleaded with Stacey one last time to just walk out with me, and I would carry the record. I thought maybe if his mom saw me holding the record with Stacey next to me, she might not make a big deal about us trading. I was grasping at straws. Stacey just told me again that his mom wouldn't stop me and it was OK for me to walk out the front door with the *Destroyer* record. Bottom line is he didn't want to walk me to the front door because he knew his mom would cut our plans short. I considered dropping it out of the window and then picking it up when I got outside. I changed my mind in fear that dropping it from three stories up might damage the record.

I came up with an alternative plan. *I'm gonna go for it*, I thought. Maybe not those exact words, but that was my mindset. I took a deep breath, made the sign of the cross on my chest (just kidding), and while gripping that record tightly in my hands, I ran to the front door as fast as I could. It was the longest run of my life. You know that feeling you get when you think the monster is chasing you from the downstairs laundry room? That's the kind of run it was. I was getting closer to the front door, and as my left hand reached for the doorknob to freedom, I felt a hand grab my right arm. It was the Mother Police. "I told you two you couldn't trade anything. Now it's time for you to go home!"

She took the record out of my hand and put me out of the apartment. The door closed loudly behind me. It was the loudest I had ever heard a door close in my life. And that beautiful *Destroyer* record was on the other side of it. So close. I was so disappointed that I didn't even think to ask for my boat and other toys back. My *Destroyer* dream was shattered. If only his mom knew how much that record meant to me.

I ran into Stacey when I was in my mid-twenties. It looked like life had been a little rough on him, drug abuse and all. We talked for about fifteen minutes, and out of curiosity, I asked him, "What did you ever do with all of that Kiss merchandise you had?" He responded, "Oh, I threw all of that stuff in the trash a long time ago."

## FIRST *DESTROYER*

I was in the third grade. There was a kid in my class named Ian who got on my nerves, so I told him that I was going to beat him up at recess. He got scared and told his cousin Katelyn, who was also in our class, that I had threatened him. As the class was getting ready for recess, Katelyn approached me and asked me not to beat up her cousin. I told her I was going to anyway because he was talking shit to me. She responded, "Anthony, I know how much you like Kiss. My mom's boyfriend has a Kiss tape at our house. If I give it to you, will you leave Ian alone?" "Which one do you have?" I asked excitedly, and all of a sudden, forgot all about beating up Ian. "I don't know what it's called, but the cover is a painting of them and they're standing on rocks with fire around them." She didn't have to say any more; I knew exactly what it was. *Destroyer*! "OK" I said, "bring it tomorrow, and I won't beat up Ian."

That night, I was so excited knowing that in the morning, I would actually own my very own *Destroyer* tape. Sure, I liked the records with the big pictures better, but a tape was better than nothing. I woke up the next morning full of anxiousness, and when I got to school, my eyes were fixated on finding Katelyn. When I finally saw her walking into class, I saw her hands were empty, so I thought she must've had the tape in her book bag. I ran up to her excited as hell and said, "Where's the tape?" She said, "I don't believe that you'll leave Ian alone once I give you the tape." I tried to assure her that the only thing I gave a damn about at that point was the *Destroyer* tape and couldn't care less about her stupid cousin. Katelyn didn't believe me, so she said to me, "If you can prove to me that you'll leave my cousin alone for the rest of the week, then I'll give you the tape." I was pissed off, but what could I do. She had me. And for that *Destroyer* tape, I would have done just about anything, including letting her cousin kick my ass. The things I do for Kiss.

Katelyn was on me every day at school. Not just about her cousin but everything I did. If I cussed, she would give me a disapproving look; if I teased the other girls in class or during recess, she would give me a disapproving look. She would say to me, "Anthony, do you want that tape or not? Then stop being an asshole." She knew Kiss was my weakness, and she was having fun exploiting my love for the band. She actually told me that she would make it another week if I didn't stop being so dumb. I had to man up because I had to have that *Destroyer* tape; it was for Kiss. So for the next few days, I was going out of my way to be nice to everyone.

Especially around her. When Katelyn and her cousin Ian were eating lunch together, I walked over to him and offered him my chocolate milk. I loved my chocolate milk, but I loved Kiss more. And when another kid was being mean to Ian, I actually defended him and scared the other kid off. That was the icing on the cake for Katelyn.

The next day at school, while sitting at my desk, I saw Katelyn walk in the class. She was smiling as she approached me. She put her hand inside her book bag and pulled out something more valuable than gold, my *Destroyer* tape.

Later that afternoon, while the teacher was talking, I was hypnotized as I continued to stare at the beautiful *Destroyer* tape that I now possessed. Then before I knew what happened, my teacher snatched it out of my hand and said to me, "Since you don't know how to pay attention, you can have this back at the end of the week!" I turned and looked at Katelyn with fright in my eyes, and she just smiled at me, shrugged her shoulders, and shook her head. Once again, the planets were against me.

## GROWING UP WITH *DESTROYER*

While growing up, I listened to *Destroyer* all the time. It was full of great songs from beginning to end. Eventually, I would possess the actual album. Cassettes were OK, but as a child, there was nothing like actually owning the big record itself, with the pullout inserts. To this day, I think it's their best studio album. I used to think it was their best '70s album, but listening closely to it, production wise, I believe it's their best studio album overall.

I know I was only two when it came out and don't know the mindset of Kiss fans back in those days, but to this day, I can't understand why fans complained, not liking it when it was released. How was it that much different from the first three studio albums? There wasn't one song on the first three studio albums that sounded better or as unique as "Detroit Rock City," "King of the Night Time World," "God of Thunder," "Flaming Youth," or "Do You Love Me." Up to that point, Kiss never sounded so good in the studio. Now just so we're clear, I'm not saying that there weren't songs on the first three studio albums that were better than the songs on *Destroyer*. I'm just comparing it production and quality wise.

*Destroyer* was also criticized for not being a heavy album. Well, neither was *Dressed to Kill*. The first Kiss album and *Hotter Than Hell* weren't that heavy, either. They may have been a little darker than *Dressed to Kill*, but they weren't heavy albums. And "God of Thunder" is darker than every dark song on the first three Kiss albums put together, in my opinion. Did fans back then complain that much about the crappy production jobs on the first two Kiss albums? I know they made remarks like "Kiss sounds so much better live," but was there the same amount of protest. Did "Great Expectations" and "Beth" really take away from the rest of the songs on *Destroyer* that much back then, or was it just the initial reaction? I assume besides not liking those two songs, they were also comparing it to the success and the sound of *Alive!* And fans wanted more of that raw energy meat and potatoes rock from Kiss back then. Those fans who were disappointed with the first three studio albums may have felt that Kiss finally found their sound with *Alive!*, then were disappointed when Kiss turned around and went with the sound of *Destroyer*.

When it comes to *Destroyer*, I don't see anything wrong with that record at all. It's just another Kiss record with more songs about partying and sex. Actually, if I'm correct, there are only two songs on the album about sex: "King of the Night Time World" and "Sweet Pain." That might actually be a record for Kiss, if you don't include *The Elder*, since it was a concept record. I just thought of another one, *Carnival of Souls*. There could be more, but I'm not gonna think that hard about it right now. OK, thought of another one, *Psycho Circus*; now I'm done.

## THE SONGS

## DETROIT ROCK CITY

As a kid and even today, I like to listen to "Detroit Rock City" for the drums. Peter's drumming makes that song for me. I hated the way they remixed it for the *Smashes, Thrashes & Hits* album. The drums sound so flat and dull. I also hate it when rock stations play that version. I get mad when Kiss isn't represented right on the radio. Once I called a classic rock radio station and spoke to the DJ because I didn't like the Kiss songs the station was rotating. One of the songs was the studio version of "Deuce." They always played that song, and I hate that version. So I said to them, "Kiss has a shitload of records and a ton of off the chain songs. Why does your station keep playing the same tired ass Kiss songs over and over again that don't represent how good and heavy the band really is? Why don't you guys play 'Keep Me Comin',' 'War Machine,' 'All-American Man,' 'Young and Wasted,' 'Unholy,' etc. This is why rock fans don't take Kiss seriously, 'cause rock radio stations like you guys keeps playing stupid songs like the studio versions of 'Deuce,' 'Cold Gin,' and 'Christine Sixteen.'" His response to me was "If you don't like it, don't listen!" What could I say?

Back to "Detroit Rock City." My older brother Andrew, who was strictly into what we now call old-school rap and R&B, wasn't into Kiss or rock at all. But he loved Gene's bass line on "Detroit Rock City." That was his favorite part. He thought it was really funky.

I think it's a brilliant Kiss song. Not one I listen to a lot because it's so redundant, but no other Kiss song sounds like it.

## KING OF THE NIGHT TIME WORLD

Such an awesome song, and something about the chorus has a good feel, especially the end of the song when the chorus is going with the lead guitar. It always takes me back to my childhood. And Peter's drumming on the chorus just sounds great. I think this album displays Peter's most unique drumming style. Thanks to Ezrin, of course.

## GOD OF THUNDER

As a solo rapper and in my rap group, I've sampled the intro voice at the beginning of "God of Thunder" at least three times. I never gave much thought as to what the chipmunk voice was saying in the intro. However, one day in the studio while sampling that part, it played loud over the speakers and my boy Jimmy repeated it and said "OK, y'all can start singing." I tripped out. *That does sound exactly like what the intro voice of "God of Thunder" is saying,* I thought. I said to him "I've heard this song a thousand times for years and never figured out what that voice was saying. But you figured it out the first time you hear it?" Maybe you and other Kiss fans are smarter than I am and knew that years ago and it's old news. But to me, my boy who wasn't even a Kiss fan figured it out on his first listen and had to bring it to my attention. Jimmy also figured out before me in '89 that Tone Loc's "Funky Cold Medina" used a sample from "Christine Sixteen." I just happened to be playing the *Love Gun* album one day when he came over. When "Christine Sixteen" came on, he said, "That part's from 'Funky Cold Medina.'" He was right. I had a good ear, but he figured out two Kiss samples before I did. I figured out that the main guitar sample from "Funky Cold Medina" is "Hot Blooded." And the cowbell is from the Rolling Stones' "Honky Tonk Woman." If you ever want to hear all of the rappers who have sampled Kiss songs or used Kiss music, or sampled from your favorite artist period, just go to a website called whosampled.com. It's pretty cool to hear Kiss music mixed in rap songs.

Back to the song. I think "God of Thunder" is brilliant, though I don't play it that much. I can never listen to that song and just enjoy it; I always have to dissect it and pick apart all of the sounds and special effects. I always think *What was Bob thinking when he came up with that part? That's genius!* As a kid, I loved the drums before the solo. I used to play that part over and over. And the silly voices going in and out of the song is brilliant! Why hard-core rock fans never embraced this song as they do "Highway to Hell" or "Iron Man" is beyond me.

## GREAT EXPECTATIONS

I love this song! Always have, always will. I think everything about this song is brilliant! Love the piano. I love the lead guitar solo, and how it's short and simple. It's a feel good song.

## FLAMING YOUTH

This has always been my favorite song on the album because it has a sentimental memory attached to it that I will never forget as long as I live. As a kid, traveling from Anchorage, Alaska, to Fairbanks, Alaska, with my mom and brother Mark, my mom got tired of driving and needed to rest and roll a joint. We pulled into a truck stop/hotel, got a room, and then went to the diner to eat.

I went straight to the jukebox to see if it had any Kiss songs. It had one, "Flaming Youth." I played it about eight times until some woman asked me to stop playing it. "OK, I'll stop," I said, but I kept plunking in quarters and playing it. The woman approached me again, saying, "I thought I asked you to stop playing that song." My mom walked up behind her and said, "How would you like me to put your head through that jukebox, bitch?" The woman became frightened. "I'm sorry, but your son was playing that song so much that my kids were getting tired of hearing it." My mom responded, "Fuck you and your kids. Keep playing that song, Anthony!" I did just that. The woman went back to her table and didn't bother me anymore, and I kept jammin' to "Flaming Youth."

It's such a brilliant song to me. I don't know what that instrument is called that makes the carnival music, but it's such a unique sound to put in such a great song. Again, how did Bob Ezrin come up with this stuff? The intro of the song is magical, one of the most unique Kiss song openers in the band's history.

## SWEET PAIN

This is a song I like to sing along with. I love the rhythm guitar and the solo. I love how Peter plays faster after the lead solo, then they slow the music back down. Brilliant! The female vocals at the end are an awesome touch. So is the constant lead guitar at the end. Still, I think this song is probably the throwaway on the album. It's not really strong and doesn't have a lot of presence. But I love it!

## SHOUT IT OUT LOUD

An awesome pop rock anthem, but I usually skip past it.

## BETH

I think "Beth" is brilliant, and sometimes, I'll play it just to appreciate the instrumentation. I think the strings are beautiful. I also like when I'm driving and it comes on the radio. Or when it comes on the radio when I'm at work. I'll ask my coworkers if they know that "Beth" is a Kiss song. They usually say no and look confused. Peter's voice complements this song so much. To this day, I still don't think it's as big a song or as appreciated as it should be. You might not agree with me, but I think it should be as big as "Hotel California" in a retro sense. It's not just an underrated Kiss song but also an underrated song in general. Oh well.

I think it's funny when I read Peter's interviews and he tries to take credit for the success of "Beth" or makes comments like "I gave Kiss their biggest hit." No, Bob Ezrin gave Kiss their biggest hit! "Beth" wouldn't have been shit without Bob Ezrin's genius and touch. Without Ezrin's production, "Beth" would have been another Peter song with mediocre lyrics and production. It wouldn't have sounded anywhere as near as good as what the end result is.

## DO YOU LOVE ME

I remember as a kid, toward the end of "Do You Love Me," when the church bells would play, the sounds of those bells would scare the hell out of me. So I would always stop the song before it got to that part. They sounded so spiritual and dark. I love the part during the breakdown where the lead guitar comes in, also during the last chorus, where you can hear a woman's voice in the background quietly singing along. The drums are tight, too. It's definitely the best song on the album to sing along to.

## ROCK AND ROLL PARTY

This piece would have me quickly walking out of the room. This scared the hell out of me. Mark would purposely play it to scare me, and it would always work. He knew I would haul ass out the room when it was on. As a kid, I thought Paul was saying "Paul Stanley of Kiss, tour of '76, a rock and roll party!" And of course, we all learned later that the singing in the background was "Great Expectations" played backward.

## ALBUM COVER

I think it's Kiss' second best album cover after *Alive!* It just captures the imagination. I remember introducing a classmate to Kiss, and he came to school one day so happy because he'd gotten his first Kiss record, which was *Destroyer*. He said he saw the cover and thought, "It was soooo badass!" He had to have it.

As a kid, I used to think that Paul's left hand was cracked in half. I also hated how Paul's right arm was so short. I think Peter looks the best on the cover, especially the way his hair is painted. Because of the way his fists are positioned, I used to imagine that he was the person driving the car on "Detroit Rock City." I also used to think that Peter's wings on his right arm were razor sharp and stabbing him in his side. Ace's fingers on his left hand used to remind me of hot dogs split in half. His legs look too long for his body. Gene's left leg is way too long. I know I'm picking it apart, but we're just having fun.

FAVORITE SONG: "Flaming Youth"
FAVORITE RHYTHM GUITAR: "Sweet Pain"
FAVORITE LEAD GUITAR: "Flaming Youth"
FAVORITE BASS: "Flaming Youth"
FAVORITE DRUMS: "Sweet Pain"

THROWAWAY: "Sweet Pain." I love it, but compared to the other songs on the album, it's not as strong production wise.

MESSING UP THE LYRICS:

"God of Thunder," first verse intro, after the first two lines: "Start my amplifier, kneel my word fancy kill."

"Great Expectations," third verse: "And you wish you'd freed them lines."

"Flaming Youth," chorus: "Our second flight is higher!"

"Shout It Out Loud," Gene's first verse: "Do or say, it's the fastest thing you ever saw."

# Chapter 6

## ROCK AND ROLL OVER

The first time I ever saw *RARO* was around the age of six. I was at my friend Shawn's house. His two older teenage sisters and their friends were hanging out in their room. I had a crush on his red-headed sister, Tonya. Hearing all the laughing and noise they were making, I wanted to get in on the fun and went in the room to hang out with them, or to get in the way or whatever. Not understanding the language or humor of white teenagers at that time, I decided I was bored and I went to go back into the living room. Before I could make my way to the door, I saw Tonya reach under her bed. As she was doing that, she said to her boyfriend, "Look what I bought," and she pulled out a record. It was *RARO*! When I saw that it was a Kiss record I had never seen before, my eyes got big, my heart began to race, and I got that shaky feeling. My eyes were drawn to the cartoon picture of Gene sticking his snake-like tongue out. It was beautiful!

Her punk ass boyfriend took it out of her hands and arrogantly just looked at it. His attitude was "Big deal, a stupid Kiss record." And he handed it back to her. Why was she showing it to him? He didn't have a clue about how special and magical Kiss really was, how they were the greatest thing in the world. And how dare he just briefly look at it and disregard it like it was some cheap TV guide. It was a Kiss record, damn it! Fuck him and his momma!

I guess my real problem at that time wasn't that she was showing it to him as much as she wasn't showing it to me. He handed it back to her and went on laughing about something else, and she put it back under her bed with my heart attached to it. I don't know why, but I didn't have the nerve to ask to look at it. I thought she might reject me in front of all of her friends and just tell me to leave the room. So still shaken, I kept my mouth closed for the moment. But I was planning to get my hands on it. Not to steal it but so I could look at it and be in awe of its magnificence.

One day, while Shawn's family was having a barbecue outside their apartment, I realized that no one was inside their house. Now was my chance to spend time with the *RARO* record! I told his mother I had to use the bathroom, and of course she told me to go into the house. I quickly ran in, locked the front door, and bolted to the girl's bedroom. I ran to Tonya's bed and looked underneath it, but there was no record. I lifted up the mattress with my little hands, and again, there was no record. But underneath the mattress, I did find a long balloon that hadn't been blown up yet. I picked it up and looked at it. I had never seen a balloon that looked like this before, so I put it back. Yes, it was a used condom. I knew that I needed to hurry, so I looked in the closet, their drawers, underneath their dirty clothes, and among the records they had lying around. I was coming up with nothing and was going to give up when I saw something sticking out of the blanket on the bed. I pulled the blanket back, and there it was, *RARO!*

It was the longest bathroom break in the history of bathroom breaks. I sat crossed legged on the floor for at least an hour and just stared at the record. I didn't care if I was caught or got in trouble for being in their room because I was spending time with Kiss. After a while, I put the record back where I found it and went outside with a big smile on my face, like after eating a good steak dinner. I was content for the rest of the day and evening.

## MY FIRST *ROCK AND ROLL OVER*

I was about seven when I got my first *RARO* record. I don't remember if Mark brought it home or if I acquired it in some way. I do remember that the tip of the album was broken off, so with "I Want You" and "Love 'em and Leave 'em" starting sides one and two, I would have to wait almost another four years before I would get my hands on another copy of the album and hear what they actually sounded like. I played it all the time.

I don't remember what songs stuck out to me or what I liked to play. I think I was fond of "See You in Your Dreams" and "Ladies Room." I don't remember being in awe of the songs at all. They were just basic Kiss songs to my young ears. It wasn't like listening to "Detroit Rock City" or the *Alive!* version of "Deuce" for the first time. Musically, *RARO* just didn't have any magic for me. But hey, it was still a Kiss record!

Around the age of eleven, I went with my dad to his friend's house. While there, I quickly made friends with his two daughters who were about Mark's and my age. I couldn't shake the idea that the oldest sister looked very familiar to me. Anyway, we hung out in their room and listened to their records. Their walls were covered in teen heartthrobs of the day, especially Menudo. Going through her stack of records, I found the *RARO* album. I got excited and without hesitation, asked the oldest sister if I could have it. She said no, with a smile. I was trying not to show her how much I really wanted it, so I put it back to work on plan B, whatever that was.

Later, as I was still working on my plan to possess the album, I had a moment of remembrance. I realized how I knew the oldest sister. One day, I saw her and Mark making out after school. I brought this up to her, and she began to act nervous as hell. She took me into the other room and said, "Please don't say anything about it in front of my sister. She can never know. My dad would beat my ass if he ever found out about it." She was scared about being caught. I couldn't care less about what she was talking about, so I quickly changed the subject and asked her, "What about the record? I want it!" She said, "Fine, you win, you can have it." At the time, I didn't know what she was talking about when she said, "Fine, you win." I wasn't trying to win anything, I just wanted the record. In retrospect, she thought I was trying to blackmail her, but I wasn't doing that at all or was even aware of the concept at that time. But in the end, I walked out with the record. All I could think about on the car ride home was how I was going to finally get to hear what the mystery song "Love 'em and Leave 'em" sounded like. When we got home, I didn't even take off my jacket. I rushed upstairs to my bedroom and put the record on. Having already possessed Kiss *Alive II,* I wasn't impressed with the *RARO* version of "I Want You." And when I finally heard "Love 'em and Leave 'em" for the first time, it didn't leave an impression on me.

## WHY DO KISS FANS LIKE *ROCK AND ROLL OVER* SO MUCH?

I have to be honest, I don't get it. I don't understand why so many Kiss fans like *RARO* so much. So many Kiss fans say that out of the three sister albums, *Destroyer, RARO,* and *Love Gun,* that *RARO* is the better of the three or their best studio album ever. To each his own, and everybody has a right to their opinion. Still, I can't help but wonder what album they are listening to. I just can't understand how some fans can defend this album so strongly. Even when I was younger, I used to think that *RARO* came out before *Destroyer* because of the poor production. But I played it all the time because, after all, it was still a Kiss record, right? One Kiss fan tried to explain to me that what makes it great is that Eddie Kramer went back to his old basic production style and sound. He said that it was a sound that classic rock fans and guitar players could really appreciate. I don't know if you agree with that are not, and it doesn't change the way I hear the album, but for years, I've tried to keep an open mind about my prejudice toward this album. Sometimes I'll drive around and play it loud in the car just to see if my perspective changes in the way I hear it; unfortunately, it doesn't. Believe me, I really want to like this album and appreciate it the way other Kiss fans do, but like being at the dentist with a mouth full of Novocain, I just don't feel anything.

## TO ME, EDDIE KRAMER DROPPED THE BALL ON THIS ALBUM

The production and mix down on it alone are blah. Keep in mind that Boston's debut album was released the same year with an ahead of its time production. Their producer did his job. Then that same year, Eddie Kramer turns in *RARO* for Kiss. Boston's debut record sounded like a look at the future for pop rock, and Eddie's Kramer's production style on *RARO* was way dated, even for 1976. The guitars sound horrible. And yes, I know they recorded the drums in the bathroom because they were experimenting with a new sound, but for me, the drums are the biggest turn off about this album. They just sound loud and cheap, and I can't stand the snare drum.

I don't know of Eddie's previous studio work that he's done with other artists or what he did in the '60s. I can understand, with the success of *Alive!*, Kiss and their management wanting to work with him again, especially to pick up the slack from *Destroyer* since they thought *Destroyer* was such a disappointment. I would always wonder why Kiss and their management just didn't sit down with Bob Ezrin and say, "Look, Bob, you're an awesome, phenomenal, well-rounded producer. But now that the *Destroyer* tour is over and Kiss is going back into the studio, this time we just want a hard rock album. No strings, no piano, and no special effects or over-the-top production. We just want the next Kiss album to be balls to the walls rock. Now take 'em in the studio and do it!" They could have easily put that into the contract and Bob could have easily delivered the goods. Even if Bob had other obligations, I think he would have been worth the wait to postpone the album for a few months. I've heard different stories about this, Kiss tried to get Bob for their next studio album but he had other obligations. Also, Bob was insulted that he wasn't asked to do the next studio album. I guess only Bob and Kiss know what really happened then. It's funny to me how Kiss fans and management had a problem with *Destroyer* when it was released. I'm wondering if they had a problem at all with the sound of *RARO* when it was released.

I understand that in some ways, it's a heavier album than *Destroyer* and *Love Gun,* and I'm assuming that's why a lot of fans are drawn to it more. But other than that, I'm just not getting the attraction to this record. I think with a better producer, those songs could have sounded a lot tighter, but then again, with a different producer, I doubt a lot of those songs would have even made it on the album. Maybe that wouldn't have been a bad thing. I'm also keeping an open mind that I'm not a follower of rock music, especially from the '70s, and because of that, I don't have other rock music or albums from that era to compare it to. When it comes to those Kiss fans who are rock fans who can appreciate the *RARO* sound, maybe they know something that I don't. Or as one Kiss fan on Facebook said to me, "If you don't like *RARO,* then you're not a real Kiss fan. Get the fuck off this page!" Duuuuhhhh.

## GENE DROPPED THE BALL ON THIS ALBUM

For such a beloved Kiss album, *RARO* has the worst Gene songs than any other '70s Kiss studio album. I'm not a fan of the *RARO* version of "Calling Dr. Love," but it's not a bad song and does make for a decent single. But the other three tracks, "Ladies Room," "Love 'em and Leave 'em," and "See You in Your Dreams" are complete throwaways. The writing and production on these three songs are simple, generic, and blah. If you think I'm wrong, then just say—don't sing—the second verse to "Ladies Room" in your head. That's probably the simplest question mark of a verse Gene's ever written on a Kiss album. Lyrically, "See You in Your Dreams" doesn't get much better. In fact, "See You in Your Dreams" is the biggest throwaway on the album, performed by Gene. These songs are a long way off from "God of Thunder," "Watchin' You," and the upcoming "Almost Human." Was Gene too busy trying to break into acting/Hollywood as early as 1976 to contribute any good, strong songs for *RARO*? Or was he just being too lazy to up his game at that point and thought he could just throw anything into the pot to cook and people would still eat it. I love Gene's '70s songs because they're Kiss songs. But I have never thought that Gene was a great songwriter/producer. In fact, I think out of the original band, Gene is actually the weakest. Paul is definitely a better writer/producer than Gene. Both Paul and Ace are great but just have different styles. I think Peter can be dangerous when he digs deep.

Let's do an *Animalize* comparison. Paul's songs on *Animalize* are what save that album, what make that album good. In the case of *RARO,* Paul's and Peter's songs are what made that album good. Some fans didn't just go nose blind but also makeup blind to *RARO*. The point is, when Gene delivers throwaway songs with no substance or backbone on a '70s Kiss album like *RARO*, with makeup and with the original members, it's OK and gets a free pass. When Gene delivers throwaway songs on an '80s Kiss album like *Animalize*, without makeup and with non-original members, fans are quick to say that those songs suck and then they become the worst Gene songs ever, or in some opinions, the worst Kiss album ever.

## THE SONGS

### I WANT YOU

The production could be a little tighter. Musically, it's just sloppy to me and a little off beat. I always loved the way Peter's hitting the ride cymbal. I never liked Paul's soft voice or the acoustic guitar; it always sounded corny. The acoustic guitar sounds exactly like the acoustic guitar on the studio version of "Black Diamond." But it's still a strong song. I don't think it's an album opener; maybe an opener for side two.

### TAKE ME

I always thought that "Take Me" is the strongest song on the album and should have been the album opener. I think if more songs on the album were heavy like this, I would have liked it a lot better. Also, I think it should have been on *Alive II*.

### CALLING DR. LOVE

I've never liked the *RARO* version of "Calling Dr. Love." Even when it comes on the radio, I'll turn the station to see what else is on. It's slow and drags as well. I think a different producer could have made it sound a lot better.

### LADIES ROOM

This is a throwaway, at least to me. Why was this song recorded so slowly and why does it drag? I would always get annoyed with the sound of Peter's cowbell and the tom-tom roll on that song because they were so damned slow. I used to think *Couldn't they hear how slow this song was when they were mixing it down?* Gene sings it as if he's going on twenty-three hours with no sleep, especially when he says the word "Rooooouugghh." How did they go from the up-tempo, kickin' it beats of "Room Service," "Love Her All I Can," "Detroit Rock City," and "Do You Love Me" to the slow and dragging beats of this and "Calling Dr. Love?"

## BABY DRIVER

I think "Baby Driver" is one of the most underrated Kiss songs ever recorded and the most unique song on *RARO*. I would have loved for Kiss to record more songs with Peter screaming and being more vocally aggressive with his raspy voice. My favorite song on the album. I loooooooooooovveee it!!

## LOVE 'EM AND LEAVE 'EM

This song is a joke. What producer in his right mind would let such a stupid song like this on an album? Personally, I love the song. I'll say it again; I love this song! Growing up, I never really cared much for it until I saw the video for the first time on *Kiss X-Treme Close Up*. When I saw the way that Kiss was jammin' to it and the way Gene was rockin' his head back and forth, also seeing Ace pretending/performing the solo for the first time, just made me fall in love with the song. My point is, in 1976, as a producer, would I have put that song on an album? Hell no! The song is just stupid. There are many Kiss songs I love, but there are also many Kiss songs that I love that I would have never put on a Kiss album or even recorded if I was their producer. But it's a song that I love singing along to in the car and rocking my head back and forth like Gene in the video.

## MR. SPEED

I don't make it a point to listen to "Mr. Speed." It doesn't do much for me. But I recognize that it's a strong Paul song. It always seems to be the fans' favorite from this album.

## SEE YOU IN YOUR DREAMS

"See You in Your Dreams" is a complete throwaway with throwaway lyrics. The lyrics sound like something Gene quickly wrote on a napkin while having lunch and said to himself "Here's a new Kiss song!" So why do I still love to listen to it and the lead solo? To me, it doesn't serve a purpose on the album at all. Those minutes could have been better spent for a heavier Gene song, or they could have put "Mad Dog" in its place. Speaking of stupid Gene songs, I love "Mad Dog!"

## HARD LUCK WOMAN

•

This is a great Peter song. It is what it is, but again, the drum track needs to come down some.

## MAKIN' LOVE

"Makin' Love" is another throwaway, and so is the title. I can't stand the snare drum on this song; it's just too loud in the mix. Too bad the drums couldn't have been recorded differently on this album. I know I'm being redundant about the drums at this point. But at the end of the day, "Makin' Love" is fun to listen to.

## ALBUM COVER

I don't like the album title at all. *Rock and Roll Over* just sounds boring. It doesn't jump out at you, and it doesn't make a statement. I don't even know what it means. I guess I've always assumed it means Kiss is going back to a basic heavier sound.

It's one of my least favorite '70s album covers from Kiss. Unlike the *Alive!* and *Destroyer* covers, it's not threatening or dangerous. It's always been too cartoonish for me with the bright colors and the heads going in a circle. It seems like the artwork would have been good for one of the first three album covers, but at this point in their careers, it seems like Kiss should have gone with something a little darker/mysterious and kick-ass!

I used to think that Peter had long grass leaves behind his head. I don't know, maybe it is grass. Still, I always thought it was weird that he had grass behind him. *What does grass have to do with the cat man?* I would think.

When I got my second *RARO* record, I made a Kiss board game out of my first *RARO* record. I cut it up around the heads and made a hole in the middle for spinning. "Spin the heads and see what it lands on." I forgot the point of the game, but I do remember playing it with neighborhood friends.

Now that I beat this record up, I will say that sometimes I like to put *RARO* on and just listen to and enjoy it for what it is. For me, it's not one of the best Kiss studio albums, but it is a unique and signature Kiss album. And among the three sister albums, *Destroyer*, *RARO*, and *Love Gun*, the *RARO* songs are more fun to sing along to.

FAVORITE SONG: "Baby Driver"
FAVORITE RHYTHM GUITAR: "Take Me"
FAVORITE LEAD GUITAR: "Love 'em and Leave 'em"
FAVORITE BASS: "Ladies Room"
FAVORITE DRUMS: "Baby Driver"

THROWAWAY: "See You in Your Dreams"

MESSING UP THE LYRICS:

"Hard Luck Woman," "Meg, the sale is only a dollar."

"Take Me," second verse: "Didn't know she was dead."

"Calling Dr. Love," chorus: "I got to cure your thinking up!"

## Chapter 7

# LOVE GUN, OR SHOULD I SAY THE HAPPY DAYS ALBUM?

I don't remember how I came to own the *Love Gun* album, but I remember owning it around '82. I do remember around the age of five, in '79, being at a drug store with my dad and I saw the *Love Gun* album in the record department. I ran up to my dad with it in my hand and asked him to buy it for me, but he just said, "Maybe next time."

A couple of years later, I went on a field trip with my second grade class. After visiting the milk factory, we went to McDonald's. I went to the bathroom in one of the stalls, and on the wall was a *Love Gun* album cover sticker without the women. I had to have it. I stayed in that bathroom for over an hour trying to slowly peel it off. One of my friends came in looking for me, so I pulled my feet up so as not to be seen. I knew I couldn't leave without this awesome sticker. By the time I pulled half of it off, I ended up ripping it. All that patient work for nothing. In the end, we were late getting back to the school because everybody was looking for me. I got detention for holding up the field trip.

### KISS SOLD OUT MUSICALLY WAY BEFORE *DYNASTY*

People always talk about Kiss selling out and jumping on the disco bandwagon with *Dynasty* or calling it the disco album. I never hear fans criticize Kiss for doing the same thing on *Love Gun*. In the '70s, '50s and '60s throwbacks were a popular fad. There were hit shows like *Happy*

*Days, Laverne and Shirley,* and the *Sha Na Na* variety show. And let's not forget the popularity of the movie *Grease* that came out a year later. Kiss, as usual, were clearly also jumping on that bandwagon with songs like "Christine Sixteen," "Then She Kissed Me," "Tomorrow and Tonight," and "Hooligan," which is definitely borderline. Why didn't fans criticize Kiss for going in that direction or call *Love Gun* the sell out or bubble gum/throwback album? Yet they've attacked Kiss for the "disco record." I've mentioned this online a few times. The answer I hear the most is "I Was Made for Lovin' You" sounds like a disco song. But "Christine Sixteen," "Tomorrow and Tonight," and "Then She Kissed Me" still have a rock edge to them. I don't buy that because in *Dynasty*'s defense, it only had one "sell out" song on it, where *Love Gun* had three and one borderline. And even though some fans say it is, "Magic Touch" wasn't a disco song. At least not to my ears. But I guess any way you slice it, "I Was Made for Lovin' You" was a disco song, and in 1979, a band like Kiss doing a disco song was totally unacceptable. The point is why does Ezrin get criticized for doing songs like "Great Expectations" and "Beth," and why does Vini Poncia get criticized for "I Was Made for Lovin' You," but when Kramer does the same thing on *Love Gun* with "Christine Sixteen," "Tomorrow and Tonight," "Hooligan," and "Then She Kissed Me," the fans nor Kiss criticize him. I'm not saying that those *Love Gun* songs were even Kramer's idea, but he was still the producer, right? And since we're on the subject, let's not forget that under Kramer's production guidance, "Any Way You Want It" ended up on side 4 of *Alive II*. Again, why doesn't Kramer get criticized for that, but Bob and Vini are seen as the bad guys who "almost ruined Kiss?"

## ONCE AGAIN, EDDIE KRAMER DROPS THE BALL

I don't think it's as bad as *RARO,* but it's still a poor effort. For me, the guitars and drums sound horrible, but at least the drum tracks aren't loud on this record like on *RARO*. But the mix down and engineering are blah. I can't help but wonder why they went with Eddie Kramer again. Were they content and happy with the sound of *RARO*? I cringe at the way some of the songs on *Love Gun* sound. Also, what I don't like about this album is there aren't enough Ace and Peter songs. That's my problem with '70s

Kiss albums; it's too much of the Gene and Paul story. I'm not blaming Gene and Paul for that, but *Love Gun* would have been a perfect album to highlight Ace and Peter more. Up to this point, Peter was averaging one to two songs an album. But *Love Gun* would have been perfect to give Ace and Peter two and two. Maybe another "Baby Driver" type song and feel. There are not a lot of highlights on this album for me. It's also not an album that I play from beginning to end a lot. Not in my top five at all.

## THE SONGS

### I STOLE YOUR LOVE

Sometimes, I can stomach the studio version, and other times, I can't. To me, the rhythm guitar to this day sounds like an old school electric can opener. You know, that grinding noise they make when you're opening up a can of cat food or tuna. Whenever I hear it, I can't get past that. Peter's snare drum sounds too distorted to me. The only way I can really appreciate this version is if I play it loud.

### CHRISTINE SIXTEEN

I love the piano on this song. I used to think that this song was a leftover from *RARO*. It just has the same sound. Of course, I've heard the stories about how Eddie and Alex played on this version and not the band. And other stories say just the demos. I never bothered to look into it or read any comments from Eddie or Gene about it. Or maybe I have read about it and just forgot.

### GOT LOVE FOR SALE

I love everything about this song! I love the way Gene sings it. He uses his "Almost Human" voice. I love the drums and Ace's solo is the shit and the acoustic guitar that's mixed in. I also love Ace's playing at the end. I always do that part with my mouth. But can someone tell me what the hell they're saying on the chorus? Again, I need to look up the lyrics on that. I love this song!

## SHOCK ME

I can't stand the rhythm guitar on "Shock Me." It's that can opener sound again. But what the hell, Eddie Kramer thought it sounded good enough. We all know the story about Ace singing that song on his back in the dark in the studio. It shows, especially when you just focus in on Ace's singing. It sounds flat and monotone. Just listen to the way he says the words "Shock Me." You can actually visualize him on his back just by the way it sounds, short winded. I don't like this recording or version.

## TOMORROW AND TONIGHT

I don't listen to this version a lot, but when I do, I enjoy it. I always thought that it was Katey Sagal singing on the breakdown. It sounds like her to me. I especially enjoy the last chorus, where the female vocals are louder and mixed with Paul's voice. The snare drum sounds weird to me, though.

## LOVE GUN

To this day, I've never cared for the studio version of "Love Gun" itself. I always skip past it. I don't think it's a bad song by any means, but it doesn't do anything for me whatsoever. The only version I like is the one they did on the *Revenge* tour. That version is bass heavy, and I like watching Gene play his bass to it onstage. But the bass line on the studio version is funky, too.

## HOOLIGAN

I played "Hooligan" a lot when I was a kid. It was my jam back in the day. But I do remember having a personal problem with it even back then. One day when I was younger, while listening to it, I thought Peter said, "If I had a nigger." Did the cat man just say nigger? Does Peter or Kiss have a problem with black people? Why would he say nigger? My feelings were hurt. So for a long time, I couldn't listen to the song. But at the same time, I loved it. I would skip past "Hooligan" whenever it came on, but everything in me wanted to listen to it. After a while, I decided to bring it to Mark's attention and ask him what he thought. Because if Kiss were a bunch of racists, we might have to rethink this obsession. After asking Mark his opinion on the matter, he looked at me in silence for a couple of seconds and then said, "Are you fuckin' stupid? He's sayin' nickel, not nigger." He rolled his eyes and walked out of the room. Boy that was a big weight off my shoulders. I was happy once again knowing that Kiss wasn't using the N word and I could continue to listen to "Hooligan" without a guilty conscience.

## ALMOST HUMAN

"Almost Human" is a tease song. What I mean is Gene puts out the sister song to "God of Thunder" but we rarely got to hear that side of him on '70s albums. Why couldn't all of his songs on this album have been like "Almost Human?" This song is the shit in every way, shape, and form, and I think it's the best song on the album. Whenever I would play it, I would look at his picture on the album cover, with his mouth open, and imagine that's what he was thinking of. As a rapper, I always wanted to sample the guitar intro from "Almost Human" and put a funky beat behind it. I never got the chance to.

## PLASTER CASTER

The song title and lyrics always get criticized but fans love it, and so do I. It seems like if it didn't end up on *Love Gun,* we probably would have heard it on Gene's solo album. Even though it's about Gene's dick, there's something sincere about the way this song sounds and the way he sings it. It just has a good feel to it.

## THEN SHE KISSED ME

I like this version a lot, especially the rhythm guitar. I remember as a kid when my mom told me that this song wasn't a Kiss song, I got really defensive because it seemed like she was accusing Kiss of stealing. I argued, "Yes, it is!" Almost in tears, I told her how Kiss doesn't copy other people's songs. I knew my mom had to be wrong. But one night while we were driving, the original version came on the radio, and my mom turned around to me and calmly said, "See, I told you." I was still in denial.

## ALBUM COVER

I don't think *Love Gun* is a good title for a Kiss album. It doesn't make a statement, and it just sounds boring; *Love Gun*? It's a song title not an album title. You don't name your album title after a dick. I think the album should have been called "Almost Human" or something with aggressiveness.

I don't know why, but I never cared for the album cover. Yes, it's a nice iconic portrait of Kiss, but I think my problem with it, like *RARO,* is it's just not badass enough for me. They're too calm. Having them look more dangerous and edgier would have been better. As a kid, it used to remind me of the Hall of Justice from *Super Friends*. And the back, like *Destroyer,* is just basic and boring. Why didn't they just put something cool on the back?

Ace has the same haircut from the *Alive!* cover.

FAVORITE SONG: "Got Love for Sale"
FAVORITE RHYTHM GUITAR: "Almost Human"
FAVORITE LEAD GUITAR: "Got Love for Sale"
FAVORITE BASS: "Almost Human"
FAVORITE DRUMS: "Hooligan"

THROWAWAY: "Then She Kissed Me," but I like it a lot.

MESSING UP THE LYRICS:

"Got Love for Sale," intro of second verse: "You got Calrissian (from *The Empire Strikes Back*) in between the lights."

# Chapter 8

## *ALIVE II*

The first time I saw *Alive II* was around the age of seven. One afternoon, the neighbor kid who lived in the apartment below us went to the dentist. And because he was such a big boy and didn't cry, his mommy bought him a new Kiss record, *Alive II*. When they arrived home, he came right over to show it to me. What was weird was he watched me look and drool all over it, but he wouldn't let me play it or play it for me. After that, I harassed him every day, and he always said no. For some reason, he was just being weird about it. I got so mad at him that I stopped talking to him altogether. He knew how I felt about Kiss. I wouldn't actually have my own copy of *Alive II* until two years later. I don't remember how I even got it, but I remember loving it to death. I wish they could have found a way to put "Take Me" on the album, though.

### THE SONGS

To contradict myself, the songs I couldn't stand or care for on *RARO* and *Love Gun* come alive for me on this album. I can't explain it, but sometimes, listening to a song live can make you hear or think of it in a totally different way.

### DETROIT ROCK CITY

I think this is the best live version of "DRC." I like all of the stuff that Ace is doing in the background on this version.

## KING OF THE NIGHT TIME WORLD

I love Ace's solo on this version.

## LADIES ROOM

I love the *Alive II* version of "Ladies Room" to death; it's one of my favorite songs to sing along with on this record.

## MAKIN' LOVE

"Makin' Love" is a major highlight for me as well. I love the rhythm guitar, Ace's solo is the shit, and you can actually hear him picking the strings.

## LOVE GUN

I still can't get into "Love Gun," so I usually skip past it.

## CALLING DR. LOVE

This version is one of my favorite songs to imitate Gene to when I'm in the mirror. Peter's drum breakdown is what made me love it as a kid.

## CHRISTINE SIXTEEN

I like how Gene's bass is really loud on this version.

## SHOCK ME

"Shock Me" was always one of the songs I played a lot from this record when I was growing up. It's got a really good feel to it. The rhythm guitar live is what makes the song for me. I like Ace's vocals a lot and I love how Gene's bass is loud in this version.

## HARD LUCK WOMAN

Whether it's the studio version, live, or pretend live, this is always a great song. Love Peter's voice.

## TOMORROW AND TONIGHT

I always listened to "Tomorrow and Tonight" from this album a lot, but it really didn't do much for me. It was just a happy, fun song. I would later learn that it was one of the songs that wasn't recorded in front of a live audience. What was weird about finding out that information was even as a kid, I thought the audience track was too loud in the mix. Well, now we know why.

## I STOLE YOUR LOVE

This version is the shit, too. I like the way Peter's kickin' the bass drum.

## BETH

I usually skip past this version.

## GOD OF THUNDER

I like how this version is faster and more up-tempo. All of the guitars sound good here. Personally, I never liked the idea of Peter's drum solo in the middle of "God of Thunder." I always thought his solo should have its own separate place in the show. Like Peter's drum solo on *Alive!*, when I watched the *Alive II* drum solo on video for the first time, I thought *What in the hell is Peter doing? This solo sucks.* That hi-hat solo he does is so ridiculous. Disappointing.

I also thought Gene should breathe fire at the end of "God of Thunder" instead of "Firehouse."

## I WANT YOU

I love Gene's bass and the way Peter's hitting the ride cymbal in this version.

## SHOUT IT OUT LOUD

I remember as kids, the first time Mark and I heard this version and how tight we both thought it was when we heard the way Peter was kicking the bass drum on the breakdown. We looked at each other and were like, "Oh, yeah!"

FAVORITE SONG: "Makin' Love"
FAVORITE RHYTHM GUITAR: "I Want You"
FAVORITE LEAD GUITAR: "Makin' Love"
FAVORITE BASS: "I Want You"
FAVORITE DRUMS: "Calling Dr. Love"

THROWAWAY: "Christine Sixteen"

MESSING UP THE LYRICS:

"Shock Me," intro: "We're gonna turn up the thermometer, Ace Frehley, Shock Me!"

## SIDE 4

## THE SONGS

As a kid, I used to listen to side 4 and wonder how come Kiss' earlier studio records don't have the same heavy rock sound like side 4 of *Alive 2*. The guitars sound like guitars, and the drums sound like drums. To me, it was the way Kiss records in the '70s should have always sounded.

## ALL-AMERICAN MAN

I always loved the hi-hat on this song, and the lead solo is the shit! If you looked up the word underrated, you would see "All-American Man" in the definition.

## ROCKIN' IN THE USA

I wish Kiss and Kiss cover bands would perform this more.

## LARGER THAN LIFE

I played "Larger Than Life" all the time. It was the bass guitar on that song that made it my jam. I like how Gene's dragging his voice on it. It's a style rarely done by him. I think the song could have been better if they would have made the arrangement of the song verse, chorus, verse, chorus instead of two verses first, then the chorus. I always thought the intro of this song would have been good if they used it on the movie *Friday*. The part when you first see Deebo, and if they did an up shot starting from his feet. Just having fun with the thought.

## ROCKET RIDE

It's funny, because I never really listened to "Rocket Ride" that much as a kid, but I always remember singing it a lot at school. Is Ace's solo on that song his best solo up to that point? I'd have to think about that a little more, but it just might be.

As a kid, I used to visualize Animal from *The Muppets* was playing the drums at the end of "Rocket Ride."

## ANY WAY YOU WANT IT

This song was always my jam-to when I was a kid. Again, Kiss was jumping on the *Happy Days* bandwagon. I always loved the way Paul's voice sounds and echoes when he says "Hey, hey, hey!" I used to also love the way Gene's voice sounded when he said, "It's all right." He just sounds so different. My favorite thing to do with that song was wait for the bass line at the very end so I could do it with my mouth.

## ALBUM COVER

The faces on the cover and blown up on the back used to be so mysterious, I thought. And the picture of Gene drooling blood officially made him the baddest mutha fucka in the world to me. I have that blown up into a life-sized poster. As a kid, the live shot in the middle of the album, with Kiss being levitated around fireworks and flames, was the most amazing picture

I had ever seen. I would think, *How could anyone not like Kiss?* I couldn't wrap my mind around the fact that someone could say, "Kiss sucks." They wouldn't think that if they saw the *Alive 2* album. The reason I think the cover isn't that great is because unlike *Alive!*, it's not that exciting. It just has the big words "Kiss Alive II" with small pictures at the bottom. I think the cover would have been better if they had used the blown-up picture from the back instead. That way, the pictures, especially Gene's awesome picture, would pop out more and jump off the shelf at you. Put the band's logo in the top left corner and the words "Alive II" in the top right corner. And that picture on the record sleeve of the live audience should have been the back of the album jacket with the song titles and credits.

FAVORITE SONG: "Larger Than Life"
FAVORITE RHYTHM GUITAR: "Larger Than Life"
FAVORITE LEAD GUITAR: I'm trying to decide between "All-American Man" and "Rocket Ride." I guess I have to give the edge to "Rocket Ride."
FAVORITE BASS: "Larger Than Life"
FAVORITE DRUMS: "Larger Than Life"

THROWAWAY: "Any Way You Want It," but I still love it.

MESSING UP THE LYRICS:

"Larger Than Life," first verse intro lyrics: "Do you wanna make fun of me."

"Any Way You Want it," "Don't want a dime or three, hey, hey, hey!"

## Chapter 9

# *KISS MEETS THE PHANTOM OF THE PARK*

To this day, Mark has a clear memory of the TV commercial for *Kiss Meets the Phantom* that aired a few weeks prior to the movie. What I remember is my mom telling me that it was coming on in a few days.

I also remember the night it aired. My brother Mark and I were going to run errands with our dad. Before we left, we told our dad in whiny voices that we would have to hurry up and get back or we would miss Kiss on TV. My dad said in a calm voice, "Don't worry; we'll be back in time for the Kiss show."

We drove around town as our dad made one stop after another. In our minds, he was taking too long and dragging out his conversations with the people he was talking to. "Dad, we have to hurry up and get back home; we're gonna miss Kiss!" we whined. "I told y'all don't worry," my dad repeated. When we went to the store, he was taking too long picking out the beer he wanted. When he pumped the gas, the gas wasn't coming out fast enough. And if the speed limit was fifty-five, it felt like we were going twenty-five. My brother and I just wanted to get back home to see *Kiss Meets the Phantom*. Like kids in the back seat who keep annoyingly asking are we there yet, are we there yet, we were in the back seat crying "Dad, we're gonna miss Kiss, we're gonna miss Kiss!"

As time went on, it was getting darker outside. We drove around all over the city. We were getting tired. Our complaining, whining voices were getting weaker. "Dad, we have to get home, we're gonna miss Kiss!" we said for the thousandth time. Finally, my dad said, "OK, let's go home."

## LOOKS LIKE WE MADE A WRONG TURN. THERE DOESN'T APPEAR TO BE ANY RIGHT ONES.

When we finally made it back to our neighborhood, our dad gave us some horrible news. He said he was lost and couldn't remember where we lived. Could this night get any worse for us? Of course, he was messing with our heads.

My dad drove around the neighborhood for what seemed like forever, trying to find our house. Mark and I were in the back seat yelling at my dad to turn this way and turn that way, trying to guide him. Our dad continued to pretend as if he didn't know what we were talking about. He was doing his best to hold his laugh in. "Dad we're gonna miss Kiss!" we continued to whine and shout.

Then our dad really started messing with us. He drove past our house at least three times, and each time, we would yell, "Our house is right there!" Of course, he would look in every direction except at the house itself. "Dad, you passed it again!" we shouted. At this point, my dad was like a volcano waiting to erupt with laughter. Him pretending like he couldn't find our house and had forgotten where we lived was killing us. But of course, we really believed that he was lost.

Finally, after torturing us, he pulled into our driveway. Being the humorous guy he was, he said, "Oh here it is. Why didn't you guys tell me this was where we lived?" I don't think the car even came to a complete stop before we jumped out and ran into the house.

The truth is our dad knew how much we loved Kiss and he wouldn't have let us miss *Kiss Meets the Phantom*. He got us back with plenty of time to spare. Thanks, Dad.

## ARMAGEDDON IS COMING TO TV TONIGHT

As I watched the opening scene, it was mysterious to me that Gene was a giant standing over the roller coaster. I thought that those two girls who were walking below and looking up at him were so lucky to be that close to

Gene, even if he was a giant. At that young age, I really didn't understand the plot of the movie. I didn't get that the Phantom was creating robots and zombies to destroy Kiss or that his plan was to take over the park. Or when the fake Gene was beating up the security guards, I thought it was the real Gene beating up the guards because he was mad. In the end, all I saw was Kiss kickin' ass and using their super powers at the same time.

I thought the house where they were staying was Kiss' real house. As a kid, I wanted to go there so bad and see the inside. I wanted to see their cool bedrooms and I assumed that Gene's bedroom was some kind of a dungeon below the house. I thought that was their real pool and that when Kiss wasn't onstage they were always sitting on those high chairs talking to each other. As a kid, seeing Kiss in that pool element was really mysterious to me. Another scene that was cool to me was them sitting on the merry go round. Because of who they were, something about Kiss sitting on fake horsies was just unique to me. I also thought that scene where they jumped over the fence was real. I really thought they could do that. "Dead center!"

I do remember after it was over having to go number two really bad. I was so scared of Gene from the movie that I asked my older sister Denise to stand outside the bathroom door until I was done. Every few seconds, I would yell out, "Denise, are you still out there?" She'd yell back, "Yeah, don't worry." I imagined that if she left, the same Gene who beat up the guards would walk into the bathroom and grab me. For real!

## THE SECOND TIME

The next time it aired on TV in Alaska was in '80–'81. My brother Mark and I were all set to watch it on the living room floor, wrapped up in our sleeping bags and pillows. Our older brother, Andrew, and sister, Lorraine, were also in the living room, arguing with each other about who knows what. From the moment the movie came on, they kept going back and forth with each other. My mom, who liked to party, was in bed trying to get some rest from an all-day hangover. She didn't hear that they were arguing, she just heard a bunch of noise coming from the living room. By the time we got to the scene where Kiss were going to fight the werewolves, my mother got tired of all of the noise. She came out, yelled at everybody, and made us turn the TV off. Just like that, our Kiss night was over. We didn't even get to see the first fight scene. I cried myself to sleep.

## VHS

It aired a few more times in Alaska between '85 and '86. But it wouldn't be until early '90s when Mark and I would own our very own copy. I remember how my jaw dropped when I was at Musicland and saw that they were actually selling VHS copies. Mark bought it for us a few days later. It was cool for us to know that we owned our very own copy of *Kiss Meets the Phantom*. It was ours to watch anytime we wanted to. At that point in my life, I was stealing cars, selling drugs, and sleeping with a lot of women. But at the age of sixteen, I still got excited like a little kid over *Kiss Meets the Phantom*.

## IT'S NOT FOR EVERYONE

One night in '91, I brought it over to my new girlfriend's house to watch it. Her parents were supposed to be out that night for the rest of the evening. So by the time we get to the scene where Devereaux is being fired, her parents walked in the door along with her dad's friends, roughneck type of guys. Before I knew it, all of us were sitting in the living room watching *Kiss Meets the Phantom*.

It was so awkward. They were all staring at the screen like "What the fuck are we watching?" I'm sure they all thought it was the worst movie they had ever seen in their lives. I could feel the uncomfortable silence in the room, so I made up some excuse about having to go somewhere and took my movie out of the VCR, jumped in my lowrider Monte Carlo, and left. It was one of those times when I realized that people just don't get Kiss. Or great cinema, lol.

By the way, I like the U.S. version better. I don't like the one that was on *Kissology*. I don't like the way they added the music from the solo albums on there. Some of it is OK, but other songs that appear in certain places, I don't care for. I love seeing all of the extra deleted scenes they added, but the movie and story line just doesn't flow well to me. Not that it's such a great sophisticated story line to follow, but I just like the U.S. version better.

Also as a fan, I wish that Kiss would do more obscure songs live and be more spontaneous onstage. I think it would be so cool if they did something unique like perform "Rip and Destroy" on their next tour. Not because it's such a great song, but for nostalgic reasons. And while Kiss is performing it, the die-hards in the audience can yell out, "Let's tear this place down!"

By the way. I wonder if Chopper and Slime ever went back to night school to get their GED's.

# Chapter 10

# GENE SIMMONS SOLO

It was 1978, Mark's seventh birthday. My mother told him he could pick a few presents from under the tree for his birthday gifts. One of the presents he went for was obviously shaped like a record. He anxiously opened it up, and to his amazement, it was the Gene Simmons solo album! He held it high in the air for the first time, like Mufasa holding up Simba. Or was it the monkey that held up Simba? It's been a while since I saw that movie.

Instantly, I was jealous and ran to my room crying. While I was in the room throwing a tantrum, Mark came running in, screaming, "Look, Anthony, it has a cartoon poster of Gene inside of it!" Now I was even more furious and jealous. I began crying even harder. Life wasn't fair at all. I should be the only person in the world to ever receive a Kiss record. They were my first love. I remember watching the commercial on TV for the solo albums and how much I wanted one so bad, but instead, Mark got one before me! Again, it just wasn't fair. My brother was a really good sport about it. He tried to calm me down and said, "It's no big deal, Anthony, we can share the record. It'll be both of ours. And we can hang the poster up together." That was really cool of him to say and he was sincere, but it didn't matter because the next words that came out of my bratty mouth was, "No!" I wanted the album and poster to be all mine, not his! I didn't want to share at all.

## WE WERE OBSESSED WITH LISTENING TO THIS RECORD

To us, this record meant Gene had something to say and we should listen, and we did. From the time we got our first Gene Simmons solo record in

'78 to this very day, Gene's has always been my favorite. When it comes to all Kiss members, I've always considered myself more like Gene in personality. I can be a very evil and wicked performer, or I can be kind of square and obscure in taste and imagination. His solo record captures all of that for me. But it's not just because he took chances and risks with his song selections that makes it a great album for me but the fact that, in my mind, he executed them well. No one song sounds like the other and it continues to go in different directions. Again, I love this record. My favorite of the four. I'm not saying it's the best, but I listen to it more than the others.

I understand that there were a lot of fans from that era who wanted to hear more of the demon than the Lennon/McCartney side of Gene. But for me, either it is or it ain't. And for me, this record is!

## GENE IS SO MYSTERIOUS

For me, every song on this album has a sense of mystique. They're spiritual in a dark way and even funny. But there was something about this record that, as a kid, made me believe Gene was really on another level in his thinking. When I would listen to these songs back then, I would always think of him when he was wearing sunglasses and a handkerchief around his mouth. I used to think that when Gene wasn't wearing makeup, that was what he wore twenty-four, seven. And that in real life, he did all of the things he talked about in his songs. Like he'd be walking down the street and a random pay phone would ring and it would always be some woman asking for him. Seriously, I thought that happened to him all the time.

## THE SONGS

### RADIOACTIVE

I remember how Mark and I used to think that the laughing in the beginning of "Radioactive" was a dog. I always visualized it as a German Shepherd. Mark told me that Bolo from *Enter the Dragon* was one of the people on the scary intro to "Radioactive." He said he was the person saying "Sonchu!" Of course, I believed him. I love the piano on this song as well as the rhythm guitar at the beginning.

I also remember when *American Bandstand* played "Radioactive" and watching all the cool people from the '70s dancing to it on TV. I thought they were so lucky to be dancing to a Kiss song on TV.

## BURNING UP WITH FEVER

As a kid, this was my jam. I must have played this song a million times. I thought the acoustic intro was so clever and funny. And when the drums kicked in, it was time to get serious. Back in the day, I never heard it as a song about sex but more as a song about Gene being the man, a badass. He was just the shit in this song. I love the slap bass at the end.

Am I the only one who sings along with Donna Summer?

## SEE YOU TONITE

This was also a song I played a lot. I like the way Gene's voice is soft and how it blends in with the strings.

## TUNNEL OF LOVE

I remember as a kid listening to "Tunnel of Love" and thinking Gene was being mean to the woman he was talking to. That line where he's talking about telling the woman to jump off the roof, I would always imagine him on top of our apartment building with a frightened woman and making her jump off. I thought it was so weird that he would make a woman jump off a roof. I took that line literally. I love the female vocals in the background on the chorus. I love this song.

## TRUE CONFESSIONS

I love it! Despite my earlier protests about the *Dressed to Kill* version of "Rock and Roll All Nite" sounding like a church choir, I especially love the breakdown with the solo choir vocals. There's also something about the drums, piano, and women singing the chorus that pulls me in. Also, the way Gene hits that high note at the end. Is Katey Sagal on this song? I swear she's the woman on the last chorus saying "Truwa uwa truuuueee confessions." I could be dead wrong I'm just having fun here. When the women go, "Sway, sway" or whatever they're saying at the end, Mark and I used to say "Safeway," the grocery store.

## LIVING IN SIN

I remember liking the part where Gene answers the phone. I used to look forward to that part so I could say along with him "Helloooo, baaaabe." I thought that it was so cool he was talking on the phone in the middle of the song. "Wow, only Gene Simmons can do that!" Duuuhhh. As kids, Mark and I used to think the woman on the phone (Cher) was saying, "Is it true what they say about you used to give your friends a horse ride." We didn't know then, and I still don't know what she's saying. As a kid, I thought the same guys from the beginning of the song "Hooked on a Feeling" by Blue Swede, where it goes "Ooga chaka, ooga ooga," etc., were doing that on the chorus of "Living in Sin." I used to think that Gene was just friends with them and asked them to be on his album to do that same line.

## ALWAYS NEAR YOU/NOWHERE TO HIDE

"Always Near You," "Man of 1,000 Faces," and "Mr. Make Believe." These songs are what officially make this album the shit to me. When "Always Near You" came on, I would stop what I was doing and just listen. I would imagine that Gene was sad and trying to express himself but no one was listening. How can you deny Gene when he hits those high notes at the end? I even came up with a video idea when I was a teenager. The video starts and all you see is Gene's face surrounded in black like the *Dynasty* album cover. He sings the song sadly throughout the video. Then the background vocals come in. Then at the same time the vocals come in, the curtain behind him goes up and the camera pulls back and all of a sudden you realize that Gene was singing on a theatre stage and there are a bunch of stage people and actors behind him getting ready for the performance and moving around behind Gene quickly. At the same time, Gene is still singing seriously and emotionally and hitting the high notes, but still, no one is even paying attention to him. Then the video ends. It was more like an '80s video idea. I love this song to death! My second favorite song on the album.

## MAN OF 1,000 FACES

"Man of 1,000 Faces" is tight all the way. It's probably one of my top two songs to sing along to from the album. The instrumentation on this song with the strings and horns is phenomenal. I think the drums on this song are a little louder than the rest of the songs, but it's not a bad thing. I like the breakdown and the way the horns come in and out. I also like when Gene starts talking after the break without the drums, and the way the strings and horns sound behind him. It's a great production.

## MR. MAKE BELIEVE

For this album, the song of the hour has and always will be "Mr. Make Believe." It's my favorite song on this record. I love the acoustic guitar and Gene's soft voice. It almost has a Bob Dylan feel to it. To me, this song is brilliant. I like it when the background vocals are saying "make believe;" it just takes me back to being a young Kiss fan.

## SEE YOU IN YOUR DREAMS

To me the solo album version of "See You in Your Dreams" is a hundred times better than the *RARO* version. I didn't really appreciate this song until I was in my twenties. Again, it sounds like Katey Sagal on the chorus. At least to me. I always wondered why Gene remade this song for his solo album. I may have read the answer a long time ago, but if so, I forgot. Oh well. I like the guitar part at the end of the song, when the drums and the singing stop.

## WHEN YOU WISH UPON A STAR

I like to sing along with this song. I have no problem with this song except I wish the breakdown with the singing could have been longer. The only way I can describe the instrumentation on this song is "beautiful." I used to imagine the video would be like this: In the beginning, with the high-pitched flute, you would see the mice from *Cinderella* and other small Disney characters running across the screen really fast and sloppy. Then when the strings come in, you would see Cinderella and her prince walking and dancing by. Then as the music gets higher, you would see Gene's back, wearing that big black and red cape he wears in the '70s dungeon photos as he's slowly turning around. Then he starts singing. Then in the breakdown, Gene is playing with the cartoons animals and a little bird lands on his finger and so on. The idea of this video is more for the shock value to critics and Kiss fans of the demon acting sensitive in a Disney style music video.

## THE COVER

Gene's face on that album cover was so mysterious. And that blood drooling down his lip was the icing on the cake for me. The cover is flawless, including the back. I remember how I would always watch Gene's head going round and round when the record spun on the turntable. His solo record was the only one I would do that with.

I remember one Halloween when I wanted to be Gene. My sisters said they would paint my face for me, so I gave them Gene's solo album as a guide. When it was all said and done, they swore to me that it looked like the makeup on the album. When I looked in the mirror, I saw that all they did was draw these weird circles around my face. My sister Michelle actually said, "Stick out your tongue and see if that makes a difference." I didn't even go out trick or treating that night because if I couldn't look like Gene, then I wouldn't be anything. Instead, I stayed home and pouted. I should have at least been grateful that they tried. Thanks, Michelle and Denise.

FAVORITE SONG: As a kid, "Burning Up with Fever." As an adult, "Mr. Make Believe."

FAVORITE RHYTHM GUITAR: "Tunnel of Love"
FAVORITE LEAD GUITAR: "Burning Up with Fever"
FAVORITE BASS: "Burning Up with Fever"
FAVORITE DRUMS: "Burning Up with Fever"

THROWAWAY: To me, there aren't any.

MESSING UP THE LYRICS:

"Burning Up with Fever," end of first verse: "Baby, I'll give you Ajax."

"Tunnel of Love," chorus: "Take my temperature, tunnel of love."

## Chapter 11

# PAUL STANLEY SOLO—OR SHOULD I SAY THE SHAUN CASSIDY ALBUM?

I can't tell you why, but growing up, I never had a desire or need to own the Paul Stanley solo record. It was nothing personal against it, but as a kid, when I would flip through the Kiss records at the store, I would always skip past it to buy another Kiss record. Mark and I didn't even get our first Paul Stanley solo album until 1985. I just remember when we got it, we played it every day over and over again. One time in '85, Mark and I got into a big argument over something, I can't remember what. We decided that the best way to settle the argument was to see who knew more of the songs and lyrics to Paul's solo record. So we played it and started singing. Neither of us won because halfway through the record, we started arguing again. I can't believe we were that stupid?

### THE KISS SOUND

Like *RARO,* I don't get it. I don't know what's supposed to be so special about this album. From what I've read and talked about with other fans, when you ask them what their favorite '78 solo album is, Paul's always seems to be second and Ace's first. But I have heard a lot of fans say that they like Paul's over Ace's. When you ask them why they like Paul's solo album the best, the common response is "It sounds more like a Kiss record." I suppose they're talking about that basic sound and feel of previous Kiss songs. All of the songs on this album follow the simple arrangement style of verse, chorus, verse, chorus, breakdown/guitar solo, back to verse or chorus. The album is just too safe and predictable to me, and every song is about a girl except "Goodbye." This album shows no real imagination or depth from Paul.

Out of all four solo albums, Paul's probably comes closest to the "Kiss sound." Notice the quotation marks. Liking it for that reason is fine. And if that sound is your preference, that's also fine. But saying that Paul's solo album is the best is something entirely different. Gene's solo album is my personal favorite, and I enjoy listening to it more than the other three, but I don't think it's the best. Bottom line is Paul didn't make a rock album but a pop album; If Andy Gibb's song "Shadow Dancing" had appeared on this album, it would have easily fit. That's how much of a pop album it is for me. This album is the prelude to *Unmasked*. I'm not saying that making a pop album was or is bad, I'm just saying that the production is weak and mediocre. I'm just calling it like I hear it, it's pop overkill but not in a good way. I also call Paul's '78 solo album the "Shaun Cassidy album," because the sound of it always reminds me of Shaun's debut album. I forgot the title of that album but it's the one with his face on the cover and he's wearing the white cap.

I think its Shaun's delivery and vocals on that album that I find similar to Paul's. When I was in the first grade, my teacher used to play the Shaun Cassidy album for the class during project time, that's how I know what it sounds like...OK, I admit it, my teacher played the Shaun Cassidy album so much that I started liking it and finally asked my mom to buy it for me...Hey, stop clowning! I was in the first grade; what do you want from me? All of you can kiss my black ass!

Getting back on the subject before I lose all credibility, fans are always trying to argue what the Kiss sound is, when in reality, they're just talking about the sound they like best. I don't believe Kiss has a sound. Some will argue that the first three albums were the real Kiss sound. I believe that's what they started out as, but they later evolved into something else. Great fighters like Bruce Lee and Muhammad Ali weren't polished when they started out and used to actually get their asses kicked in street fights. But eventually, with hard work and a lot of sweat, they evolved into the badasses they became. My point with that perspective is that during the era where Lee and Ali were getting their asses kicked and pushed around, would you say because that is what they started out as, that was their original style of fighting and that they should have stuck to that style even though it wasn't getting them anywhere? Or would you have encouraged them to dig a little deeper to try to take their fighting style to the next level and become what they eventually became? Same thing with Kiss. Imagine if Kiss had kept the sound of their first three albums throughout the late '70s into the '80s…aaauuuggghhh, they wouldn't have lasted. And right or wrong, meaning albums that fans love and hate, they had to evolve. And as fans, like Lee and Ali, we would have been the ones getting our asses kicked and pushed around daily for defending that sound. Well maybe you guys, but not me.

You will hear a large group of fans say that they love the *Creatures* and *Revenge* sound, and how *Revenge* made them a fan all over again. But the *Creatures* and *Revenge* sound could hardly be considered the Kiss sound. Those albums sounded nothing like anything from the '70s, the era that many fans love to defend. That was just a sound they evolved into for that period. Then there are the fans who love the Kramer *RARO*/*Love Gun* songs and feel those albums are the real Kiss sound.

Another problem I have with Paul's record is the recording and sound. It's too muffled. To use studio terminology, the sound is not sharp or bright enough. It's dull. Also, there's not enough depth to the music or songs. Basic bland rhythm guitar, basic solos, and the songs and choruses don't jump out at you or are memorable. Again, yes, it has that basic Kiss sound, and there's nothing wrong with a basic production, but there is good basic and bad basic. A lot of Kiss records have a basic produced sound, like *Creatures* and *Lick It Up*. But those basic produced records still have a lot of depth to them. Even Paul songs that a lot of fans like to bash, such as "Sure Know Something," "Shandi," "What Makes the World Go 'Round," "Tomorrow," and "The Oath" have more depth and backbone than most of the songs that ended up on his '78 solo record. For me, this record is full of throwaways. What I would want from a 1978 Paul solo record is a rock album, not a pop album. What this album needed was more "Detroit Rock

City," "Do You Love Me," "Take Me," "Mr. Speed," "I Stole Your Love," and "All-American Man," and less "Move On" and "Love in Chains."

I'm not saying he was wrong for making his album the way he did, I just wish he would have dug deeper. Say what you want about Gene's album, but at least it sounds like there was some thought behind it, while Paul's sounds like he just wrote some quick songs and recorded them quickly in the studio. To me it shows. Or to make the "makeup blind" comparison, '70s "makeup" Paul, while still a part of the original Kiss, admits to recording a bunch of demos, polishes them up, and throws them on his '78 "makeup" solo album. Afterward, fans praise the album as brilliant and genius. Now fast forward to '89. Paul does the same exact thing on an '80s Kiss album, *Hot in the Shade*, without makeup and with non-original members and now it's the worst Kiss album ever? Again, some Kiss fans have gone makeup blind to the way they listen to Kiss music. In other words, if Paul is wearing makeup, songs like "Tonight You Belong to Me" and "Goodbye" are brilliant '70's songs. But if he's not wearing makeup, songs like "Silver Spoon" and "You Love Me to Hate You" are stupid '80s songs? So what we've just learned is if Kiss is wearing makeup then somehow that makes listening to their music more appealing. Obviously I'm just pointing out the hypocrisies in the way some of us fans critique and judge certain Kiss songs, albums and eras.

I don't remember if I read this in a magazine or a book, but Paul was asked to rate the solo albums 1 out of 5, and he gave Ace's a 3 and his a 5. I don't know if his answer was coming from a perspective of ego or if he was under some illusion. For Paul to like his album better than Ace's is understandable, but to actually believe his is better than Ace's is out of touch with reality. But then again, this is the same person who bragged about how great his production was on *Sonic Boom*.

## WHAT'S GREAT ABOUT THIS RECORD

What I love about this album is that out of the four, it's my favorite to sing along to. Maybe it has something to do with Paul's voice that makes you want to sing along with him. It also has a good '70s pop rock feel to it. It's a sappy mediocre feel good album. Sometimes it's cool to put it on and just listen to it.

## THE SONGS

### TONIGHT YOU BELONG TO ME

This song is so corny. It's like the kind of song you write when you're a young teenager just starting out as a musician/writer, that long cheesy acoustic guitar intro with Paul quietly singing those corny ass lyrics. And the rhythm guitar throughout the song is so elementary and simple. Shoot me now! Imagine if he didn't open with this song and opened with a song that was like "Take Me," a balls to the wall rock song. But it's still fun to listen to.

In his book, Paul said that this song and "Wouldn't You Like to Know Me?" were about his girlfriend, if you want to call her that, Carol Kaye. What's sad is when you look at the picture of them together in his book, she looks distant, as if she could take or leave their relationship. Paul's facial expression looks like he's trying too hard to give the impression that they're in a happy, committed relationship. He's not really smiling, but it's in his eyes. Poor confused guy.

### MOVE ON

I'd have to double check, but in my mind, I think "Move On" is probably the dumbest Paul song he's ever recorded. I know some of you are saying, "what about 'Read My Body'?" If you really think about the lyrics and style, "Move On" seems like something Peter should have recorded for his solo album. And that's not a shot at Peter, but to me, it always sounded like a Peter solo song, even the title. The lyrics make no sense. I would listen to the first verse, and even as a young man, I would think, *Why would a mother be telling her baby about women trying to control him?* And he ends the verse with his mother telling her infant that he's not aware of his surroundings and doesn't keep his eyes open. Are these normal conversations that mothers have with their infant babies? I thought at that age, babies only understood "No! hot!" And "Bah bah." Stop reading this for a moment, close your eyes, and actually say the lyrics to the second verse to yourself very slowly. There are four sets of lyrics to the second verse, and you will see that they make zero sense. Like he's talking about four different subjects in one verse. It's like the kind of cut and paste together lyrics Gene would write.

The first time I watched them perform this on the *Dynasty* tour on VHS, it confirmed that it was a horrible song because even doing it live couldn't save it. I cringed. But on this album, it's my favorite song to sing along to, and I always sing it loud.

## AIN'T QUITE RIGHT

Growing up, Mark would always play this song. I didn't care for it as a kid, but as an adult, I love it. It's got a little bit of an R&B feel to it. I like the ending lead guitar solo.

## WOULDN'T YOU LIKE TO KNOW ME?

This is another song off the album I played a lot. I've always loved the drums on the break.

## TAKE ME AWAY (TOGETHER AS ONE)

Mark and I both played this all the time. It's probably the most sincere and best song on the album. I like Paul's voice and the lyrics on the chorus. I also like the instrumental music as the song is ending. But it's also the most muffled song on the album. That's too bad because it's such a great song.

## IT'S ALRIGHT

"It's Alright" is another jam and my favorite up-tempo song on the album. Really fun to sing along to. More great singing from Paul on this chorus.

## HOLD ME, TOUCH ME, (THINK OF
## ME WHEN WE'RE APART)

This was my favorite song when we first got the album. When I was young, I thought, *I could definitely see Shaun Cassidy singing this.* It also reminds me of "Beauty School Drop Out." The verses have the same feel.

## LOVE IN CHAINS

This seems like one of those songs where they needed to kill a few more minutes on the album so they micro waved this song really quick and threw it on there. To me, it's just as much an album filler as "See You in Your Dreams" is on *RARO*. Still, it's a fun song.

## GOODBYE

"Goodbye"? Oh, how creative of Paul to make that title the last song on the album. Duuhhh! I'm just being stupid. This is my favorite throwaway on the album. I love the chorus on this song. The verse lyrics are annoying to me. I hate it when Gene and Paul write with that particular style, mostly Gene. It's that same style Gene uses on "Confess" or the song "I Walk Alone" from *Carnival of Souls*. Poor Bruce? I'll just make up some lyrics that are similar. "I look in the mirror but I can't see my face," or "The sun is out but it's dark outside," or "I'm walking fast but my feet won't move." That writing style always annoys me. It's like they're trying to be deep but it's so elementary. Aside from the lyrics, I like the song.

Also, let me add that off the top of my head, I don't know if Gene actually wrote "Confess" or "I Walk Alone." I'm just picking on him because it sounds like his writing.

## ALBUM COVER

As a kid, I would always wonder why the artist made Paul's hair so frizzy. I think it's the weakest of the four.

FAVORITE SONG: "Take Me Away (Together as One)"

FAVORITE RHYTHM GUITAR: "It's Aright"
FAVORITE LEAD GUITAR: "Ain't Quite Right"
FAVORITE BASS: "Goodbye"
FAVORITE DRUMS: "Wouldn't You Like to Know Me?"

THROWAWAY: If I can only pick one, I'd have to say "Move On."

## Chapter 12

# PETER CRISS SOLO

I believe it was around '82 when Mark and I got our first Peter Criss solo album. Thurston was a friend of my dad's and she had a cool long-haired teenage son named Crash. He was a badass guitar player. I remember how much Mark and I enjoyed going over to their house because Crash would always plug in his guitar and play for us. He played like Vinnie Vincent, always shredding and playing loud, heavy notes. He was, to use the words of the time, "totally awesome!" That loud guitar was powerful. Mark and I loved every minute of it. Of course, us not knowing anything about rock music or rock groups, we would always shout out for him to play Kiss songs. "Play 'God of Thunder,' play 'Hotter than Hell.' Do you know how to play 'Hard Times'?" Of course, he didn't know how to play those songs, but he could play Zeppelin, AC/DC, and Van Halen without effort.

One day, while going through his record collection, we discovered he had a Peter Criss solo album. One of us asked if we could have it, and he said yes without hesitation. Maybe he thought Kiss sucked or just wasn't that much into them, I don't know. But Mark and I couldn't have been happier. We were both grinning from ear to ear. That's how we got our first Peter Criss solo album.

Speaking of Crash, I've always had this memory of him playing the AC/DC *Back in Black* album a lot when I was at their house. So every time I hear songs from that album on the radio, I think of Crash and wonder how he's doing.

## SHAWN'S BIRTHDAY PARTY

One afternoon around '84, our friend Shawn called us up and said it was his birthday, and his mom was going to pick us up and take us all to Chubby Chuckles, a generic version of Chuck E. Cheese. Anyway, we didn't have time to buy a gift, so at this time, we had two Peter Criss solo albums, and we came up with the idea that we would wrap one of them up in cheap paper and give it to Shawn as a birthday gift. It was the best we could do. So after stuffing our faces with pizza, cake, and ice cream, it was time to open the presents. Shawn was unwrapping all these cool action figures and expensive remote control cars as all the other kids looked on in awe and jealousy as one gift was cooler than the last. Family members snapped pictures and proudly pointed out which particular gift came from them. Then the big moment came when Shawn reached for our present. I couldn't speak for Mark, but I stood there with a fruit punch smile with cake and pizza crumbs around my mouth. Shawn unwrapped his present and the more paper that came off, the more his smile faded. Finally, it was completely unwrapped—behold! It was a used, beat-up Peter Criss solo album. Everyone in the room got quiet really fast. Shawn just looked at the album as if he didn't know whether to say thank you or ask what he was supposed to do with it. The adults looked confused to, like our gift was a sandwich bag full of weed or something. But I was smiling from ear to ear like I had just given him the keys to a brand new cool motorcycle with fire and lightning stripes on the side. He said thanks and put the record down. And that was it. I think our gift actually took some of the sail out of the party. I expected much more fanfare for our awesome gift, the gift of Peter's music. But our gift was the least favorite. Nobody cared. It was almost as if our gift was offensive.

## SOME FANS JUST NEED TO GET A GRIP

Since its release, this album has always gotten negative or not so favorable reviews from fans. What's stranger is the fans I've come across who actually like it seem scared to admit they like it. Like heavy metal fans I went to school with in the '80s who were closet Duran Duran or Culture Club fans, they didn't want anyone to know. Then there are the Kiss fans who openly like Peter's album but act as if they have to be pardoned for liking it. They admit they like it but in a hesitant tone of voice. Fuck the dumb shit! Since the day we brought that record home in '82 and put the needle on it, Mark and I have always said it loud and proud that we **LOVE** Peter's solo record! We played it all the time. It's a powerhouse record. Peter's voice on this album is great from beginning to end. Out of the four solo records, it's my second favorite to listen to. There are no throwaways on this album.

I'm still amazed that fans who are my age or older say things like "Peter's record is the worst of the four solos; Peter's record sucks," and "Peter was on drugs when he made that record!" I guess it amazes me because you're supposed to grow up, mature, and evolve as a Kiss fan. First of all, there's nothing at all bad about this record. Let's get the obvious out of the way and say that it doesn't sound like a Kiss or rock album at all. Having said that, even if it's not your type of music or you're not into blues, country, R&B, disco, and everything else it's mixed with, that still doesn't make it a bad record. I also challenge any fan who doesn't like it to tell me musically where this album has failed in production, writing, or arrangement? You can't because it doesn't fail at all. It would be like playing Bob Dylan's 1979 album *Slow Train Coming* and saying that it sucks because it has an R&B and gospel sound to it, unlike his earlier work. *Slow Train Coming* is an amazing album even it's not your cup of tea when it comes to your style of music or what you want as a Bob Dylan fan.

You also have some other fans who trash Peter's album not because they actually think deep down that it's a bad album, but because they feel a little cheated and wanted to hear the cat man deliver the goods. When the album didn't live up to expectations, not musically but style wise, they turned on the album and still carry that grudge thirty plus years later, with "Peter's album sucks" and so on. What I've always found a little strange was if there was any member of Kiss who went completely off the deep end musically, it was Gene. In addition, yes, many fans complain about the sound or song choice from Gene's solo album, and he has some songs that are way out there and not at all what most fans wanted or expected, yet fans don't bash or reject Gene's album the way they do Peter's album. Is it because of the love for Gene and the demon character? If anything,

Peter actually stayed closest to his style and sound from his songs off Kiss records. Songs that we loved and songs that made him uniquely stand out in Kiss were "Mainline," "Beth," "Hard Luck Woman," and "Hooligan," even though he may not have written most of them. Yet when he delivers those same types of songs on his '78 solo album, everybody rejects and trivializes the album. Maybe the problem was that album just had too much of those types of songs and it was overkill.

As much as I love the album, if I had my way, I think it would have been better if Peter would have put some heavier songs on there. Example, just keep the four love ballads and make the other six songs like "Baby Driver," "Hooligan," "Strange Ways," and "Dirty Livin'," etc. Yes, I know "Dirty Livin'" came after the solo albums. I'm just saying in a perfect world, with the four ballads and six heavier songs, it would have given the album a better feel and balance. Instead, Peter had six soft pop rock songs and four ballads, so the result was the album doesn't have much of a backbone. There's no edge to it, and he didn't let his sharp claws out on this one. Does that make it a bad album by any means? Not at all. I personally would have just loved two or three heavy rock tracks from Peter on this album. But at the end of the day I love this album from beginning to end.

Because I like Peter's album better than Paul's I guess that means I'm not a real Kiss fan or know anything about Kiss music? Duuuhhh!!!

## THE SONGS

### I'M GONNA LOVE YOU

I always have to play this song loud. It always makes me want to sing along with it. Perfect opener for this album. It's a jam. I always loved the way the music breaks down right before the chorus. I don't know why, but the snare drum always sticks out to me on this song, in a good way.

### YOU MATTER TO ME

As a kid, this was probably my least favorite song on the album. Sure, I listened to it but it didn't grab me. I appreciate and love it as an adult, especially the background vocals. I always whistle the keyboard melodies from this song.

## TOSSIN' AND TURNIN'

This used to be my favorite song on the album. It was the cowbell that sucked me in. I've always loved cowbells in rock songs. Then again, I'm not a hundred percent sure if that is actually a cowbell on that song or something else. Whatever it is, I love it. I also like the saxophone and the background female vocals as the music is fading.

## DON'T YOU LET ME DOWN

This song could have easily been a big hit for this album. It's one of those great songs that was released years ago that will probably stay buried in the sand like a treasure chest. It's a shame it's never gotten its due. Background vocals are awesome. Good work.

## THAT'S THE KIND OF SUGAR PAPA LIKES

I remember when we were kids, Mark played this song all the time. Because of that, I probably learned the lyrics to this song first. Awesome song!

## EASY THING

"Easy Thing" is not only a beautiful song but also some of Peter's best vocal work.

## ROCK ME, BABY

This is the most up-tempo song on the album. A fan once said online that they should have done this song live during the *Dynasty* tour. At the time, that sounded really stupid to me, but now when I think about it, I believe they could have pulled it off and made it great. Of course, Peter couldn't be high onstage. But they could have done it. I love everything about this song. The sax, the drums/hi-hat, background vocals, everything. I'm noticing that I'm stressing a lot on the background vocals on this album. They're great!

## KISS THE GIRL GOODBYE

Peter's vocals blended with the acoustic guitar makes "Kiss the Girl Goodbye" just a beautiful song. I believe if any Peter song was going to be the next "Beth," "Kiss the Girl Goodbye" was it. I remember as a teen, when I was visiting family in Junction City, Kansas, I was always missing my girlfriend, Megan. I wrote the lyrics to "Kiss the Girl Goodbye" on a piece of paper and mailed it to her, saying it was a poem I wrote. She loved it.

## HOOKED ON ROCK 'N' ROLL

I always loved the piano on "Hooked on Rock 'n' Roll." "Hey momma, *gling, gling, gling, gling, gling.*" Is that what a piano played in a high key sounds like, *gling, gling, gling, gling, gling*? This song would be good in a '50s or '60s throwback musical.

## I CAN'T STOP THE RAIN

And the award goes to, "I Can't Stop the Rain!" I don't need to say too much about it. I love the strings on the chorus. It's the greatest song on the album. And the second greatest Peter song ever recorded after "Beth."

## ALBUM COVER

I think Peter's album cover is the best. He has the most mysterious look of the four. Is he cool, nice, evil, approachable, threatening? Who knows. Well, you get the answer when you listen to the album. The green outline around his head and shadow on his face is cool. I think the green colors on his solo album look the best of the four colors.

FAVORITE SONG: "I'm Gonna Love You"
FAVORITE RHYTHM GUITAR: "Kiss the Girl Goodbye"
FAVORITE LEAD GUITAR: "Kiss the Girl Goodbye"

FAVORITE BASS: "That's the Kind of Sugar Papa Likes"
FAVORITE DRUMS: "Tossin' and Turnin'"

THROWAWAY: I don't think there are any throwaways on this album. But If I absolutely had to choose one, I'd have to say "Hooked on Rock 'n' Roll."

# Chapter 13

## ACE FREHLEY SOLO

I don't remember how Mark and I got it, but I remember owning Ace's solo album around '81. I also remember as a kid only liking "Rip it Out," "Speedin' Back to My Baby," and "Wiped Out" on the album. Back then, I didn't care for his solo album that much because it was too heavy of a rock sound to me. I was used to the softer Kiss sound, like from *Dressed to Kill, Destroyer, Love Gun,* etc. But back then, Mark played it all the time. Even though Mark was always Gene when we would pretend and play Kiss or have a Kiss concert in the bedroom, in a lot of ways, he was equally an Ace fan. I suppose I had the same issue, too. I was always Paul when we pretended and acted like Kiss, but when Eric Carr joined, I found myself liking the fox character a lot.

### ACE'S SOLO IS THE BEST OF THE FOUR

It wouldn't be until years later that I would learn to love and appreciate the album in its entirety. Now as an adult, I can listen to it and say it's brilliant! Even though I like Gene's solo album the best, I think Ace's is the best solo album of the four. I also believe that *Destroyer* and Ace's solo record are the best '70s studio albums with the Kiss name on them up to that point. Paul once said in an interview that Ace's '78 solo record came closest to the Kiss sound. Shiiiitttt!! Paul's trippin'. There's not a Kiss studio album before that record with the balls, unique guitar riffs, and leads that Ace's record has. It was almost as if it was Paul's way of admitting how good Ace's album really was but at the same time trying to connect it to Kiss somehow. What makes it the best for me is because Ace was the only member who made an actual balls to the wall rock album. Well produced, well written, and like Jimmy Page, it has unique guitar riffs and leads. Also, every song isn't about a girl, and every song has the Space Ace signature, but at the same time, each song doesn't sound like the last. With the success of Ace's solo album, I wonder why Kiss didn't push more in the direction of Ace producing or coproducing more on Kiss albums, or at least have him come up with more unique guitar riffs or leads. That would have been great. I'm sure the reasons were keeping control, order, and politics on Gene and Paul's part. Not because they were being assholes but more because Ace was just too out of control and had to be put on a short leash, so to speak.

## OUT OF EDDIE KRAMER'S MOUTH

Ace obviously likes Eddie Kramer's production style a lot, so I assume that's why he picked him to produce his album. With the production and sound of *RARO* and *Love Gun*, I think each member of Kiss should have been running away from Eddie as fast as they could. Yes, I know he did a great job on *Alive!* and side 4 of *Alive II*, but *RARO* and *Love Gun*…cringe. Eddie once said in an interview that he actually didn't produce Ace's '78 solo album. He actually said that Ace produced, arranged, and came up with everything on the album, and all he did was just reply yes or no and tell Ace whether he liked something or not. But he confirmed that Ace actually produced his own '78 solo album. I'm sure if you go online and dig hard enough, you can find other interviews that contradict that. I guess in the end, only Ace and Eddie know who did what on the album.

## THE SONGS

## RIP IT OUT

The drum breakdown on this song is what made me love it as a kid, especially the way Anton was kicking the bass drum.

## SPEEDIN' BACK TO MY BABY

I always liked the opening lead guitar. It's what makes the song for me. I love the lead guitar solo. Ace was really creative. I remember as a kid Mark telling me that Ace's wife was the woman who was singing at the end of the song. Of course, I believed him.

## SNOW BLIND

As a kid, this was my least favorite song on the album. I would always skip past it. The rhythm guitar intro sounded really annoying and angry to me. It wasn't until I became a teen that I began to appreciate it more. And I also thought it was cool and creative how the music picked up during the solo then dropped back down again during the verse. When I was rapping in my teens, I wrote a rap song called "Danger Zone." I took the Ace Frehley solo tape to the studio and had my producer sample the guitar intro to "Snow Blind" and put a beat behind it. With my rap lyrics over it, "Danger Zone" became a tight ass song. I wish I still had that demo. That was maybe 1990.

## OZONE

"Ozone" was another song on the album that I would skip past as a kid. It had that long intro, and it seemed slow and dragging. It was too dark for me. Not a good dark like "God of Thunder," but more of a dazed and confused dark. Now as an adult, it's my favorite song on the album. I think it's brilliant! It has so much feel and passion to it. I love the lead guitar in it. The intro is tight, and so is the drumming on the chorus. The way he says "Ozone" on the chorus just sucks me into the song even more. It's probably my favorite Ace song of all time. I think I'm gonna take some R&R and listen to it right now.

## WHAT'S ON YOUR MIND?

Even as a kid, I didn't know what a throwaway was, but for some reason I felt that "What's On Your Mind?" was a filler song for the album that really didn't serve a purpose. I never cared for it growing up. It wasn't special or jumped out at me. Then one day a few years ago, while looking up Kiss footage on YouTube, I came across the group Medieval Knievel covering "What's On Your Mind?" I thought they did such a good job covering it that it made me appreciate the song more. And now I love to listen to it. Go on YouTube and check out their version.

## NEW YORK GROOVE

The only version of this song that I ever cared for was on the *Unmasked* tour. I loved the way Eric Carr played drums on it during that tour. The album version then and now has never done anything for me. Yes, it's a great song and I will listen to it, but it just doesn't have that spark to me. I had a part-time job at a Burger King in the mall when I was fourteen, and I remember how cool I thought it was to hear it played over the mall's intercom system when they would rotate '70s and '80s music.

## I'M IN NEED OF LOVE

This is another jam to me. That lead guitar lick he plays throughout the song is the shit. I would always imitate that noise with my mouth when I was at work. Also, the guitar solo. I especially like the way the lead guitar goes higher at the end of the song. I also like the bass lick that comes in and out during the song.

## WIPED OUT

It's brilliant! The rhythm guitar, drums, bass, Ace's vocal delivery. It's one of Ace's most unique songs. As a kid, it was my favorite song off this album. I don't understand the obvious Surfaris intro rip-off of their song "Wipe Out." I wonder if it was intentional on Ace's part to do it that way. The differences on the intros are:

Surfaris version:

1. The laughing is first.
2. Then he says "Wipe Out."
3. Then the drums come in.

Ace's version is backward:

1. The drums are first.
2. He says "Wiped Out."
3. Then he laughs.

My common sense tells me between the title and intro that there's a connection. Or was it just one hell of a coincidence? I guess the reason I question it is because if it was intentional, then why didn't Ace just do it in the same way and order the Surfaris did it since people would see the similarity regardless. Then again, maybe Ace has already spoken on this subject and I'm just way behind on my Kiss trivia.

## FRACTURED MIRROR

Fractured mirror is as genius an Ace song as they come. Still it's a song I only listen to from time to time. But I do love it. The way the song builds up and fades from beginning to end is beautiful.

## ALBUM COVER

Ace's head always looked a little lopsided to me.

FAVORITE SONG: "Ozone"
FAVORITE RHYTHM GUITAR: "Wiped Out"
FAVORITE LEAD GUITAR: "I'm in Need of Love"
FAVORITE BASS: "Wiped Out"
FAVORITE DRUMS: "Speedin' Back to My Baby"

THROWAWAY: Paul's solo record-LOL.

MESSING UP THE LYRICS:

"New York Groove," first verse: "I am in the Mississippi."

## Chapter 14

# WHAT IF THE SOLO ALBUMS WERE ONE RECORD?

Like many Kiss fans, over the years, I've always wondered what if the songs for the solo albums were used to make one record. What would it sound like and what songs would be used to create this album? I've decided to see if I could create one album from the song choices. I thought of the idea of a double album, but I thought it would be too much music, so I narrowed it down to ten. I also had a system and a way of doing it. When it comes to picking song choices, here's what I could and couldn't do:

1. I couldn't pick songs based on my personal favorites.
2. I couldn't pick songs just because they were singles or considered the best songs on the album.
3. The songs have to sound like they could actually be Kiss songs.
4. They have to be songs that give the feeling of a mid/late '70's Kiss album.
5. How many songs each person gets to have. Paul's average 4. Gene's average 3–4. Peter's average 1–2. And by the late '70s, Ace's average 1–3.
6. What order the songs will go in and what songs will be on side 1 and side 2. Also, the way one song ends and leads into another.

Now again, remember, this is not based on my personal favorites or what songs I think are the best. I'm just using the songs from the solo albums to create an album that flows like a mid/late '70's Kiss album. My choices aren't written in stone. Here's what I've come up with:

SIDE 1

IT'S ALRIGHT
BURNING UP WITH FEVER
AIN'T QUITE RIGHT
TUNNEL OF LOVE
OZONE

SIDE 2

LIVING IN SIN
TOSSIN' AND TURNIN'
WOULDN'T YOU LIKE TO KNOW ME?
I'M IN NEED OF LOVE
TAKE ME AWAY (TOGETHER AS ONE)

"It's Alright" would be the first single. "Living in Sin" would be the second single.

# Chapter 15

## DOUBLE PLATINUM

I can't tell you why, but to this day, I have never owned *Double Platinum*. I don't ever remember seeing it in stores or on the shelves. I never had a desire to own it or was curious to hear what it sounded like. Not because I expected it to be bad but probably because I knew it was just another greatest hits album. Songs I already had, just with new packaging. I have heard "Strutter '78" and "She," and I know that some of the other songs have been remixed as well. Still it wasn't enough for me to go out of my way to possess it. Now maybe if I had actually seen it in stores, I would have bought it. But since it wasn't in my face, it was out of mind.

# Chapter 16

# *DYNASTY*

One day in 1980, Mark had to stay home from school for whatever reason. My mother had some errands to run, so Mark had to go along for the ride. While they were at the store, Mark went to the record department, where he had a life-changing experience. He saw with his own eyes something better than money on the ground, he saw the *Dynasty* album—a Kiss record he had never seen before! He was so excited. He grabbed it, ran back to our mom, and begged over and over again for her to buy it until she finally said yes. The new generation of Kiss fans might not understand this, but back in the '70s and '80s, there was something magical and exciting when you accidentally stumbled upon a new Kiss record or one you'd never seen before. It was just an awesome feeling. Unless you were from that era, I can't explain it.

I remember coming home from first grade later that day and hearing Kiss music playing that I had never heard before. I walked into our room where the music was blasting to see Mark with a huge grin on his face. He held the record up to me and smoothly said, "Look, Mom bought me a new Kiss record." To me, that meant Mom bought *us* a new Kiss record. Then he pointed to the wall at the new Kiss poster hanging up proudly, like the American flag. It was the foldout poster that came with the album, where Kiss' bodies were covered all in black. I got my first glimpse of that poster, and it blew me away. Mystique is what it was. On that day, we were introduced to the *Dynasty* era, even though it was 1980 and we were a year behind.

## MY FAVORITE

*Dynasty* is my favorite '70s studio album from Kiss. The songs are really good, and for me, it's one of their better engineered albums. Even though it was recorded with so much treble and highs, it still sounds great to me. Like *Destroyer*, *Dynasty* has a powerful production but in the more modern style of its time. I like all of the weird sounds on *Dynasty*. Ace once said in an interview that when they were close to finishing the *Dynasty* recordings, the band felt like there was nothing special about the material. The songs were just not there. I suppose coming off their solo albums, I could understand that perspective. For me, it's not a matter of the songs not being there but maybe they weren't edgy enough. What I mean is a year earlier, the name Kiss had just had a great album added to their catalogue, Ace's solo. The band knew what a great album it was, and so did the fans. So when it was time to go back into the studio, why didn't the band have a meeting and discuss the new direction they should go in for the new album and use Ace's solo album as a starting point? Anyone with ears could hear that not only did he deliver a great album but he delivered a great *rock* album. It seemed like that would be the logical thing to do. Or maybe they felt with the '80s just around the corner, they had to go with a more commercial pop sound. As a fan, I'm just speculating. And maybe Gene and Paul had already talked about this before in interviews that I haven't read or seen.

## DID VINI PONCIA DESTROY OR SAVE KISS?

The story fans have heard for years was Peter threatened to leave the band if they didn't use the producer from his studio album, Vini Poncia. I don't know if I ever bought that. What I mean is they weren't happy about *Kiss Meets the Phantom*, the solo albums weren't financially successful, and at that time, they felt that Peter's solo album was the worst, so why *would* they use his producer? Obviously, they weren't hurting, since they were already the biggest band in the world. But then again, it was around this time that Paul said the band was becoming lazy and unfocussed. Still, if they all felt that Peter's album was the worst, then why would they turn around and use his producer for their upcoming studio release? It doesn't make sense, marketing wise or business wise. I mean, if my objective is to sell records, I'm not going to use a producer who I believe just had a major flop. At least this is how it seems to a fan looking in from the outside. Also, let me add that I don't know anything about Vini's history as a producer. For all I know, he may have produced many successful albums that went platinum. Who knows what really went on behind the scenes during that era? In the end, they made their decision and went with Vini anyway. And even though it wasn't a "balls to the wall" rock album like Ace's solo, I believe Vini delivered a great album.

## THE SONGS

### I WAS MADE FOR LOVIN' YOU

I don't usually listen to "I Was Made for Lovin' You." It doesn't do much for me. I think it's a great disco song, but I usually skip past it if I can help it. The only version I really like of this song is the one on the *Unmasked* tour with Eric Carr. I love watching Eric play drums on that version. It's fast, and they're just jamming to it.

I remember as a kid going roller-skating almost every other weekend, and the highlight of my night would be when the DJ would play it. And if he was taking too long putting it in rotation, I would skate up to his booth and nag him about playing it.

### 2,000 MAN

For most fans that I've spoken to, "2,000 Man" is their favorite song on the album. It's not my favorite, but I like it. My favorite part of this song is the guitar intro.

### SURE KNOW SOMETHING

I remember even as a kid, I thought the guitar on the chorus was too loud. I used to think it would be so much better if they turned it down a little. I must have been right, because that's exactly what they did on the *Smashes, Thrashes, and Hits* version. It sounds so much better that way. It's weird because I love this song and it's great, but again, I usually skip past it. But when I do listen to it, I think it's the shit. I remember the first time I watched *Kiss X-treme Close Up* and saw the video. I thought that part in the video after the lead solo, where their heads are together and in reverse motion, was just the shit! The way Gene stuck out his tongue and how they're just looking at the camera making faces was so mysterious to me.

## DIRTY LIVIN'

As a kid, I didn't like to listen to "Dirty Livin'." It was too dark and depressing to me. It was just something about the lyrics and the sound of the music that seemed angry, like the character was being rejected by society and life. It's very sincere sounding. I used to imagine that Peter was really hurting or in real trouble. I guess I took it too personally because I felt sorry for him while he was singing it. I think it's too bad that this was Peter's last studio song with the band from that era, because as an adult, I believe it's the best song on the album. I love that bass guitar lick that goes throughout the song. The lead guitar solo is tight. The background vocals are great, so is the drumming and the melody. It's definitely one of the top five underrated Kiss songs of all time. I can't stress enough how great this song is.

## CHARISMA

As a kid, this was my favorite song on *Dynasty*. I played it a lot. It's probably a throwaway and a continuation from Gene's solo album. It has the same vibe as "Living in Sin." I can't say why I loved it so much, but there was something about Gene's voice, the chorus, the basic rhythm guitar, the whole song in general that was just great to me! I love the last part of the lead guitar solo. I'd have to think about it, but it's probably his most unique recording on a Kiss studio album since "God of Thunder," not including his solo record.

## MAGIC TOUCH

I would always skip past "Magic Touch." I just didn't like it then and even up until my adult years. It was just slow, and Paul's voice was just too pouty and whining. He would duplicate this singing style a few years later with "Thrills in the Night." It wasn't until Paul's "Live to Win" tour, when I heard him and his band play "Magic Touch" live on YouTube, that I fell in love with it for the first time. They did a great job on it and gave it new meaning and life for me. Now I play the *Dynasty* version all the time.

## HARD TIMES

"Hard Times" has always been my second favorite song on the album. Ace's lead solo—forget about it! If you forgot exactly what it sounds like, go listen to it again. It's so creative and has so much feel to it. Ace always makes you feel what he's playing, and this solo is a perfect example. For me, this song is killing you and healing you with the same knife. He's telling you a serious story about his life and hanging out in the streets, but between the funny sound effects in the background and cartoonish rhythm guitar, it comes off silly. It's tight.

## X-RAY EYES

This has always been my favorite song to sing along to on this album. When I do sing it, I go into serious Gene mode. My eye's bulge out, I stick my bottom lip out, and I start doing Gene's head nodding. And when I actually say the words "X-Ray Eyes," I always cross my eyes and grin at the same time. Gene sings it with so much passion that I can't help but get sucked into it. He wouldn't sing with this much passion again until "Rock and Roll Hell." The lead guitar solo is a little reminiscent of the lead guitar solo on "Ladies in Waiting."

## SAVE YOUR LOVE

This song has always been an album filler to me. It's weak and so is the chorus. But I love it! It's fun to sing along to and mock Ace's voice. I always do the funky bass lines from this song with my mouth when I'm driving or just hanging out. I have comments about the two breakdowns. The first one is on the first breakdown that leads into the guitar solo, that guitar melody always reminded me of Batman and Robin driving really fast in the Batmobile. Seriously, listen to it, it sounds like Batman and

Robin music. The other thing is on the second breakdown, where Aton is getting busy on the drum break. I always hated the way it jumps back into the ending chorus. The transition isn't smooth at all. Ace's voice and lead guitar playing are what make and save this song. Again, I love it!

## ALBUM COVER

It's their third studio album title at that point that begins with the letter D, LOL. *DTK, Destroyer,* and now *Dynasty.* I'm OK with the title *Dynasty* because it represented where the band was at this point in their careers, livin' large! I just think that the Kiss logo and album title don't pop or stick out on the cover. They're just both on top in the corners in plain red. When you think of the word "dynasty," you think of something a little brighter with a pinch of flash.

I don't like the picture on the cover either. It's too boring and basic. Kiss was at a point in their careers where they were bigger than life. They should have gone with something more dangerous or electrifying. Yes, I get that it's one of their signature iconic '70s photos of the band, and we love it because it brings back memories from when we were younger, but it's still way too plain for as big as they were at that time. Paul looks mad, Gene looks cool but constipated, and Ace and Peter just look bored. Also, at that point, they had too many album covers with just their faces: the first album, *RARO, Alive II,* and the solo albums. We know what they look like; we didn't need another plain album cover with just their mugs. I always thought that picture from the *Dynasty* photo shoot where they're wearing the straitjackets would have been a cool album cover and they could have called the record *Asylum.* I also thought that the picture from the poster that came with the album, where their bodies are all in black, would have been the best choice for the album cover. That picture just has a lot of mystique and they look very cool, especially Gene and Paul. That same photo was on the record itself, and I became obsessed with always staring at it as it went around in a circle.

What also bothers me about the cover is for some reason, Ace's lower face seems fat and bloated to me. Also, Peter's green makeup on his right eye is much higher than his green makeup on his left eye. I know it sounds trivial, but that always bothered me. *How could he not have caught that?* I would wonder. I never thought it looked good when Peter would loop his green makeup like that. I thought it looked better when he would wear it smaller, thinner, and more rectangular over his eyes, as he did a few times during the *Love Gun/Alive II* era.

As for the back, again, that photo that was used as the poster where they're all covered in black would have been perfect for the back, if not the front. Song titles on top and credits at the bottom. It's another wasted back cover to a Kiss album.

FAVORITE SONG: "Dirty Livin'"
FAVORITE RHYTHM GUITAR: "Hard Times"
FAVORITE LEAD GUITAR: "Hard Times." But "Save Your Love" is a close second.
FAVORITE BASS: "Save Your Love"
FAVORITE DRUMS: "Hard Times"

THROWAWAY: "Save Your Love." But I love it.

MESSING UP THE LYRICS:

"Dirty Livin'," chorus: "Can't wait in an ogger," whatever an "ogger" is!

"Sure Know Something," second verse intro: "I was Sarah Jean you were."

# Chapter 17

## PETER'S DEPARTURE

In all of my years as a Kiss fan, I've never questioned or gotten upset when a member left or was fired from the band. I always just accepted it and moved on. As a kid, I had the *16 Magazine* with the title "Kiss Cracks Up!" I remember the rumors of Peter leaving but didn't take them seriously. It was just all talk to me. I guess my young mind couldn't see Kiss ever breaking up or not being around. But the first time I saw Eric Carr, on *Kids are People Too*, I didn't panic or even think, "Wait, what happened to Peter?" I just accepted that Kiss had a new drummer and we were moving on. As long as it didn't mean the end of Kiss, I was OK with it. That's not to say that there weren't others, especially older fans, who didn't take issue with his departure.

# Chapter 18

# UNMASKED

I love '70s Kiss albums, but I'm IN LOVE with '80s Kiss albums. My must have '70s albums are *Dressed to Kill*, *Destroyer*, the solo records, and *Dynasty*. If I didn't hear the other '70s albums for the next twenty years, honestly, I could live with that for the most part. Most '70s Kiss albums, like the debut, *HTH*, *RARO*, and *Love Gun*, I don't like as a whole. Each of those albums has about two to four songs that I really like and the rest of the songs on those albums or the overall sound really don't do anything for me. I compare those albums to *Kiss Meets the Phantom* because that movie has a cheesy, corny production and wasn't executed well. Neither were those albums. But for the record, I love *Phantom*! As for *Alive!* and *Alive II*, I love the sound and energy of those albums, but *Alive!* is so redundant to me that over the years, I've grown a little tired of it. The truth is all I need off of *Alive!* are "Got to Choose," "Parasite," "She," "Watchin' You," "100,000 Years," and "Rock Bottom." Those are my go-to songs off that album. Yes, the rest of the album is great, but again, when you've played it as much as I did growing up, it gets old. It's like when you tune in to watch reruns of one of your favorite TV show and they're showing an episode you've seen a million times so you decide to see what else is on. When it comes to *Alive II*, I'm actually more into side 4 of that album than the live versions of sides 1, 2, and 3 themselves. My go-to songs off the live sides are "Ladies Room," "Makin' Love," "Shock Me," and "God of Thunder." The rest I could take or leave. If I've "Got to Choose," I choose *Alive!* over *Alive II*.

The fact of the matter is I'm bored with '70s Kiss music. The sound and productions off of those albums just don't do it for me as much as they used to. As a kid, I played those albums a million times—before I went to school, when I got home, and before I went to bed. Yes, those songs and albums appealed to me as a kid, but as an adult, they're not as motivating or get my blood going. They no longer have the same excitement or appeal, except for the songs off of *Dressed to Kill*, *Destroyer*, solos, and *Dynasty*. Point is, I need and love '80s Kiss music/albums. I don't necessarily need Peter's drumming, but I definitely need Eric Carr's drumming. Out of all of the Kiss lead guitarists, I believe that Ace has the most feel to his playing, but again, the older I get, the more I'm drawn to Vinnie's and Bruce's lead guitar playing. Those '80s albums come alive for me in a way the '70s studio albums don't.

## "I NEED MORE SYNTHESIZER." LOL. I NEVER GET TIRED OF THAT SKETCH.

I have never been one of those Kiss fans who thought that Kiss' music was good only if it had loud guitars and drums. But if it had keyboards, strings, or other effects mixed in, then it wasn't a good song or album. To me, that's bullshit. Either the songs and recordings appeal to me or they don't. I've definitely never been the kind of Kiss fan who felt Kiss was only at their best or musically great when they were in the '70s, with the original band. I don't understand the blind loyalty some fans have to that era of Kiss music. Some of them have a smugness just because they think liking only the original band makes them more of a fan than people who like the '80s or the Tommy and Singer versions. They have the same self-righteous attitude of some of the granola people who drive a Prius instead of a Chevy, or people who drink soy milk instead of two percent. "I'm saving the planet and my body! My shit don't stink."

As a fan, I don't try to convince myself or create the illusions in my head that when they were recording those '70s studio albums, the heavens opened up and shine down on the recording sessions. Or the angels blessed their hands so they could write brilliant masterpieces like "Deuce," "Let Me Go, Rock 'n' Roll," "Ladies Room," "Christine 16," and so on. Some fans who like the '70s sound want to believe that when Kiss was in the studio creating these '70s "masterpieces," they were brothers at arms, totally focused, they hadn't lost their way yet, and they made calculated decisions for each verse and riff, had long, drawn-out discussions about everything they were recording down to the plink of a string and hit of a Pearl Tom, and the planets had lined up for them as musicians and songwriters. In other words, because some fans like '70s Kiss so much, they try to create this magical image in their heads of how they think the creation of these songs and albums came to be. When in reality, or my opinion, Peter was already threatening to leave the band as early as '74, Ace was so drunk most of the time, he probably didn't even know he was at a recording studio—like Paul said, they had to hurry up and record his part before he passed out on the couch. By '77, Gene already had his eye on Hollywood and his focus was out the door. And Paul probably spent most of his time in the studio's bathroom talking to himself in the mirror, repeating the words, "I am worthy, I am somebody!" As a fan, I don't think those '70s songs are magical or the planets had lined up for them. I love those '70s songs, not because I think they're so great but because they represent a period in my life growing up as a die-hard Kiss fan. Personally, I think those songs and albums could have been so much more under the right producers' guidance. Some fans want to believe that if someone else had joined Kiss instead of Ace, it wouldn't have been the same. Or if they had signed to another label instead of Casablanca, they wouldn't have lasted. Or if they had other producers instead of Kramer or Ezrin, then it wouldn't have sounded as good. My point is, if these particular things had been changed, different lead guitar player, different label, different producers, managers, and so on, it might have been the best thing to happen to Kiss. They might have been twice as big as they were in the '70s. Musically, they probably could have blown away radio groups like Boston, Foreigner, and harder bands like Zeppelin. Or these particular changes could've been the worst thing to ever happen to '70s Kiss and ended their careers before they even started. None of us know what could've been. What I'm saying is just because I love '70s Kiss music doesn't mean I'm musically stuck in only '70s Kiss music or have gone ear blind.

I've never understood Kiss fan's prejudices against '80s albums. I don't get this idea that songs like "Love 'em and Leave 'em" and "100,000 Years" are so genius, but songs like "Love's a Deadly Weapon" and "I've Had Enough (Into the Fire)" are just stupid '80s songs. I don't get that calculation. As a die-hard, I feel there's no such thing as a bad Kiss album. There are just some albums I like more than others, and there are some songs, sounds, and eras I like more than others. That's it. But just because I don't care for a particular Kiss album doesn't mean I think it's a bad album. I don't care for *Sonic Boom* but there are a lot of fans who love it, and good for them if that's the sound they like. I said earlier that I'm not a big fan of the *RARO* and *Love Gun* albums, but sometimes I'll take those two albums and play them every day for two weeks straight, because at that time, I'll be in the mood for the Eddie Kramer sound. The truth is I would be bored of Kiss' music if every album was a hard rock album. I love the idea that Kiss' music has all of these different flavors and sounds. I love hearing their voices on different styles of music. One minute, Paul is singing "What Makes the World Go 'Round" then "Odyssey," and then turns around and sings "Danger." One minute, Gene is singing "See You Tonite" then "Mr. Blackwell," then turns around and sings something like "Dance All Over Your Face" or "Boomerang." The point is, I love all of those different colors and flavors in Kiss' music. I wouldn't have it any other way. But at the end of the day, my loyalty is to '80s Kiss albums.

## MOVING ON TO *UNMASKED*

The first time that I would learn of *Unmasked*'s existence was around 1981. I was at a mom and pop store buying candy when I came across this square packet of bubble gum. It had the Kiss *Unmasked* album cover on the front. Of course, at that time, I didn't know that it was supposed to be the cover of a Kiss record. I just thought it was a strange looking pack of gum with cartoonish images of Kiss. I bought the gum, chewed the whole pack, put it behind me, and didn't think of it again until a year later.

## SIDE 1: SHANDI

## SIDE 2: SHE'S SO EUROPEAN

Around '82, I went to visit my favorite used record store, Robert Joe's. I just so happened to be looking through the singles selection and came across a record that said Kiss on it. It had two songs on there that I had never even heard of, "Shandi" on side 1 and "She's So European" on side 2. I bought the record and couldn't wait to get it home to listen to it. When I put it on the turntable and turned it up, I immediately knew something wasn't right. "Shandi" was playing and I remember actually thinking to myself, *It sounds like Paul's voice but this doesn't sound like Kiss at all.* When the song ended, I flipped the small record over and played the other foreign song I had never heard, "She's So European." Again, I was stuck; I said to myself, *This can't be Kiss.* I thought that maybe somehow the company put the Kiss label on the wrong record. This had to be some other group. It kinda sounded like Kiss, but it couldn't be. Not that I thought the songs were bad, they were just weird. I was confused!

I went outside to find Mark to tell him about this weird discovery. When I finally found him hanging out with his buddies on the corner, I told him, "I bought a small Kiss record with two songs on it, and even though it says Kiss, I don't think it's them."

After he listened to it, he became just as confused as I was. Now we both didn't know what to make of or do with the little record with these two supposed Kiss songs on it.

## THE MYSTERY IS SOLVED!

A few months later, I went to the downtown JCPenney's with my two sisters. As usual, I had to check out the music department to see what Kiss records were in stock. While flipping through them, I came across a Kiss album that I had never seen before. It was titled *Unmasked*! The words that came out of my mouth were "Whoooooaaaaa, what the?" It was actually a Kiss album cover with comic book pictures. Immediately, I thought back to the pack of gum I had bought with the same *Unmasked* image on it.

*So that's where the picture of that pack of gum comes from*, I thought. I also read the song titles on the back and saw the titles "Shandi" and "She's So European." *So this is where those songs come from*, I again thought. The record was $8.00. I was a couple of dollars short, so I ran to my sister Michelle, showed her the record, and begged her for the $2.00. Knowing my love for Kiss, she just smiled at me and said "Maybe." She wanted to give me the money, but I had been a bad smartass all day, and she told me if I behaved while we were in the store, she would give me the money.

From then on, I was on my best behavior, dotting all my Is and crossing all of my Ts. Even though I hadn't paid for the record yet, I held onto it like it was mine and I had the receipt in my hand. I had never even seen or heard of such a Kiss record with comic book pictures on the cover. It was so fascinating to me. Trust me, if I had to run out of that store with that record in my hands because of lack of funds, I would have. In the name of Kiss! Also because, to me, it was the only copy of *Unmasked* that existed in the whole world, the label only released one copy, and I was holding it in my hands.

## MOVING ON

For the rest of our time there, my sister Michelle kept fuckin' with me about giving me the money. Every time I would do the smallest thing to upset her, even when I didn't know I was doing it, she would threaten me by saying, "Put the record back, you're not getting it!" Of course, I would just grip the record tighter and say, "OK, I'm sorry!" I really wasn't doing anything wrong, she was just having fun with me. I love my sis.

After a while, I decided that I needed a little insurance. You know the old saying "You break it, you bought it?" I decided to rip off the protective plastic. I don't know if they would have made me buy it because of that, but it was the best plan I could come up with. After I did that, I peeked inside the jacket and saw a thick piece of paper inside. I couldn't believe when I pulled it out that it was a big foldout poster. I opened it up and laid the big Kiss poster out right there in the middle of the aisle floor. I stared at it in amazement as if it was the map to the Ark of the Covenant. It was great! A big cartoon poster with Kiss, each member holding a mask of his own face. To my young eyes, it was beautiful. I wanted people who walked by to notice how great this big Kiss poster was, too, so when they passed by, I would say excitedly "Look at my new Kiss poster!" A few women gave me courtesy smiles, but most of the men looked at me like I was just some stupid kid. "Was I the only one here at JCPenney's who could recognize how amazing this Kiss poster was?!

As my sisters were wrapping things up, Michelle was really mad at me for opening the album so that now she felt like she really had to give me the $2.00, but now she wasn't going to take me to McDonald's for being sneaky. Fuck McDonald's, I just got a new Kiss record, and its name is *Unmasked*!

## I STILL SAY THEY STINK?

A few days later, I took the *Unmasked* album to school for third grade show and tell. I proudly showed all of my classmates the new Kiss album. I read off the album title, the song titles, and finally, importantly, I read off the cartoon captions like I was reading a book for the class. Nobody, including my teacher, seemed to care until I got to the part that said, "I still say they stink!" That got everybody's attention. That's when everybody started laughing and smiling. Then all of my classmates wanted to see the record, so I let them pass it around the classroom. At that time, I thought they were sharing my love for Kiss with me by wanting to see the record. However, it turned out that they couldn't care less about the Kiss album or the songs, they just wanted to actually see the words "I still say they stink!" on the cover so they could mock Kiss and me as well.

As the weeks went by, it turned out that bringing *Unmasked* to school had been a bad idea. At recess, kids were coming up to me and saying, "Hey, Anthony, I still say they stink!" Then one time, when I came back from a bathroom break, someone had written on my notebook, "I still say they stink!" It just didn't stop. I would have to whip a few asses out of frustration and to protect the Kiss honor, but boy was I ripped on by my schoolmates. Here I am, every day in school, trying to convince these kids that not only is Kiss the greatest band in the world but that they're the greatest thing in the world. And what does Kiss do to validate my point? They put in writing on their own album cover, "I still say they stink"!

## YES, I LOVE *UNMASKED*

It seems like whenever Kiss wants to go into a different direction musically, they always do a great job in execution. *Unmasked* is a great pop album from beginning to end. Whether you like the album or not, or think Kiss was stupid for making this type of music with no hard rock edge or backbone, it's still a very good, excellently produced Kiss pop record. I love to listen to it. There's not one bad song on this album. I know there are fans who love to trash this album, especially older fans, but I was a kid when this album came out, so as a kid, as long as it had Kiss' faces on the cover, it was all good to me. I appreciated and loved it. There are some Kiss fans who don't seem to know the difference between something being bad and not personally liking something. Sometimes I'm guilty of that myself. Just because certain fans don't like *Unmasked* doesn't mean it's a bad album. It just means it's not what you want in a Kiss album. But again, songwriting and production wise, this is a great pop album. One of the things I really love about this album is Anton's drumming. I believe his drumming played a major part in this album being as good as it is.

## THE SONGS

## IS THAT YOU?

I was so surprised when I found out a few years ago that Kiss covered "Is That You?" and it wasn't a Kiss song. I also like the original. I love everything about this song, especially the breakdown and the way Paul's voice sounds with the drumming. I never get tired of hearing it.

## SHANDI

The sound of the guitars is really unique and one of the reasons I appreciate this song so much. Why this song isn't featured on *Smashes* is beyond me.

I remember a sista I was dating back in '90 came over to my house and I was playing the *Unmasked* tape. "Shandi" was on, and she instantly fell in love with the song. She went out, bought her own tape, and played it nonstop.

## TALK TO ME

I think Ace's songs are the most dominant on this album, and "Talk to Me" is one of the reasons why. It's an underrated Ace song. I love Anton's drumming on this song. I wish Kiss cover bands would do this more.

## NAKED CITY

I love singing and imitating Gene's voice on "Naked City." I love the lead guitar on the outro of the song.

## WHAT MAKES THE WORLD GO 'ROUND

My favorite song on the album. I love singing along to the chorus. I also love the guitar solo.

## TOMORROW

I think "Tomorrow" could easily be played on '80s retro radio stations. The chorus just feels good. I love the way the lead guitar sounds on the solo.

## TWO SIDES OF THE COIN

Another awesome Ace song.

## SHE'S SO EUROPEAN

Another song on this album I love to sing along to. This song always makes me think of not the demon, but the business side of Gene. Or his international side. Or at least the international side he portrays.

## EASY AS IT SEEMS

I would usually skip past it. But one day ten years ago, while I was playing *Unmasked* at work, "Easy as It Seems" came on, and my boss rushed in and said he really liked the song that was playing and asked who the band was. Long story short, for the rest of my time there, he would come in my area at least three times a week and ask me to play it for him. I thought it was all right, but I never thought it was all that great, so I found it weird that he liked it so much.

## TORPEDO GIRL

"Torpedo Girl" was probably the song I played the most from this album as a kid. The funky drums and bass line intro sucked me in. As a teen, I even sampled it for one of my rap songs. I remember my producer at the time had a hard time making a beat to match the beat Anton was playing. However, he finally did, and the song came out tight.

## YOU'RE ALL THAT I WANT

I love it. But I kind of think it would have been better if they went with the demo version that appears on the box set. Just tighten it up a little bit more. I play the demo version all the time.

## ALBUM COVER

I don't have a problem with the comic book cover. I think it's unique. If I had the final say on it, would I have done it that way? No! What I would have done is kept the title *Unmasked* and the picture that appears at the bottom of the cover of them holding their masks; I would have made that picture the whole album cover.

I think it's like what Paul said about *Creatures of the Night*, "Sometimes people listen with their eyes." I believe if they had made the album cover more edgy, older fans today would consider the songs more. Even if the songs are a little light in the ass. Or maybe not. But the bottom line is with Kiss making a pop album coming off of a "disco album," there was bound to be consequences for both of these albums, short and long term.

FAVORITE SONG: "What Makes the World Go 'Round"
FAVORITE RHYTHM GUITAR: "Torpedo Girl"
FAVORITE LEAD GUITAR: "Tomorrow"
FAVORITE BASS: "Two Sides of the Coin"
FAVORITE DRUMS: "Torpedo Girl"

THROWAWAY: "Easy as it Seems"

MESSING UP THE LYRICS:

"Two Sides of the Coin," end of second verse: "Cause they expire, all of Space Ace, all of Space Ace!"

# Chapter 19

# THE ELDER

One night in 1981, Mark and I went with my mom to the Pay 'N' Save store to purchase some items. Out of the blue, my mom told us that she would buy us both a record. It was out of character for my mom to just volunteer to buy us records, but on that night, she was being very generous. Mark and I looked at each other and grinned, then hauled ass to the record department. Instead of following me to where the Kiss records were, Mark had something else in mind. He went to where the Journey records were and immediately pulled out Journey *Escape*. It was a hot record at that time. Every time "Don't Stop Believing" came on the radio, Mark would always make a big deal about the drumming and the ride cymbal on the song. It didn't really do anything for me. I will admit that after a while, I did start to like the song "Stone in Love."

While Mark was excited to have the Journey *Escape* album in his possession, I was still flipping through Kiss records. There were two rows of Kiss records, and when I got to the first album in the second row, I saw that there was a strange record with a hand on it. Obviously, it wasn't a Kiss record. I pulled the record out to put it aside, and that's when I realized that it had the Kiss logo on it. I looked a little closer and realized it actually was a Kiss record, one I hadn't seen before. The cover was a weird brownish color. I wasn't excited or anxious about it at all, as I usually was when I saw a Kiss record that I had never seen before. My attitude about this strange Kiss album was more "What's this all about?"

I showed it to Mark and he seemed just as puzzled about it as I was. We were both in the middle of the store staring at this supposed Kiss album with confused looks on our faces. As weird as the cover was, it didn't matter because it had the Kiss logo on it, and that made it OK.

## FIRST LISTEN

I put the needle on the record, and when the intro of "The Oath" came on, I got excited. Then when Paul began to sing, I was hooked. I continued to listen to "Just a Boy," "Dark Light," "Only You," etc. I sat in my room and completed the album from beginning to end. And when the album was finished, I had to say I loved it! I thought it was great! I have to admit that even I'm surprised that a year later, while listening to the singles "Shandi" and "She's So European," I thought those two songs were more odd and strange Kiss songs for me. But as for *The Elder*, I didn't have a problem with it whatsoever. I think the reason that I didn't have a problem with *The Elder* at that young age of seven was because to me those *Elder* songs were just a continuation of songs like "Great Expectations," "Beth," and Gene's solo album. I'd already heard Kiss songs with big productions and strings, piano, horns, etc., and I loved those songs. So it wasn't as if *The Elder* was some kind of strange shocker for me. What I didn't do at that time and age was read into it as a concept album or a bunch of songs that were telling a story. Honestly, it was just another Kiss album to me. This was also the first album that Mark and I got on track with their releases.

## WHAT I DON'T LIKE ABOUT *THE ELDER*

The majority of the songs on the album musically have no real depth to me. What I mean is if you listen to the instrumentation, production, and arrangements on songs like "Great Expectations," "Man of 1,000 Faces," and "Beth," they all have a lot of depth and sounds going through them. This album all around doesn't. The only songs with depth to them on *The Elder* would probably be "Just a Boy" and "Odyssey." The rest don't have it. Also, like Paul's '78 solo album, the recording and mix down of *The Elder* also sounds a little muffled, flat/dull, and needs to be brighter.

## THEIR NEW OUTFITS WERE COOL!

When *The Elder* look came out, I really didn't have a problem with it. Yes, their hair was shorter and they weren't wearing the big outfits or high heels anymore. But I didn't question it. I actually thought it was cool, especially Paul's look with the purple scarf wrapped around his head. I also thought Paul's outfit looked a lot like the three villains' outfits from my favorite super hero movie *Superman II*, the original. I also remember liking Eric's zipper outfit and wanting one of my own so I could wear it to school. In my mind, I actually saw myself walking into school wearing it and being surrounded by all my classmates, who were in awe of all the cool zippers I was wearing. I did like the version of Gene's outfit with the chain silver pants. But those pants always looked like they were heavy, and hard to wear or walk in.

## I'LL DIE FOR *THE ELDER*?

I took *The Elder* to show and tell about a week after buying it. I remember thinking that because *The Elder* was such a serious looking album, I needed to be serious when showing it to the class. I acted more like an art dealer showing a new sculpture or painting than a second grader showing a new Kiss album. First, I presented the cover, then the title. I opened it up and displayed the picture inside the middle; in a serious tone, I named off the songs on the back and talked about which ones were my favorite. Then when I was done talking about the album, I pulled out the latest *16 Magazine* with Kiss wearing *The Elder* look and talked about their hair being shorter, their new outfits, and to use my exact words, "Now Kiss has smaller boots." I was a complete professional when presenting *The Elder* to my class. Afterward, the most amazing thing happened. My classmate Bryan raised his hand anxiously and asked, "Can we listen to it?" Then all of the other kids started saying, "Yeah, let's listen to it, let us hear it." It wasn't the response I was expecting at all. My teacher, Mrs. Paige, said we couldn't listen to it that day but we could make some extra time to listen to it the next day during our special projects hour.

When the next day came and Mrs. Paige put *The Elder* on for the class, I felt like I had accomplished something big, like a protester who finally had his day to be heard. I had talked about how great Kiss was at school all the time, but now, they were going to get to hear it for themselves. My attitude was "Yes, Kiss does have songs other than 'Rock and Roll All Nite'!" All the kids sat quietly and listened while each song played. I spoke a little during each song and talked about which member was singing and what the song was about. My classmates just worked on their projects and listened quietly. They could have easily been talking to each other and carrying on, but they weren't. They were actually attentive to *The Elder*. During the listening, someone would ask me a question about the band or the makeup. Like a professor, I was happy to help and answer all of their questions.

By the time the record got to "Mr. Blackwell," Murphy's Law set in. Alaska is known for its almost monthly earthquakes. We had earthquake drills all the time in school. Every time there was an earthquake, the entire state would wonder if it was going to be the big one, like in 1964 when the whole city and state were practically destroyed. So while Gene was telling Mr. Blackwell to "Go to hell," the classroom began shaking violently! Like we were taught in drill, all the kids quickly hid under their desks—all the kids except one, the only black Kiss fanatic in Alaska. I ran toward the cheap record player, quickly pulled my *Elder* record off it, grabbed the album cover, and *then* ran under my desk.

I will never forget it as long as I live; while the whole room was shaking violently and everybody was hiding under their desks screaming, my teacher was hiding under her desk and giving me a stare that would cut through glass. Her eyes said, "Nigga, have you lost your mind?" Because I sacrificed my life for *The Elder*, I got in trouble and was given extra homework assignments.

## 16 MAGAZINE

From what I remember, no other magazine promoted *The Elder* era like *16 Magazine* did. I was always at the bookstore at the nearby mall trying to get a copy of the latest issue so I could admire Kiss and *The Elder* look.

One of my favorite photos was where Gene and Paul are standing next to each other with a reddish background. I believe Gene's arms were folded. Another *Elder* photo I like is of Ace and his black Les Paul at his waist. I think it was the black Les Paul. Maybe it was the red. But I bought every *16 Magazine* with those *Elder* photos in them.

I thought it was so cool when the *16 Magazine* editors would put fan letters in the magazine. The fans would say how great Kiss was and how much they loved the new drummer, Eric Carr, etc. I would think how kids in Alaska didn't appreciate Kiss, but those kids in *16 Magazine* did. I believe *The Elder* was the last era of Kiss that *16 Magazine* really highlighted. By the time *Creatures* came around, Kiss' pictures became smaller and their stories were reduced to short articles. Obviously, Kiss wasn't a hot item to put into the magazine anymore. I remember a few full-page color photos of Kiss during the *Lick It Up* era. Maybe the magazine was trying to cash in on the Kiss without makeup hype. I could be wrong, but I barely recall seeing Kiss on the cover of *16 Magazine* during the *Creatures* or *Lick It Up* eras.

## FRIDAYS

I remember the night Kiss was to perform on the comedy show *Fridays*. It was the same night my best friend at that time, John Stanley, was having his birthday slumber party. Yes, I wanted to go to the slumber party, but no way in hell was I gonna miss a Kiss performance on TV. At school earlier that day, I asked John if he was sure his mother was going to let me watch Kiss on *Fridays* at their house, and he said yes. I didn't feel too reassured because it was a slow yes. "You sure you asked your mom?" I asked again. Annoyed, he replied, "Yeah, she said you can watch it!" I wasn't satisfied, so when I got home after school, I asked my mom to call his mom and explain how important it was for me to see Kiss on TV that night. My mom said that she would call her for me. When it was time for me to go over there, I asked my mom if she had called John's mom yet, and with a "get out of my face" tone, she assured me she had.

While at John's house, all the other kids, including Mark, were playing and roughhousing, I joined in, but at the same time, all I could think about was seeing Kiss on TV. Mark had asked me a couple of times if John's mom was going to let us watch *Fridays*, and all I could do was shrug my shoulders. I didn't know John's mother at all. John and I were best friends at school, but this was the first time I had been to his house and met his family. I decided that I had to confront this situation because if I didn't, it could mean that I would miss Kiss on TV. I gathered up all the courage I had, went upstairs, and asked his mom, "Did my mom call you?" She looked at me, smiled, and said "No." I blurted out, "Well, Kiss is coming on TV tonight, and I want to watch it." She gave me a confused look and said, "Well, we're not watching Kiss tonight, OK. Now go play with the other kids." My feelings were so hurt and I felt so betrayed by my mom and John. They both lied to me when they knew how much I wanted to see Kiss on *Fridays*!

I didn't want to be there anymore. I had to get out of there. My plan was to slowly and quietly put my winter gear on and when nobody was paying attention, bolt out of the front door as fast as I could. I even had the route picked out in my mind that I was going to take so they couldn't track me down. It was through a dark wooded area that I hated being in, especially in the dark cold Alaskan night, but for Kiss, I would do it! It was about three miles to my house in the snow, but I knew I could make it. I had been lied to about Kiss, so I knew that my anger and frustration would motivate me and guide me home. While the other kids were still playing, I was preparing myself for the great escape. I was so ready that I don't even think I blinked while waiting. What's funny is I didn't even know what time *Fridays* came on or if I would miss it by the time I got home. I just knew it was coming on that night.

A considerable amount of time had passed, and when I was about to make my move to my winter gear and out the front door, Mark came running downstairs and said, "Anthony, his mom is watching *Fridays* upstairs!" A look of excitement came over my face and a bolt of joy went through my body. As I ran up the stairs, Mark was telling all the other kids to come upstairs to watch Kiss. We all sat on the living room floor watching the magic that was Kiss. It was so awesome for me to watch Kiss in their *Elder* outfits performing *Elder* songs on national TV. I was ecstatic throughout the whole episode. I especially loved the end, when Kiss and the cast were saying good-bye to the camera and audience; it was a funny silly side of Kiss that I rarely got to see as a kid. When it was all over and all of us kids went back downstairs, Mark and I pulled out *The Elder* album to play the songs that Kiss had just played on the show so the other kids could hear what the songs sounded like on the album. For some odd reason, Mark and I always felt like it was our job to educate other kids about the things of Kiss. But *Fridays* will always be a significant Kiss TV appearance for me.

## THE SONGS

By the way, I hate the way *The Elder* songs are rearranged on the remasters. To me, the songs don't flow right.

## THE OATH

To me "The Oath" is a much-underrated Kiss song. It's special. It always makes me feel good when I hear it. To this day, I've never read the lyrics to "The Oath," but I love singing along to it. I'm always doing Eric's drumming on that song with my mouth. Because they wanted to put *The Elder* behind them after its failure, of course, they weren't going to play any of those songs live anytime soon afterward. When Kiss was doing those long sets on the *Hot in the Shade* tour, it would have been great if they had added "The Oath" onto the set list. The only time I heard "The Oath" live was when a Kiss tribute band performed it at the Hard Rock Cafe during a Kiss tribute band contest.

## JUST A BOY

I remember instantly liking this song the first time I heard it. I've always liked the fanfare at the beginning. Concept or not, it's just an awesome Kiss song! I don't think I've ever described a guitar solo as beautiful, but it is. It should easily be on a greatest hits. I always thought that it would have been a good song for the *Lion King* movie.

## DARK LIGHT

"Dark Light" feels to me like "Hard Times." I'm not saying it sounds like "Hard Times," it just has that same type of comical feel to me. Maybe it has something to do with Ace's voice and the way he is speaking in between singing. I love the way his voice sounds on the chorus. It's not my favorite Ace lead guitar solo, but it's off the chain. It has a lot of feel to it. I think it's cool how out of the three sister albums, *Dynasty, Unmasked,* and *The Elder,* it's the third album where an Ace song comes before a Gene song.

## ONLY YOU

It doesn't really do anything for me but I like it. I also like the heavy rhythm guitar that ends the song.

## UNDER THE ROSE

As a kid, I would usually skip past "Under the Rose." As an adult, I love it and listen to it more. I don't know why, but as a kid, I thought it was Eric Carr singing on the chorus in that monstrous voice. I also thought he was singing that way because he was the new guy and was trying to impress Gene, Paul, and Ace. The lead guitar solo is tight!

## A WORLD WITHOUT HEROES

To this day, I still skip past "A World Without Heroes." It's nothing personal against the song, I just don't care to listen to it.

## MR. BLACKWELL

"Mr. Blackwell" was my favorite song on the album as a kid. I loved the way Gene's voice sounded on this song. In the early '90s, my rap group sampled the music in the breakdown of this song and used it for the intro to one of our songs. It was background noise for a robbery scene.

## ESCAPE FROM THE ISLAND

As a kid, the first time I heard Ace making those scratching noises or whatever he's doing with his guitar throughout this song, it was love at first listen. I played this song a million times back in the day. Ace is so creative. My favorite thing now about "Escape from the Island" is the bass guitar in the background. Having it on record and tape for so many years, I had never heard it clearly until I bought *The Elder* on CD. On CD, you can hear the bass line clearer, and it's just funky as hell.

## ODYSSEY

Like so many other Kiss fans, I was surprised when I found out a few years ago that Kiss covered "Odyssey" from the artist Tony Powers. I think the original sounds horrible, but I still love to listen to it. I even have it saved to my favorites. The Kiss version is much better. I think it's the best song on the album, and from the time I was a kid till now, I love to sing along to it. Of course, I had to make up my own lyrics, because who can understand what Paul is saying on that song? I always thought that it would have been a great song for the *Titanic* soundtrack. Instead of "Odyssey," it would have been called "We Met Along the Way" because of the two lovers meeting on the boat.

## I

As a kid, I thought "I" was great and played it a lot. Now as an adult, I still play it, but now it sounds so damned corny to me. Still, I wouldn't mind Kiss surprising the audience and playing it on the next tour just to do something different. I love it when, after the breakdown, the music gets mellow and that funky ass bass line is playing. I always thought that "Fractured Mirror" would have been a great way to end the album if, of course, it wasn't already on Ace's album.

## ALBUM COVER

I never really cared for the album cover. Not that I think it's a bad picture. There were just so many directions that they could have taken it in. For me, it just didn't capture the experience of the *Odyssey* quest they were going for. The door always reminded me of the kind of wooden doors I would see inside apartment buildings that were built in Alaska in the '50s. The knocker had no kind of authority to it. It was plain with a rose at the bottom. The table in the middle of the jacket looked like our dining room table that we used to have at our old house. We also had the tall wooden chairs. The album jacket could have been so much more. I don't think the concept of the door and knocker was bad, but the execution was. Shouldn't the door be bigger and have more authority? And why would it have such a tiny little knocker?

## "A WORLD WITHOUT HEROES" VIDEO

I'll never forget the day our big brother, Andrew, told Mark and I that he saw the new Kiss video and said, "At the end of the video, Gene cries." Of course Mark and I were in disbelief. No way does Gene cry! I tried to actually imagine Gene crying in a video, and all I saw in my mind was Gene being really pouty with tears rolling down his face. The image didn't make much sense to me, so I just rejected what Andrew was saying. Mark asked him what song they were singing, and Andrew, not really knowing Kiss' music, said "Gene was singing a slow song." At that time, I wasn't even thinking of any songs off *The Elder*. Bottom line is it just didn't seem possible or even realistic that Gene would be singing a slow song and crying in a music video at the same time. Andrew was wrong! Imagine my surprise when I found out he was actually right!

FAVORITE SONG: "Odyssey"
FAVORITE RHYTHM GUITAR: "The Oath"
FAVORITE LEAD GUITAR: "Under the Rose"
FAVORITE BASS: "Escape from the Island"
FAVORITE DRUMS: "The Oath"

THROWAWAY: "Mr. Blackwell," but I love it!

MESSING UP THE LYRICS:

"The Oath," first verse: "Like a plane I have saw on these broad wings way, fire is hot! Temporarily I am frightened till the night I'm there, acid hot!"

The chorus: "You're birthin', I swear a world on you, the hour, I trust and want your shoes, the servin', I hey, hey bumper share air Paul Stanley!"

I would actually sing it passionately this way.

# Chapter 20

# KILLERS

Mark and I found this tape while browsing at a record store in the late '80s. At that time, we didn't know of its existence. We didn't think anything odd or special about it, it was just a greatest hits package with an *Elder* image and four new additional songs. So for the sake of owning those four new songs, we bought the tape.

To this day, I have no memory of our first listen or how we initially felt about the four added songs. I guess at that time, it couldn't have made that much of an impression. I'm sure if Paul made a solo album during this time, this is what the songs would've sounded like. Instead, they ended up on a greatest hits package.

In the end, *Killers* isn't a bad album that you try to explain, defend, dissect, or turn other rock fans on to. It is what it is; a throwaway greatest hits album that only a Kiss fan could appreciate.

## THE SONGS

### I'M A LEGEND TONIGHT

I always thought because of the beat of this song that it could have been used in the movie *Flashdance*. It has that early '80s dance pop sound to it. The title and chorus are really stupid. But I love singing along to it.

## DOWN ON YOUR KNEES

I love it! Another great song to sing along to.

## NOWHERE TO RUN

This would have been a great song for *The Elder*. The chorus to this and "Under the Rose" sound similar. They could have kept everything else but changed the lyrics and made it about the boy trying to get away from the dark powers that be, "Nowhere to Run"! But I like this song. I especially like the breakdown where Paul is singing in a soft tone with the acoustic guitar behind him.

To me, part of this song was a rip-off of the Supremes song "Back In My Arms Again." It even has the same lyrics in some spots. One day, someone on a Kiss Facebook fan page asked if anyone else noticed the strong comparison to the Supremes song. I always thought I was the only Kiss fan who noticed the plagiarism.

## PARTNERS IN CRIME

WE HAVE A WINNER! Definitely my favorite of the four. There's something about the rhythm guitar, drums, and the slow groove on this song that just sucks me into it. Bob's lead guitar playing on this track is tight.

## ALBUM COVER

Trying to use an *Elder* era picture for the cover probably wasn't such a smart idea, considering all the controversy that surrounded that album and the look. Something edgier would have been better. Especially for album sales. Like all *Elder* pictures, I like that picture a lot. I even have a big poster of it. Now that I think about it, it would have been cool if you opened up the double jacket on *The Elder* album and that picture was inside of it. Or even the cover for that matter.

FAVORITE SONG: "Partners in Crime"
FAVORITE RHYTHM GUITAR: "Partners in Crime"
FAVORITE LEAD GUITAR: "Nowhere to Run"
FAVORITE BASS GUITAR: "I'm a Legend Tonight"
FAVORITE DRUMS: "Down On Your Knees"

THROWAWAY: "I'm a Legend Tonight"

# Chapter 21

## ACE'S DEPARTURE

Again, the perspective I had with Peter leaving/fired from the band was the same one I had when Ace left. I didn't know that Ace had even left the band. I just happened to be looking in a rock magazine one day, and there was Vinnie. Again, I accepted it and moved on.

## Chapter 22

# CREATURES OF THE NIGHT

It was a couple of days before Mark's eleventh birthday, and we had been arguing and fighting a lot. I remember on this day being really mad at him for something he said to me, and not even wanting to be in the same room with him or the same house, for that matter. I stayed in my room that evening, played some Kiss records, and enjoyed my time alone. A couple of hours later, I heard some loud talking and heavy rock coming from Mark's room. I was curious as to what all the commotion was about. When I peeked out my door, I saw that Mark's bedroom door was open. The heavy rock music was now even louder. I saw that his best friend, Kalonji, was in the room with him. Mark looked at me with a big smile and said, "Look, Anthony, Kalonji bought me the new Kiss tape for my birthday!" That was the first time that I ever saw or heard of *Creatures of the Night*. Mark as well.

That dark cassette cover of Kiss looked so badass as he was holding it up for me to see. "Come in and listen to it," he said. Mark was extending his hand of healing and letting go of the argument. At that moment, I was stuck. Everything in me wanted to run in his bedroom and give the new Kiss tape a big hug. Yes, I wanted to hear it so bad. But I was still mad at Mark. Do I let my anger at Mark deter me from hearing the great new Kiss music? Or do I forgive, forget, and embrace my brother's unspoken apology? I decided to do the right thing and said to myself, *Fuck him; I'm not going in there.* I just mumbled some words to him and walked back into my room.

Boy, I was so jealous. I could hear the new Kiss music blasting away through the walls. It sounded so badass and energized. I remember hearing the lead guitar solo to "Danger" through the walls, and it was amazing. I could hear Kalonji and Mark carrying on. They were in his room laughing and talking about how cool the new Kiss tape was. I wanted to participate so badly. But even at that young age, my pride got the best of me. I just played my *Alive!* album and stayed in my room for the rest of the night. That was our introduction to *Creatures*.

## KISS VS. GARFIELD, TONIGHT ONLY!

In the third grade, during the *Creatures* era, there was a kid in my class named Arnold who was a big Garfield fan and had a lot of *Garfield* comics and merchandise. We got into a fight in class because he said that Garfield was better than Kiss. Why we were comparing Garfield and Kiss at that time, I don't know. The teacher broke us up, put us in the hallway, and gave us "listen" and "talk" cards. Whoever was talking held the "talk" card, and whoever was listening held the "listen" card. The teacher told us that we each had to say something nice about what the other one liked. I said that I liked reading *Garfield* comic books and thought that they were funny. He said that he liked the song "Shout It Out Loud." The teacher left us alone in the hallway to continue our pleasant conversation, and that's when Arnold said, "Kiss is stupid; all they do is yell and scream in their songs." I just blew up! I lunged at him and began punching him. He fought back. I had to admit I underestimated him a little. Like me, he could fight. Throwing punches, we crashed through the door of a fourth-grade classroom. The teacher from that class was trying to pull us apart but was struggling. Finally, a male teacher from another class came in and broke us up. We were sent to the principal's office, where Arnold and I both sat in our chairs breathing heavily as if we just went twelve rounds in a heavyweight fight. Then the principal came in and started drilling us about what happened and why were we arguing about something as stupid as Kiss and Garfield. Both Arnold and I noticed that the principal had a big booger in his nose. We were both doing our best not to look at it and holding in our laughter, but we just couldn't help it; after a while we burst out laughing. The principal had no clue why we were laughing, and no matter how many times he asked what was so funny, we couldn't tell him. He thought that we were just being little smartasses. But we just couldn't stop laughing.

As punishment, we had to pick up trash around the school building and parking lot for a week, and in that time, Arnold and I actually became friends. He even loaned me some of his *Garfield* comics, and I loaned him two Kiss albums and told him to just listen and see if he liked them. He liked *Destroyer* a lot.

## MICHAEL

The Michael James Jackson era is definitely my favorite sound for Kiss. It was heavier but still basic rock, and Kiss wasn't drifting too far off with that sound. It was still Kiss, just with more balls. Though I love the '80s albums as they are, at the same time, I wish they had finished the '80s with Michael James Jackson.

## I LOVE IT, BUT...

Yes, *Creatures* is an awesome album. And in my opinion, it's the second best studio Kiss album after *Destroyer*. Of course, I'm not saying it's my second favorite or that *Destroyer* is my first at all. Yes, it has a heavier balls to the walls sound, and yes, I love *Creatures of the Night*, but at the same time, when I listen to it, I can't help but feel that it reeks of effort. Kiss trying too hard to do the metal thing. That might be the minor issue that turns me off a little about this album. And even though I know it sounds great and exciting, in my heart, I never looked at Kiss as a metal band. They have and always will be a rock band to me. Still, to contradict myself once again, *Creatures* and *Lick It Up* have a style and formula I wish they would have stuck with throughout the '80s. But just as they were successful at executing a pop album a few years earlier, they were also successful at making a metal album.

## THE SONGS

## CREATURES OF THE NIGHT

I usually skip past it; it doesn't do anything for me. To me it kind of reeks of effort, as if Paul is trying too hard to be dangerous and talks about the darkness of the night. It's like, "OK, Paul, you're so dangerous now; I'm totally convinced." Some bad boy rock singers can pull that off, but I just don't believe Paul can convincingly. I can still hear the sensitivity in his voice. That's just how I hear the song.

## SAINT AND SINNER

This has always been my favorite song on the album. I love it. But I don't believe it belongs on the album. It's like at first, you're jamming to "Creatures of the Night," which is up-tempo and in your face heavy rock, then everything slows down when "Saint and Sinner" comes on. And Gene's singing is so lah-di-dah. After *Creatures* should have been another hard-hitting song Like "Keep Me Comin'" or a heavy Gene song to keep the party going. But the point to me is this song always seems out of place and simple as hell. As a producer, I wouldn't have put it on this comeback heavy metal album for Kiss.

Again, it's my favorite song on the album. I love the drumming and the way Eric is hitting the ride cymbal. I also love Gene's voice and the background vocals that go "Whooaaaahh uh ooohh." It sounds great when Gene hits those high notes "Oooww!" The lead guitar solo has so much feel to it. I always listen to the solo twice every time I play it because I love it.

## KEEP ME COMIN'

I remember loving the intro rhythm guitar as a kid. It might just be the baddest rhythm guitar on a Kiss song ever. Paul's voice with that music is perfect. And the background vocals on the chorus are perfect. I love the rhythm guitar on the breakdown, where Paul is saying "Oohh, yeah, right here." In the mid '80s there was a commercial that used to come on TV, and I forgot what it was for, but they used the intro guitar to "Keep Me Comin'". I tried really hard to find that commercial on YouTube recently, but no luck. I hope I'm not tripping over my own words, but this has got to be the number one underrated Kiss song of the band's history.

## ROCK AND ROLL HELL

Definitely, in the top five underrated Kiss songs. If I keep saying that, I'm gonna run out of top five spots. I think "Keep Me Comin'" and "Rock and Roll Hell" are musically the best two songs on the album. I also think this is the most sincere song on the album. I love the rhythm guitar during the lead guitar solo and the way Gene yells out on the solo. As a rapper, I've tried to sample that tight ass bass line in the past, but the loop would never come out right. I've had so many problems trying to sample Kiss' music. Maybe I wasn't meant to sample them.

## DANGER

It's a favorite of mine and a song I like to play a lot. Probably because of Eric's drumming. Its energy always makes me want to sing along to it.

## I LOVE IT LOUD

As a kid, I thought this song was a rip-off "I Love Rock 'n' Roll." They both even begin with the words "I love." They both have marching drumbeats and loud military chanting choruses. With the success of "I Love Rock 'n' Roll" only a year and a half earlier, I believe Kiss knew what they were doing when they made this song. They were trying to hitch their wagon to Joan's hit single. I could be wrong. Maybe it wasn't intentional, like the "I Want a New Drug" versus "Ghostbusters" lawsuit. Since we're on the subject, I always thought that "I Love Rock 'n' Roll" would have been a good early '80s Ace song. It just sounds like something he would sing. She even sounds like Ace a little on the verses.

"I Love It Loud" is not a song that I listen to a lot, and I'll usually skip past it. But when I do listen to it, I like to sing along. My favorite version is the live in Rio '83 one. The one that appears on *Kiss eXposed* and *Kissology*. I love how it's up-tempo and faster. But to my knowledge, that's the only tour where they played it faster. I've actually seen an '83 *Creatures* show where they're playing it slow, the way they do now. I thought it was odd that they would switch it up and experiment with the tempo like that in the middle of the tour. The song doesn't do much for me, but it's great. Why classic rock stations don't play it more, I don't know.

## I STILL LOVE YOU

I've skipped past this song for years. I used to feel that it was too long, slow, and dragging. It doesn't take all of that time to get the point across; we get it, Paul, you're still in love with Donna Dixon! Actually, if Paul sees what she looks like today, he'll know he came out ahead with his new wife. I think it's even worse when they do it live. Really, who wants to stand through all of that? It's a bathroom break song. I don't think it's a bad song by any means, it's just too damn long, especially when I'm in an up-tempo mood. It slows the party down on the album.

Sometimes, I do like to listen to it, and if I haven't heard it in a long time, I'll think it actually sounds great. The lead guitar solo is tight with a lot of feel to it. My favorite part of the song is Eric's drumming on the chorus. But as a producer, I wouldn't have put it on the album. I would have used those minutes for a heavier song.

## KILLER

I don't know why but this song always had a Gene Simmons '78 solo era feel to me. I can't put my finger on it. The title suggests something heavy and hard-hitting, but the music actually isn't. Even though it's one of my favorite songs to sing along to on this album, if I were the producer, I would have scrapped the song and lyrics, kept the title, and remade it to be heavier. The song is too happy. Gene is stressing that he can't tame this woman, but he also can't get enough of her; a very redundant Gene concept. I guess what kills this song for me is again the music, lead guitar solo, and his singing is too happy. It almost sounds like this song, at least the lyrics, could have been on *Animalize*. *Creatures* is not an album where I want to hear about Gene's romance and sexual issues. They could have used this time slot for another "War Machine" type song.

## WAR MACHINE

From what I can tell, it seems to be the fans' favorite from this album. I don't play it that much. I remember Mark playing it a lot when we were kids. It's a great song, and I like the lead guitar solo at the end. I like the live in Rio '83 version and the way Vinnie is playing lead guitar to it onstage.

## ALBUM COVER

Again, it's another album cover with just their faces. At least it's a hell of a lot cooler and edgier than *Dynasty*. When I saw the real photo that inspired the *Creatures* cover, I thought, *Wow, Kiss totally ripped them off.* I think it's an awesome cover and one of their best. I always thought the picture used for the poster of Kiss standing on the rocks that said Loudest Band in the World should have been used for the back of the album. Why there are so many Kiss albums with boring backsides, I don't know.

## "I LOVE IT LOUD" VIDEO

I don't remember ever seeing it on MTV or other video channels. It seemed like that video should have been big on MTV but it wasn't. I remember when I was ten seeing a quick clip of it when they showed it on *Entertainment Tonight* for a Gene interview. But I can only recall seeing it for the first time when I bought *Kiss eXposed* on VHS.

I always liked the way Gene wore his hair and makeup in that video. I think he should have worn both like that for the tour.

## THE OUTFITS

### GENE

I love the *Creatures* look. I think Gene's second *Creatures of the Night* boots that had the spikes or points on them were better than his *Love Gun* boots. In addition, the way Gene did the smaller version of his bat wings makeup was cool for that *Creatures* era. Again, onstage, he should have worn his hair the way he did on the "I Love It Loud" video.

## ERIC

The silver fox outfit was cool for Eric. I like the silver shin and ankle warmers. To me, Eric's outfit always looked good in photo shoots, but in concert photos, his outfit looked really plain. Never understood that.

## VINNIE

As a kid, before they took off the makeup, I would wonder, *Why are Vinnie's boots so big?* Of course, when you are that young, you're not thinking it's because a member of Kiss is too short. I always liked Vinnie's boots. Even though his outfit was basic, I think it was perfect for him. What I never understood was when Eric joined, his outfit was designed around his orange/red colors. But with Vinnie, instead of designing his outfit around his gold color, they designed it with Ace's silver. Of course, they changed that later on.

## PAUL

I remember when I saw *Creatures* era Paul wearing a T-shirt with his outfit. I actually thought, *When Kiss starts wearing T-shirts onstage, it's over!*" For some reason the T-shirt made him look fat. Paul has had a few different looks for the *Creatures* era. He looked his best in the "I Love It Loud" video. I also like the outfit with the black sleeveless cutoff shirt with the studs.

FAVORITE SONG: "Saint and Sinner"
FAVORITE RHYTHM GUITAR: "Keep Me Comin'"
FAVORITE LEAD GUITAR: "Saint and Sinner"
FAVORITE BASS: "Saint and Sinner"
FAVORITE DRUMS: "Saint and Sinner"

THROWAWAY: "Killer"

MESSING UP THE LYRICS:

"Saint and Sinner," end of second verse: "Without you, the place is hot."

# Chapter 23

## LICK IT UP

*Lick It Up* came out around the time the break dancing craze was becoming a phenomenon. Movies like *Breakin'* and *Beat Street* had millions of kids and teenagers breaking their necks and backs trying to learn how to imitate what they saw on TV and the movie screen. These movies and soundtracks had a major impact on the black youth of America. For the first time, hip-hop was becoming appealing to more and more kids of other races around the States. Who would have known that thirty years later, it would be as big as it is today. As for Mark and I, the only thing that was white about us was our mom and our love for Kiss; other than that, we were typical young black kids. In the early '80s, Mark and I were trying to become extreme break-dancers. We practiced in the middle of the living room with a big piece of cardboard as much as we could. It was an exciting time in music and entertainment because for the first time, with break dancing and rap music becoming more mainstream, young black kids were getting a voice and a way to express themselves. It was also a time when Kiss decided to surprise their fans around the world.

The first time I saw Kiss without makeup was in an Alaskan newspaper, the *Anchorage Times* in '83. They were talking about Kiss in the entertainment section. My mother and I were sitting on the couch, and she was reading the paper. She just handed it to me and said "Look!" At first, I didn't know what I was looking at. I saw some pictures of celebrities, entertainers, and articles on the page. My eyes even glanced over four white guys with big bushy hair looking into the camera, but I still couldn't figure out why she had handed it to me. I turned and looked at my mom with a "What am I supposed to be looking at?" expression. She pointed at the four white guys with the big bushy hair and said, "It's Kiss without makeup!" My eyes quickly darted back to the page, and when I looked closer, at that very moment, my world was quickly turned upside down. I couldn't believe what I was seeing. I thought, *The sons of bitches actually did it. They took off the makeup. Or did they? Would Kiss do such a thing? Is this some Twilight Zone shit? Is this really Kiss in the photo? It couldn't be Kiss because Kiss never shows their real faces, so what the fuck is this all about?* Maybe not in those exact words.

It was the picture taken at MTV's studios of Gene, Vinnie, Paul, and Eric in that order, holding up small signs with their names on them. I just sat there and continuously analyzed the photo. To me, the way Paul and Eric looked made a lot of sense. I could see them as the same guys under the makeup. Gene didn't look anything like I expected. Without his makeup, he had more of a caveman face. He also kind of reminded me of the singer from Quiet Riot but with more hair. I guess as a kid, I always thought that Gene would be this cool looking white guy with cool features, but in that picture he was not so much ugly but weird looking. I remember thinking, as I was obsessively staring that not only did Vinnie look like a girl, but he looked like a girl I went to school with named Kelly. I even asked her at school if she thought she could be related to Vinnie Vincent and just didn't know it. Of course she thought I was a dumbass for asking.

I must have stared at that photo of Kiss without makeup for at least two hours. *It kinda looks like them, but can this be real? Are they just some local guys trying to pull a joke?* I felt somewhat cheated, like Kiss should have at least phoned me first to let me know they were going to take off the makeup so we could at least talk about it. Instead, I had to find out through the newspaper. I guess I felt the same way Paul did when he found out that Donna Dixon had married Dan Akroyd by reading it in the newspaper.

It was a confusing time for me as a Kiss fan. Not that them taking off the makeup would ever stop me from being a fanatic, but it was just so unexpected. At that age of nine, I had more of a feeling of "OK, so as far as me being a Kiss fan, where do we go from here? I guess we're moving forward. I'm scared but excited at the same time." As a fan, it was my job to spread the word about Kiss and explain the crazy makeup and outfits to those who didn't get it. Now I had to start all over, spread the word, and promote them without makeup.

## THE FIRST TIME I HEARD KISS TALK WITHOUT MAKEUP

The first time I saw Kiss on TV without their makeup was when Gene and Paul were doing an interview on a late-night show. I tried to research it, but I can't remember what the show was. I want to say that it was *Friday Night Videos*. Again, I'm not for sure. It was so weird seeing them on TV for the first time without makeup. Again, Paul was still Paul to me, but it just wasn't Gene. Something was just off about him. Not only the look, but his voice and attitude. Of course, now we can look back and know that he was just getting comfortable in his non-makeup persona, but back in the *Lick It Up* era, his personality was really weird to me. I'll never forget what Gene said when asked a question by the interviewer and he replied, "I do it for the girls!" At that time, I thought that was so cool and only something Gene could get away with saying. "Gene gets all the girls" is what I always thought when I was younger. But the older I got, Gene talking about getting girls and laid started sounding more and more stupid. It sounded so cool when I was thirteen. But hearing that at eighteen and twenty years old, it sounded dumb.

That same show would also be the first time that Mark and I would see the "Lick It Up" video. My mother had let us stay up late to watch it. But if our dad came home, it didn't matter, we would have to go to bed. I was praying he wouldn't walk through the front door anytime soon. I had to see that video! Looking back, the "Lick It Up" video is dumb as hell, but back in 1983, it was the shit. Especially when the camera shows all of them for the first time during the chorus. Mark and I were bug-eyed watching it. When it was over, my mom told us to hurry to bed before my dad caught us still awake. While lying in bed, all I could do was stare at the ceiling in the darkness and think about that video. *Even without makeup, Kiss is still the greatest band in the world*, I thought. But in the video, Gene still looked weird to me.

## TO ME, THEY WERE EVEN MORE MYSTERIOUS

I know in '83, some fans and the public in general thought Kiss lost their mystique when they took off the makeup and revealed themselves to the world. For this particular Kiss fan, it made them even more mysterious. What I mean is throughout the '70s, Kiss wore crazy makeup, outfits, did crazy things onstage like spit blood and fire. They had drum risers, the stage floor would shoot fire into the air, and they had the coolest stage logo. What made them even more mysterious to me when they revealed themselves in '83 was it was the same guys but they just didn't wear makeup anymore. You actually got to see their real faces. Even though Vinnie and Eric were new, it didn't matter, they were all part of this thing called Kiss! Kiss taking off the makeup wasn't a spoiler; seeing the men behind the masks added a factor of mystery for me. When they wore makeup, I didn't want to see them without makeup, but now that it was off, I wanted to learn more about the men behind the makeup.

Like I said before, I'm in love with '80s Kiss. I can't get enough of it. When I'm on YouTube I'm always searching for '80s interviews and footage I've never seen before. When I found the making of the *Crazy Nights* video, I just about shit on myself. I thought it was the coolest thing. I especially love the *Lick It Up* interviews and TV appearances.

## I NEED MY *LICK IT UP* ALBUM

Our sisters Michelle and Denise were going clothes shopping one Saturday, and Mark and I went with them. I guess I should mention that they said they would each buy us a *Lick It Up* album, which was why we volunteered to go women's clothes shopping. Do you know how boring it is to go clothes and shoe shopping with your older sisters? You're just sitting there going out of your mind while they try on one thing after another. They're having the time of their lives while you're looking for a loaded gun to point at your head. But what kept us going was we knew that soon, we would each have our own *Lick It Up* album. I couldn't wait. We took the bus with them all over town going into one store after another, and every time we got close to a record store, they wanted to go somewhere else. Finally, after paying our dues, we walked into a store and Denise bought Mark a *Lick It Up* album and Michelle bought mine. It was official. I don't think that from the time I got the album until I got it home, I stopped looking at it. It was the greatest band in the world without makeup.

When we got home, I quickly put it on the turntable and just soaked it all in. Mark was in his room blasting his record. Why we didn't listen to it together, I don't know. I'll never forget after listening to it, going into Mark's room and saying, "Paul is trying to sound black." I was referring to "All Hell's Breakin' Loose." And because Paul was trying to rap, it sounded stupid to me, so initially, I hated the song. Then a month later, I was playing the hell out of it.

I loved the album when I first played it, and "Fits Like a Glove" jumped off the record at me. I took it to school every day with me for about a month. At this time, I was in the fourth grade. I wanted the whole school to know that Kiss had a new non-makeup album out and everybody should appreciate and acknowledge it. I would keep it propped up against the leg of my desk and every so often, I would look at it when the teacher wasn't paying attention. I also took it to school because I just wanted to have it close to me. I loved that record.

One day in class, I was showing the record to a classmate and making too much noise. My desk was in the back of the class. My teacher got mad at me and told a kid up front, Eli, to trade places with me for the rest of the afternoon. Eli looked at the teacher and said that he couldn't. Our teacher insisted again that he trade places with me, but again, Eli said he couldn't, and he wasn't backing down. "Why can't you trade places with Anthony?" the teacher asked him. He responded, "Because I'm not allowed to sit where a nigger sat." I was shocked by his words, and so was the teacher. The entire class was stunned and quiet. Not only did he say the N word to me, but he also said it with conviction. Filled with anger and ready to drop him, I yelled out "Fuck you, white boy!" Enraged, I quickly ran toward him, fists clenched. In an instant, in my mind, I saw his face covered in blood. I was going to beat the shit out of him. My plans were cut short when the teacher intercepted me. While I was throwing wild punches and kicking, my teacher was holding me back, and Eli was trying get away from me as fast as he could. At this point, I was a little bit older than when the racist lady wouldn't let me in her house a few years earlier, and I had become more sensitive to that word. By then, when someone would say the N word or anything racist against me, I would snap and go off. It was like being told you weren't good enough or you didn't matter because your skin was darker. Like Richard Pryor said, "Fuck skin color. It's hard enough just being a human being!" Right now, the N word is used more freely and as a term of endearment. However, this was '83. We were only a decade and a half out of the '60s, when blacks were still marching and fighting for civil rights. Now in my very own classroom, my classmate calls me a nigger?

While in the principal's office, Eli was treated like he was the victim. The office staff was comforting him and making sure that he wasn't traumatized or hurt by this experience. They even bought him a soda. Did I mention that with all the punches I was throwing and kicking, nothing landed because the teacher was holding me back. Even my teacher, who was white, said that Eli was never hit and that he had started it by calling me a nigger, but she had stopped me before I could do anything. Not once did the principal question Eli for calling me a nigger. But he repeatedly asked me why I used the F word in class. In the end, I got two days in detention for saying the word "Fuck" in class. For calling me a "nigger" in class, Eli didn't get in trouble at all. Some things never change.

I spent my two days of detention in my classroom. My teacher, Mrs. Larry, was so sympathetic toward me that instead of making me do homework, she would let me put on the headphones and play my *Lick It Up* record until my hour was up.

## MY FIRST NON-MAKEUP T-SHIRT

We were at the Fred Meyer shopping center when Mark and I saw the 1983 *Lick It Up* shirts. They had the album cover on the front, and on the back, they said, "If it's too loud, you're too old." We begged our dad to buy them for us. Our dad was always cool about our Kiss obsession, and he bought 'em for us. I couldn't wait to wear it to school the next day and show everybody. I could already see all the kids approaching me at recess, admiring my new Kiss *Lick It Up* T-shirt. Of course, that didn't happen. As a matter of fact, I don't think anyone asked me about my new Kiss shirt. Fuck 'em! But a few months later, when Patrick Adams came to school wearing his Mötley Crüe *Shout at the Devil* T-shirt, all the kids at recess treated him like he was the man. Everybody wanted to be next to him and the Crüe. A week later, many kids came to school wearing *Shout at the Devil* T-shirts. The attitude was Mötley Crüe was better than Kiss.

## I LOVE *LICK IT UP*

*Lick It Up* is my favorite Kiss album of all time. I think this album has the perfect amount of hard rock, metal, and writing. Where I think *Creatures* tried a little too hard, *Lick It Up* is heavy but still sounds more like Kiss to me. Or I should say is a sound that I appreciate.

## THE SONGS

## EXCITER

I love it. My favorite part of this song is the lead guitar solo.

## NOT FOR THE INNOCENT

Back then and today it is my favorite song on the album. I love singing to it.

## LICK IT UP

It didn't do much for me as a kid, and I would usually skip past it. I love and appreciate it so much more as an adult. I really like the basic, simple rhythm guitar. I don't know why, but I always thought it was Vinnie backing up Paul on the vocals, saying "Oh yeah, oh yeah," etc. Why I thought that, I don't know. But who knows, maybe it is. Or maybe it's Eric.

## YOUNG AND WASTED

I like singing along to it.

## GIMME MORE

Growing up, I skipped past this song the most. It was always a throwaway to me. It probably wasn't until I was in my late twenties that I started listening to it more and realizing how great it really is. Now I play it all the time. I love the rhythm guitar on the breakdowns.

## ALL HELL'S BREAKIN' LOOSE

Why this song isn't played daily on classic rock stations, I don't know. I love the lead and bass guitar, and it's fun to sing along to. Eric's drumming is the shit here. Basic but the shit.

## A MILLION TO ONE

My favorite song to sing along to on this album. I love the lead guitar solo. To me, this song has always been a continuation of "I Still Love You." In "I Still Love You," he's letting her know how much he loves, misses, and needs her. In this song, he's saying since she's not responding, he's angry and mad; "Fuck her, she'll never find anybody better than me." At least that's how I've always connected those two songs. Paul confirmed this for me in his book.

## FITS LIKE A GLOVE

I've loved this song since the first time I heard it. The lead guitar solo is tight. I especially love the way Bruce plays the lead guitar solo on the *Animalize* MTV concert. Go back and watch Bruce play it when you get a chance.

## DANCE ALL OVER YOUR FACE

I love it! To me this song always sounded like it was a leftover from *Creatures*. I always thought that because of the way the drums sounded. I guess only Kiss knows what session this song was from. It's another highlight for me on this album. I love the way Gene sings the chorus and the way he yells at the end of the song. It's great to sing along to.

## AND ON THE 8TH DAY

I love this song so much. The intro rhythm guitar, Gene's growling voice, the chorus, the marching drumbeat on the breakdown, and the lead guitar solo. I play it all the time. I go into complete Gene mode when I sing it.

I always thought it was odd that they ended this album with three Gene songs instead of mixing up side two and wondered if there was a conversation about that being a concern from Gene and Paul. I always thought that "Fits Like a Glove" should have been the second song, and "A Million to One" should have been the third song.

## ALBUM COVER

I love that picture on the album cover. I always thought that Paul and Vinnie's hair looked really good. Years later, we would find out that Vinnie was wearing a wig. I just don't think it was a good photo for something as big as Kiss coming out of makeup in '83. There were actually other photos from that photo shoot I thought might have been better for the cover, especially the ones where Gene isn't sticking out his tongue. But knowing that they were revealing their faces for the first time on an album cover, why didn't they dress better for it? The story goes that it wasn't planned and they were just trying out some non-makeup shots; I don't know. But even if that's the case, knowing how professional Gene and Paul were and how much they wanted to control the Kiss image, why did they approve the final photo to be one of them in their street clothes? You would think when revealing themselves for the first time and trying to cash in on the upcoming tour and publicity over it, they would want to look their best. But for the band, the whole *Lick It Up* era from beginning to end just had an attitude of "We look like crap but whatever." Still, I love the *Lick It Up* look and remember collecting all of the pictures out of the rock magazines. I would put the magazine pictures in comic book bags to keep them protected and store them in a three-ring binder, as if they were going to be the only pictures of the band without makeup to ever be released. Thirty years later, the album cover is a signature picture, and I love it. Again, the back of the album was wasted.

To this day, I think the title is stupid. Like *Love Gun*, *Lick It Up* is not an album title, it's a song title. I believe it's the worst album title to date. They should have called the album *All Hell's Breakin' Loose*. To me, that would have represented Kiss taking off the makeup and "All Hell's Breakin' Loose!"

Around 2005, while speaking to Mark on the phone, I said that it was too bad you can't find any more good Kiss posters anywhere. Mark said, "All you have to do is look on eBay, they have all kinds of Kiss stuff on there." Mind you, I was always late for everything when it came to what's new and trendy in technology. I didn't learn how to use the Internet until 2005, and I didn't get my first cell phone until 2010. Even when I wrote my first book, I wrote it in pencil. I'll never do that again. In 2005, I went to my friend James Conn's house, and he pulled up eBay for me on his computer. I asked him to type in Kiss posters, and when he did, I couldn't believe what I was looking at, a shitload of classic Kiss posters for sale in one place. Let's just say that first year of discovering eBay, I spent more money on Kiss than I care to admit. Now I have a ton of Kiss stuff stored in four different states. But the first thing I bought off eBay was the *Lick It Up* album cover poster.

## THE VIDEOS

## LICK IT UP

I like to go on YouTube and watch Kiss videos. Sometimes I'll click on "Lick It Up" for nostalgic reasons. But I'm not a big fan of the video.

## ALL HELL'S BREAKIN' LOOSE

Back in '83, Mark had to stay home sick from school one day and that was the first time he got to see the "All Hell's Breakin' Loose" video. When I came home, he was bragging about the video and how cool it was. He said they were fighting in the street like in *The Warriors*. I was so mad and jealous that he got to see it before me. I stayed in the house for the rest of the day in front of the TV screen waiting for that video to come on. It never did. And I never saw it rotated on MTV. It would actually be a couple of years before I would see it. I remember how funny Gene was to me in that video, and I thought that's how he really acted when he was in public.

FAVORITE SONG: "Not for the Innocent"
FAVORITE RHYTHM GUITAR: "Gimme More"
FAVORITE LEAD GUITAR: "Not for the Innocent"
FAVORITE BASS: "All Hell's Breakin' Loose"
FAVORITE DRUMS: "Dance All Over Your Face"

THROWAWAY: "Gimme More," but I like it a lot.

MESSING UP THE LYRICS:

"Not for the Innocent," end of chorus: "Let the peace court pay."

"Gimme More," beginning first verse: "I'm fire on the loose, driver's wild, we're singing Deuce."

"Dance All Over Your Face," second verse intro: "Hey baby, what's the world coming to," (drum rolls) "baby get the money where a mountains, you're strong like it loose you need another man."

## Chapter 24

# DID VINNIE SAVE KISS?

This question has been asked a lot over the years and every fan has their own opinion. But what is the real question—did Vinnie save Kiss financially, did his presence increase album or ticket sales, or did he bring morale to the band? Was the label threatening to drop the band unless they brought a shredder like Vinnie aboard for some new blood? Was it Vinnie who influenced the band to make a heavier hard rock album like *Creatures*? My personal opinion is no, I don't think that Vinnie saved Kiss whatsoever. Especially during that era.

From a business standpoint, the *Creatures* album and tour were a flop. Every real Kiss fan knows that. So no, he didn't save them there. To my knowledge, the *Lick It Up* tour didn't do well either, but the album sold better. Why did the *Lick It Up* album sell better than its sister album *Creatures*, which is obviously a superior album? I believe that it was the little bit of hype that surrounded Kiss taking off the makeup. Some Kiss fans who jumped ship after the *Dynasty* album and rock fans in general bought the album to hear what Kiss would sound like without makeup, curiosity. Also, the "Lick It Up" video did get a decent amount of attention on TV. But I wouldn't attribute that to Vinnie. I never thought of the single "Lick It Up" as a great single, especially in '83, when rock singles like "Cum On Feel the Noize," "Metal Health," "Photograph," "Rock of Ages," and the singles from all of the early '80s rock bands that were blasting out on MTV and boom boxes at that time were just dominating. To me "Lick it Up" was just a weak single. Sure, as a fan, I love it, but it just couldn't compete. At least "I Love It Loud" had an anthem feel to it. I always felt that the label should have pushed "All Hell's Breakin' Loose" as the first single.

To get back on topic, when Eric Carr joined, I remember many people talking about the new Kiss drummer, whether it was on the news, in the newspaper, magazines articles, or just word of mouth. When Vinnie joined, you could hear a pin drop. Outside of Kiss fans, I never heard anybody talking about the new Kiss guitarist, and that was mostly because nobody gave a damn about Kiss anyway at that point. I'm talking in this way because I'm just trying to cover all the scenarios I can think of for how Vinnie could have saved Kiss, and as a fan, I'm coming up short.

We all know that Vinnie is an awesome songwriter and guitarist. He's filled with talent, and in my opinion, besides being short, I thought he fit visually in the band with and without makeup more than Mark and Bruce. Vinnie always had a cool New York look about him. But I think with or without him, Gene and Paul were already in the mindset of going into the direction of releasing a heavier album with Michael James Jackson. Either way, even if it wasn't Vinnie, they would have still gotten some hotshot lead guitar player who could play fast and have shredding ability. Would the songs have been written as well? Maybe, maybe not. If Gene and Paul were already looking for or in the mindset to use outside writers, they could and would have easily found them. But the question is, would they have looked for new writers or was it being exposed to or around Vinnie himself that pushed them in the direction to use his songwriting ability for the upcoming Kiss album. The difference would have been that they would have still had a heavy album but they would have had different songs. Maybe even better songs, commercially. On the other hand, maybe not. That's up to speculation.

I guess what I'm saying is that, to the record and ticket buying public, Vinnie's presence didn't make or break Kiss. Especially when both Paul and Mark Slaughter said that Vinnie's long guitar solos live could clear a room. But what about to the Kiss fans themselves? I think because he was and is such an awesome writer, some fans think he saved Kiss in that regard. Yes, his writing on those albums was the best the band had up until that point, but I don't think that saved the band. In the end, it just means that they had two albums with superior songwriting on them. Good songwriting doesn't equal album or ticket sales at all. Some might argue that Vinnie's songwriting gave Kiss a credibility in the rock community that they didn't have before. But what good is that credibility if your ticket sales are plummeting? Which would mean that in the end, Vinnie's presence in, and songwriting for the band was relevant only to a small group of people. If anything, I say "Heaven's on Fire" saved Kiss, and Kiss did better after Vinnie's departure. *Animalize*'s songwriting was inferior to *Creatures* and *Lick It Up,* but thanks to the single "Heaven's on Fire," all of a sudden, radio and MTV were rotating Kiss again, which saved Kiss, album and ticket sales wise. Not dramatically, but it did get better.

## I LIKED VINNIE'S PRESENCE AND IMAGE

I'm not putting Vinnie down in any way. I'm just giving my opinion on a question that has been hovering around since '82. Of course I love his songwriting, and again, I wish that they would have finished out the '80s with Michael James Jackson and hired Vinnie on as their official songwriter because I love that combination. But that's just fantasy. I'm also happy that Gene and Paul kept his guitar playing under control on those albums. I like his makeup, and in some pictures and interviews, like when Kiss was on *Night Flight,* I think he looks really tight! To me, his makeup image fit the heavy metal/lead guitar master, early '80s vibe they were going for during that era.

## Chapter 25

## *VINNIE'S DEPARTURE*

Before I ever heard "Heaven's on Fire" or knew of an upcoming Kiss record, I saw Mark St. John in a magazine. One day, at the age of ten, while at the Laundromat with my mom, I ran to the 7-11 across the street to check out the rock magazines, and when I found one with Kiss in it, of course, I was happy. I turned the page and in the bottom corner, it said something like "Kiss' new lead guitarist," and it was a picture of Mark St. John. Honestly, I did not think anything of it. I didn't ask myself *What happened to Vinnie, did he die, was he in a car accident?* or *Is this Mark guy any good?* I just immediately accepted that there was a new member, and again, in the Kiss world, we were moving forward.

# Chapter 26

## *ANIMALIZE*

There was an older teenager, Steven, who lived in our neighborhood who had subscriptions to *Circus* and other rock magazines of the time. He would receive different issues in the mail monthly. When he was done with them, he would let me come over and take out the Kiss pictures. I got most of my *Animalize* pictures from him. I just wanted to take this moment and say thanks, Steven.

### AND THEN THERE WAS *ANIMALIZE*

Before we had an *Animalize* album in the house, Mark and I would hear "Heaven's on Fire" a lot on the radio. We saw the video for the first time at our friend Kalonji's house. I don't remember being as excited about that video as I was when I first saw "Lick it Up." When it ended, I remember having a weird feeling, like "This is a really good song, and a lot of people are going to like it. This is not good." I didn't know why I initially had a weird feeling from watching the video for the first time, but I did. Later, I would realize it was because Kiss would soon be somewhat popular again.

### STINGY ASS MARK

Mark had gotten the album first. Maybe it was because he was going through puberty, but he was becoming a real asshole about it. He wouldn't let me listen to it when I wanted to. I could only hear it when he played it. He would always tell me that I was going to scratch it or something. Finally, I got him to agree to let me record it on tape. At least that way, I could play the tape without hearing his mouth or him trying to micromanage me to make sure I didn't scratch it. Still, I liked to actually hold the album in my hand and stare at it while I listened. In the meantime, while I listened to it on cassette, I would just have to look at my magazine pictures of Kiss until I could figure out how to get my own copy. Ironically, I did get my own copy thanks to Mark. Mark had earned some money and gave me $10.00. The first thing I did that very night was run to the grocery store/plaza mall and bought my own *Animalize* album. Then, like a dumbass, instead of saying thank you to Mark, I came back home to brag about it with an in-your-face attitude. "Ha, ha, I got my own *Animalize* now biieeeaaatch." Actually, we didn't say "biieeeaaatch" in '84, but you get the idea; I was being an ass. Mark looked at me, shrugged his shoulders, and walked away. I felt stupid. So let me take this opportunity to say thank you, Mark, for giving me the money to buy my own *Animalize* album. One love. By the way, did I spell "biieeeaaatch" right?

## I'M HAPPY FOR KISS, BUT I'M NOT

Something was still bothering me about the newfound success and attention Kiss was getting with this new hit song "Heaven's on Fire." All of a sudden, rocker kids at school were wearing Kiss T-shirts again and playing Kiss music on their boom boxes at recess. Cars would drive by the neighborhood blasting out "Heaven's on Fire." Rocker guys I knew were all of a sudden putting Kiss pictures on their walls. So why was I so offended by this at age ten? It took a while for me to figure it out, but I did. Everybody liked Kiss again but for what I thought was the wrong reason. Just because they had a hit song on the radio, all of a sudden, rocker fans were jumping back on the bandwagon. That's why I was offended!

Where in the hell were all these fair-weather fans during *The Elder* era? Where were these so-called fans when the *Creatures* album and tour was sinking faster than the Titanic? I don't remember anyone wearing a Kiss T-shirt at school when *Lick It Up* came out or supporting the album. And what about all the so-called fans who jumped ship after Peter was fired, or when the other flavor of the month rock bands were having their fifteen minutes? I was still there and supporting Kiss, but they weren't. Now that

Kiss had a hit song on the radio, all of a sudden, everybody wanted to claim my band again? Hell nah!

## GRAPE SLURPEE/"HEAVEN'S ON FIRE"

During the *Animalize* era, one night, I went to the 7-11 by my house. A man and a woman were working behind the counter. "Heaven's on Fire" was playing on the radio, and the woman was singing along to it. Even though I had everything I needed from the store, as a Kiss fan, it was my obligation to continue to stay in the store until the song was over. But the dumbass guy behind the counter started making rude comments about the song and Kiss. "This song is so stupid, they look so ugly without their makeup, one of them is really a woman and they're just hiding it from the public," etc. I stood there in the aisle getting madder and madder with each shot he took at Kiss. The woman, on the other hand, was saying how much she loved the song. She checked out OK!

A moment later, the Kiss hater left the store, and then I walked out. I saw him getting something out of his car that was parked on the side of the building, and then he walked back into the store. Still filled with anger and offended like someone had just insulted a family member, I took the grape Slurpee in my hand and threw it as hard as I could at his windshield. I didn't even wait for impact, I just ran and hauled ass as fast as I could.

When I got home, I was out of breath and peeking out the windows to see if I had been followed or seen. I hadn't been. In my young mind, I imagined that when he came back outside to his car and found grape Slurpee all over his windshield, he would be devastated and it would be the biggest catastrophe of his life so that he would probably have to quit his job and relocate to another state. Also, he'd have to get a new identity. His whole world was ruined because he talked shit about Kiss. Well he paid the ultimate price, grape Slurpee all over his windshield!

## CAN YOU MAKE ME LOOK LIKE ERIC CARR?

In the '70s and early '80s, most black folks didn't go to beauty salons to get their hair done, but went to a friend or neighbor who did hair out of their house. My father, with his big pimp style James Brown hair, went to the house of a woman named Ms. Ward. Back then, I usually went with my dad when he got his hair done, so when he made another appointment, I asked if I could go with him and if Ms. Ward would do my hair too. I had something special in mind. I didn't even tell my dad or Mark, who came along, what I was planning.

After she finished my dad's hair, she called me into the kitchen, sat me down in a chair, and asked me what I wanted. I pulled out a magazine picture of Eric Carr from the *Animalize* era and said, "I want my hair to look like this." The look on her face was priceless. Not only did I pull out a picture from a heavy metal magazine, but her expression also said, "Why would any black child want to look like a white boy?" I was dead set on having hair like Eric Carr, and I didn't care what she thought. Let's do it!

While she fondled my hair, I sat in that chair with a big cheesy grin on my face. I couldn't believe it; I was going to look like Eric Carr. I was already imagining what it was going to be like when I walked into school and all the other kids would see my cool Eric Carr hair. I was gonna be the shit, the coolest fifth grader, the man!

About ten minutes later, Ms. Ward said she was done. *That was fast,* I thought. I couldn't wait to see it. I was going to actually look like Eric Carr. When she handed me the mirror and I saw what she had done with my hair, my cheesy grin instantly turned into sour cream. I could feel my little heart breaking into pieces. All she did was pick my hair out into a big afro. I began to tear up, I looked at my dad with fright on my face and said, "This doesn't look like Eric Carr!" My dad, trying to make me feel better, said in his patronizing tone, "Boy, you look just like him; I can't tell the difference. You look slick, diamond in the back, get down." And Mark didn't help the situation, either; he was pissin' all over himself laughing at me. He knew from the beginning that my hair wasn't going to turn out looking like Eric's, he just wanted to see the outcome. Mark's laughing made me cry harder. My dad told us to get in the car with all that noise and paid Ms. Ward and we left. I rode all the way home crying in the back seat with this huge afro on my head that I didn't know what to do with. I looked ridiculous.

# TIME HEALS ALL WOUNDS

Back then, I used to think that *Animalize* wasn't such a great album by Kiss. But as the years went by and I listened closer, I began to feel that it was just Gene's songs on this album that were horrible. I used to believe this album has the worst Gene songs in the history of Kiss' catalogue. That was too bad, considering that they had such a big breakthrough hit off of it. Also, let me add that if there was ever a Kiss album where you couldn't understand what the hell Gene was saying, it was *Animalize*. I would also wonder, because of Gene not being a hundred percent there and having his mind on Hollywood, why didn't Paul use this opportunity to let Eric record a song for the album. I always thought it was strange that he made Eric and the fans wait so long to finally give him a song. With so many of Gene's throwaways on *Animalize*, they could have easily dropped one of his songs and let Eric get one in. I understand at that point Gene and Paul had a quota of songs they each wanted on the album, but still, throw Eric a bone.

Years later, I listen to the album totally differently. Now I love Gene's songs on this album. I used to think that "Murder in High-Heels" was the stupidest Kiss song in the history of Kiss songs. Now it's my favorite song on the album. I love it!

## THE SONGS

## I'VE HAD ENOUGH (INTO THE FIRE)

Amazing song! Unlike any other Kiss song ever made. Very unique and executed well. Best song on the album. I always thought this would have been a great song for *Rocky IV*.

## HEAVEN'S ON FIRE

Awesome Kiss song. I would usually skip past it though. The hi-hat is very sharp and clean on this song. It's another Kiss song that I can't figure out why classic rock stations don't rotate it more.

## BURN BITCH BURN

To me, it's the sister song to "Love 'em and Leave 'em," meaning what the hell was Gene thinking? Remember how Ezrin took "God of Thunder" away from Paul and turned it into a heavier, darker Gene song? That's what they could have done with this song. Kept the title but made it into a heavier metal Gene song. They should have slowed it down a little, taken Paul off of the chorus, and Gene should have sung the chorus with more of a badass attitude. Give the chorus the same feel as "Dance All Over Your Face" or "War Machine." But in the end, I like it, and it's my favorite song on the album to sing along to.

## GET ALL YOU CAN TAKE

To me, this has always been the sister song to "Keep Me Comin'." Another example as to why Paul's songs were great on this album. The chorus always pulls me in. The way they're saying the lyrics in the chorus is really different and unique. I love the lead guitar solo. Songs like this are my Kiss classics.

## LONELY IS THE HUNTER

I used to think that this song had one of the dumbest song titles to ever appear on a Kiss album. But after so many years of listening to it, I've actually grown to love it. In fact, when I'm out in public, I always say the opening line to this song. I call it my Kiss Tourette's syndrome. That's when I sing a Kiss lyric, blurt out a line from an interview, concert, *Kiss Meets the Phantom*, or Gene movie for no apparent reason. I feel one coming on right now, "You're probably wondering how I did that?" The lead solo is off the chain. I love this song!

## UNDER THE GUN

When I was a kid, Mark told me that there was a new Kiss video for this song. He said that Paul was driving a classic Firebird really fast down the highway singing the lyrics, and Eric was in the back seat with girls hanging all over him. I forgot the other details he said about the video, but I believed him. Again, for the next few years, I kept waiting to see this video and inquiring about it. Of course, Mark lied. Again, another Kiss song for classic rock radio stations.

## THRILLS IN THE NIGHT

Even when the album came out, I never cared for this song. Paul's voice is just too whining and pouty. It's got a weird feel to it. And the recording sounds muffled to me. But lately, it's really growing on me. I'm starting to play it more and make it a go-to song off the album. It only took about thirty years.

## WHILE THE CITY SLEEPS

This used to be my favorite song on the album. I've always loved the feel of it.

## MURDER IN HIGH-HEELS

I used to think, *Was Gene so busy during that era that this was the best he could come up with?* I hated it in the past, but now I'm IN LOVE with it. The rhythm guitar is so funky with the drums, and the hi-hat is really clean and sharp on this song. We all know the chorus sounds exactly like the rhythm guitar on Aerosmith's song "Sweet Emotion." I always thought so. I also love the lead guitar as the song is ending. Again, I don't just love this song, I'm IN LOVE with this song!

## ALBUM COVER

The album cover never bothered me. I don't think it's that great, but I also don't think it's bad. It works. It also brings back a lot of memories of that era for me whenever I see it. I like the title, too. Way better album title than *Lick It Up*.

I love the photo on the back. I was shocked and happy to find a poster of it being sold on eBay. When I first started bidding for it, I remember trying my best to outbid everyone else. I was so disappointed when I lost. I thought I had missed my opportunity. What I didn't know was that sellers were putting up the same posters every week. So eventually, I got one. I'm so out of touch with technology.

As a kid, I would always stare at the back of the album and wonder, *What's wrong with Mark's neck?* Also, Paul's right arm seemed bent in a funny way, too. Maybe most of you Kiss fans already knew that their heads and body parts were cut and pasted from different pictures from the photo shoot. I didn't know that until I read the book *KissFAQ.* I think it's a great photo of the band and the non-makeup equivalent to Kiss standing on the cubes in '77.

## THE VIDEOS

### "HEAVEN'S ON FIRE"

I never understood or cared for the concept and the clips of them being in what appears to be a cheap hotel room. To me, those scenes make the video look a little generic. The director could have come up with something so much better. It's not a great video, but it's fun to watch.

### "THRILLS IN THE NIGHT"

I tried so hard to find the footage of the original video, Kiss in an office with the secretary and all. I never had any luck. That would be cool to put on a Kissology. I'm sure I've read somewhere the reason why it wasn't completed or released, but I've forgotten. You all might know better than me. But the outcome of the final video was generic. As an adult, I don't like it, but as a kid, I loved it.

One afternoon, when I was eleven, my mother took me to Chuck E. Cheese to play video games. I saw that there was a new machine with a big screen that played music videos for a dollar. It also had the "Thrills in the Night" video. At that time, I didn't know the video even existed. Instead of playing video games, I pulled a chair up to the big video screen and played the "Thrills in the Night" video over and over again, maybe about seven times. Then some older blonde girl who looked about sixteen/seventeen and talked with a Valley girl "like for sure, as if, totally bitchin'" voice and attitude approached me. She said, "Like, would you please stop playing that stupid Kiss video. As if anyone likes Kiss." I would get so heated when anyone said anything against Kiss, and I responded in my hardest tone, "Get the fuck out my face!" I played it four more times.

## *ANIMALIZE* MTV CONCERT

Mark bought this used on Beta years after its release. But by then, we had moved on to VHS. I tried to find friends or anybody who had a Beta machine so I could watch it, but came up empty. So all I could do was look at the pictures on the cover and wonder what this great concert on this tape was like. I wouldn't get to watch it until 1989. Then I watched it almost every day, or in bits and pieces. However, this has always been my favorite non-makeup concert. The energy, sound, and up-tempo of the music was just great. To me, non-makeup Kiss was at their best live during the *Animalize* era, and they definitely redeemed themselves from the *Lick It Up* tour.

I didn't think Kiss looked bad on the *Animalize* tour, but I thought they would have looked better if they had worn the outfits from the "Heaven's on Fire" video. To me, it was just a better look. When I would watch this back in '89, I would wonder, *Why is Gene's hair so stiff?* I didn't know anything about Gene wearing a wig back in those days. Even when *Asylum* came out, I just thought that Gene grew his hair longer. But Gene's hair/wig looked good to me in the "Heaven's on Fire" video and also in a lot of the *Animalize* photo shoots.

FAVORITE SONG: "Murder in High-Heels"
FAVORITE RHYTHM GUITAR: "Murder in High-Heels"
FAVORITE LEAD GUITAR: "Lonely is the Hunter"
FAVORITE BASS GUITAR: "I've Had Enough (Into the Fire)"
FAVORITE DRUMS: "Murder in High-Heels"

THROWAWAY: "Burn Bitch Burn" but my favorite to sing along to.

MESSING UP THE LYRICS:

"Burn Bitch Burn," first verse: "It's like a baby walkin' right into, into the fire, you're baby of a baby so let me be your dry, yeah, you're on the streets it's as easy as that times two." The lyrics go on, and wraps up verse with "My fault, yeah, just listen to this bass."

"Murder in High-Heels," first verse intro: "Breakfast by the hand."

## Chapter 27

# MARK'S DEPARTURE

One day, I was at the store looking at a rock magazine and staring at a picture of Kiss. The first thing I thought when I saw Mark was he looked different; I thought he poofed his hair out to look more like the rest of the band. Then it hit me—*Wait a minute, that's not Mark. Who is this guy? His name is Bruce. A new guitar player?*

# Chapter 28

# *ASYLUM*

In '85, at age eleven, my mother and I were watching a show on TV. I'm not sure, but I think it might have been *Entertainment Tonight* or one of those types of shows that talk about celebrities and what's happening in the world of entertainment. The topic, I believe, had something to do with "Too much sex in music videos." I was lying flat on my stomach with my face resting in my hands when they showed footage of the "Who Wants to Be Lonely" video. At that time, I didn't know it was a video. I jumped up and said "Whaaattt?" It was Kiss footage I had never seen before. What was it, where did it come from, was that a Kiss video, or was Kiss doing something special for TV? That quick clip was all they showed of Kiss. And that was the first time I would learn of *Asylum*'s existence. Well not the album, but a song from the album.

## VISITATIONS

I have a very close friend named Jamie, more like a brother. In '85, we used to live in the same neighborhood. We would always walk a mile to this grocery store/plaza mall to get two big scoops of ice cream in a cone. It was one of our weekend rituals. So one day, I go over to the record department to see what Kiss albums they have in stock. While flipping through the albums, I saw one that I had never seen before. It was Kiss' big faces drawn in cartoon form on the cover. It was *Asylum*! Once again, I began shaking at the sight of a new Kiss record. I remember anxiously thinking, *I bet that song from that TV show is on this record.* I just didn't know the name of it.

At that moment, Jamie asked me if I wanted to go look at bikes. I told him I'd meet him over there and continued to just stare at the magnificent record. I was shaking badly on the inside over this new discovery. I was so happy and thrilled that there was a new Kiss album, but with no money, I had to figure out how to get the $8.99 to buy it. I didn't want to let it go; it was the only *Asylum* album in the Kiss section. I was so afraid that if I put it back in with the records, someone else would buy it. All I could do was stare at it obsessively, trying to figure out what my options were. Would my mom give me the money, my sister, could I work for it, etc. For me to leave that record there was like purposely leaving your wallet full of hundred dollar bills on a park bench and hoping when you came back it would still be there. I was also in the weird mindset again that this was the only store in America that sold the *Asylum* album.

Nobody was loaning me the money or hiring me to do odd jobs to get it. I was so frustrated. It was like having something in pawn and only having a certain amount of time to get it out or they were going to keep it and resell it. I did the only thing I could think of—every two to three days, I would walk a mile to that store to make sure no one had bought it. I would get so nervous when I walked in the store. I would quickly flip through the Kiss albums, praying. When I would see that it was still there, I would let out a big sigh of relief.

But on one of my many trips to the store, I wasn't so lucky. As usual, I flipped through the Kiss records, only the *Asylum* album wasn't there. I panicked and looked again; nothing. I anxiously looked through all of the records of other artists to see if it was mixed in with theirs, but it wasn't. Someone had bought my *Asylum* album! I was mad and heartbroken at the same time, thinking it was probably bought by some fair-weather fan who couldn't name one song off *Unmasked* if you asked them. But the bottom line is they now possessed my *Asylum* album. Even though I didn't own it legally, I still felt that I had bought it with my time and conviction.

## I WALKED EIGHT AND A HALF MILES
## IN THE SNOW FOR *ASYLUM*

Remember my friend Shawn from the *RARO* chapter, whose sister's room I snuck into just to look at the album cover? Well, this story involves the same Shawn and sister. One day in '85, I was talking to Shawn on the phone when he happened to mention that his sister Tonya had just bought *Asylum*. Immediately, I was excited! "Can I come over to listen to it?" I asked right away. He said yes. Now even more excited, I told him I would be there the next morning. The only problem was Shawn lived across town, and it was snowing pretty heavily outside. I was hoping the snow would stop by the morning. Either way, I was taking the bus, so the snow wasn't that big of a deal.

When morning came, a monkey wrench was thrown into my plans—my mother was gone. No one was in the house to loan me the bus money I needed. Sure, I could wait, but how long would it be until someone came home? Mark was spending more time at his friend's house than at home, so there was no finding him. But I had to do something. Bottom line is I had to hear this new Kiss album. I turned the house and couch cushions upside down trying to find spare change, but found nothing. I called my friend Mike who lived close by to ask him for the bus fare, but there was no answer. My options were dwindling.

I came to the realization that if I was going to listen to *Asylum* that day, I was going to have to walk. Damn, that would be a hell of a walk. Shawn lived so far away. Maybe along the way, some miracle would happen and someone I knew would see me and pick me up or I'd find money on the ground and be able to pay for the bus. What's funny is I could've easily waited until the next day and given myself time to plan it better, but no, I had to go on that day because if I didn't, I might get hit by a car, the album might get broken by then, their record player might break down, Shawn's mom might be in a bad mood and say that I couldn't come over, etc. All sorts of crazy ideas played in my mind about what could go wrong. It had to be that day.

I began walking to Shawn's house. I recently Googled the distance between Shawn's and my old house, and it was eight and a half miles. Yes, eight and a half miles of walking in the cold and snow. But I didn't care; I was on a mission. I had looked at the album cover long enough; I had to hear what those new songs sounded like! Besides, Kiss was worth it. Like a dumbass, I was wearing gym shoes, a thin jacket, and no gloves, but off I went. Talk about being unprepared. It was my *Lord of the Rings* moment. I was on a journey, a quest if you will, to hear the new songs performed by my heroes.

After a few miles, I began to realize that no one I knew was going to stop and offer me a ride and I wasn't finding any miracle money on the ground, either. It was just Jack Frost and me. Usually, when it snows, it gets warm outside, but on this particular day, it was nightmarishly freezing. I watched people drive by in their warm cars as my ears were so frostbitten that no matter how hard I pinched them, I couldn't feel a thing. My feet were so wet and frozen, I could have taken my shoes off and probably wouldn't have known the difference. What the fuck was I thinking, attempting this journey on foot in the snow? But I knew if I hung in there, it would only be a matter of time before I could hear *Asylum*.

With about two more miles to go, I saw a car started outside someone's house. I thought to myself I could easily jump into it and be on my way. At eleven, I didn't know much about driving except what my parents had shown me, but I was down to steal a car if that meant getting out of the cold. I decided to do it. I would steal the car, dump it a few blocks from Shawn's house, then figure out how to get home later. I walked toward the car, but just when I got close to the bumper, a man came out of the house. He gave me a stern look that said, "What're you doing next to my car?" Then he said, "Get away from my car!" I just kept walking like I didn't even know he was there. I guess in retrospect, it was better, because I probably would have killed or hurt myself or someone else driving in the snow and ice.

With about a mile left, I passed by a house that had a bike on the porch covered in snow. Now when you're freezing your ass off, you'll do just about anything to get to your destination. I planned to steal the bike and ride it to Shawn's house on the snowy, icy roads. Not the smartest plan, but I was desperate. I walked up to the porch and grabbed the bike, but when I pulled it, I realized it was locked to the porch. Then the porch light came on and a mean-looking man was staring at me through the window. He opened the door, and I hauled ass out of there as fast as I could. Again, in retrospect, I guess it would have been easier walking than trying to ride a bike on the ice. But I continued on with my journey.

I stopped at a public Laundromat to warm up. The cashier was watching everything I was doing and knew I wasn't a paying customer. I had my eye on someone's heavy winter jacket that was laying on a chair. "I'll just grab the jacket and run out," I thought to myself. I know this chapter has a lot of stories of me stealing, but when you're frozen solid and going back home isn't an option, you'll do just about anything to survive. The cashier approached me and asked if I was there to do laundry or if I was warming up. She seemed really nice and pleasant, like she would offer me warm cocoa. I told her that I was warming up for a moment before I went outside again. That's when she told me I couldn't loiter and to please leave! She turned out to have a bad attitude. Again, I continued on with my journey in the freezing cold.

Finally, I had made it to Shawn's house. Thank the heavens. By the time I knocked on his front door, I was a freezing cold mess. The grease in my hair was frozen, I had frozen snot coming out of my nose, and my hands wouldn't stop shaking from the frostbite. Also, I was hacking up green spit. Still, I had made it, and my attitude was "OK, where's that *Asylum* record?!"

Shawn gave me some of his clothes while my clothes were in the dryer. He wanted to update me and show me some of the new cool shirts and pants his mom had recently bought him. He was also showing me his new remote control car, but I only had one thing on my mind, *Asylum*!

Finally, the moment came. I sat on his sister's bed while Shawn put the album on the turntable. *This is it*, I thought. I was finally going to get to hear *Asylum*. I was shaking so bad from excitement. Shawn continued

**169**

talking as he played with the buttons and knobs on the record player, and I wanted to yell out, "I can't take it anymore! Just play the fuckin' record!" Then it happened.

When Eric's drumming started on "King of the Mountain," I thought that I was going to shit bricks, it sounded so tight to me. And when the song started, I realized that it had been worth the long walk to his house. Just from listening to that first song, I knew that this album was going to be heavy and special. Then "Any Way You Slice It" came on, and again, I loved it. When that breakdown came on and Eric was beating the tom-toms, without hearing the rest of the album, I said, "This is my favorite song on this record." But my victory listen was short lived. While the intro of "Who Wants to Be Lonely" was starting, his sister Tonya came home. Shawn quickly ran in the door, took the album off, and told me to get out of her room. It's funny how both my *RARO* and *Asylum* experiences took place in her bedroom so many years apart.

She was leaving for the weekend and stopped by the house to get a few things to take with her, including the *Asylum* album. My heart was beating fast and my emotions were all over the place. *Please don't dangle the carrot in front of me and then pull it away. Not after the new great Kiss songs I just heard; please, let me just finish listening to it.* Shawn mentioned to her how I had walked all the way there from my house to listen to it, but she didn't care; she was taking it with her. But she was sympathetic to me having to walk and gave me a ride home. All that walking in the freezing cold was for nothing. I was almost caught trying to steal a car and a bike, was kicked out of a Laundromat, my hands were frostbitten, and for what? I was so sad and disappointed that I didn't speak in the car the whole ride home. I just sat in the passenger seat moping. Tonya wasn't even half the Kiss fan I was, but she got to drive away with the *Asylum* album. Life isn't fair.

## THEY NEVER PLAY A WHOLE KISS ALBUM ON THE RADIO

The next day, my friend Jamie and I stayed the night at our friend Paul's house. Paul was a wannabe stoner who always wore heavy metal shirts, ripped up jeans, and smoked a lot of pot. But the funny thing was this white boy was also a wannabe hip-hopper? He would always talk using hip-hop slang and referred to everyone as "blood." He would say things like "Blood came up to me last night acting really stupid." He was just young and having an identity crisis. Jamie and I always thought it was funny.

While they were playing some board game, I was still moping and depressed from the day before. I had been so close to hearing *Asylum*. Paul had the rock station on the radio when the DJ came on and said "And don't forget, we'll be playing the new Kiss record *Asylum* in its entirety tonight! So make sure you're tuned in." I couldn't believe what I was actually hearing. It was going to happen. *Tonight, I'll get to hear* Asylum *from beginning to end*. I had gotten my miracle! It was a day late, but I got it.

While *Asylum* played on the radio that night, I stared at the speaker in a trance. I don't think I even blinked. I remember while listening thinking to myself, *Wow, these songs are really heavy*. I loved it. I slept well that night.

## FINALLY, IT'S MINE

There was a rocker guy who lived in our building, Stan. In his mid-twenties, Stan was an OK guy. Funny and a little odd. One day, he saw me reading my comic books outside and took an interest in my collection. We struck up a conversation and began discussing a trade. He mentioned that he had some comic books and cassette tapes he'd be willing to trade. I asked him if he had any Kiss tapes and if he did, I would be willing to trade. He said he did. He brought out a cardboard box full of tapes. It was full of artists I had never heard of before, and while digging through the crappy box, I had yet to find a Kiss tape. Obviously, he was bullshitting me. Then, at the very bottom, I saw it. It jumped out at me and bit me like the black mamba snake from *Kill Bill*. It was an *Asylum* tape.

I decided to just play it cool and let him know I didn't see anything that I really wanted. After he showed me what he wanted from my comic book collection, I decided to try to hustle him a little. It wasn't that I was trying to be sneaky, but I wasn't going to let him swindle me out of a bunch of my comics for a few tapes. Truth be told, he could've had all of my comic books for that *Asylum* tape, but he didn't know that.

Remember that scene in the 1985 movie *Mask*, where Rocky Dennis was trading baseball cards with his friend? Rocky told his friend the card he had in his possession was useless but he would take it off his hands anyway. But Rocky really wanted that baseball card. I was pulling the same hustle. I lied and told Stan that I already had *Asylum* on record and it wasn't that good, but I would take it anyway and give it to my brother, plus a few other cassettes of his. And just like that, I was the proud owner of my very own *Asylum* cassette. Happy days are here again!

I don't know why, but I was obsessed with learning all the lyrics on *Asylum* as fast as I could. So every day after school, instead of doing my homework, I would play the tape and read along with the lyric sheet until I learned all the lyrics.

ERIC'S PERFORMANCE ON *ASYLUM* IS WAY BETTER THAN HIS PERFORMANCE ON *CREATURES*. ALSO, BRUCE'S PERFORMANCE ON *ASYLUM* WAS BETTER THAN *REVENGE*.

To me *Asylum* has always been the Bruce and Eric Carr album. Not only do their performances stand out on this album, but they really shine on this album more than any other Kiss album they've performed on.

FUCK *REVENGE*! BRUCE WAS BETTER ON *ASYLUM*

When fans talk about Bruce coming into his own or his best guitar work, they usually say it happened on *Revenge*. I don't believe that. To me, Bruce wasn't doing anything special on that album. Yes, on *Revenge*, his playing isn't as predictable, and yes, there is a little difference in his style and technique. Of course, I'm not taking anything away from Bruce or saying that his playing on *Revenge* wasn't great. I'm just pointing out that there is so much effects, distortion, and reverb on his mixes, I think fans have mistaken that for great or unique playing. I'm also glad that his playing on *Asylum* doesn't have all of those effects, distortion, and reverb melting over each other. On *Asylum,* I can actually hear what he's playing more clearly. When you really listen, his style on *Revenge* wasn't that much different from his style on *Asylum* or *Hot in the Shade*. I mean, the lead guitar solo on "Read My Body" could have easily been a solo on *Revenge*. Think about how that solo sounds. But there are many other solos from those albums that could have been on *Revenge* as well. I still say that *Asylum* is Bruce's best work.

## ERIC'S DRUMMING ON *ASYLUM* IS FAR SUPERIOR TO *CREATURES*

When fans talk about Eric Carr's drumming on Kiss albums, *Creatures* is the album they usually praise as his best work. I totally disagree with that. I think some fans are mistaking the way his drums were mixed and recorded on *Creatures* as great drumming. Loud thunderous drum sounds doesn't mean great drumming. The drumming on *Creatures* is actually pretty simple and basic, if you listen to it. *Creatures* is just good drumming, nothing special. I believe that Eric's drumming shines more on *Asylum* than any other Kiss album.

## IT MIGHT BE THE SKITTLES ALBUM, BUT IT'S STILL A HEAVY ALBUM

To me, *Asylum* is a heavy rock album. And even though it's heavier than *Animalize*, it's also one of the most criticized non-makeup albums ever. I personally believe that again, it's a situation of what Paul said about *Creatures,* fans listening with their eyes instead of their ears. I believe with all the Skittles colors that surrounded that era from the album cover, videos, stage outfits, stage logo, and Gene's big wigs, that some fans couldn't see or get past that.

Let me paint a scenario for you. Now imagine in 1985 that *Asylum* was released with the *Revenge* album cover. Let us also imagine that instead of the bright colors they wore on that tour, they wore the same outfits they wore on the *Revenge* tour. Now having absorbed all of that, would you still say *Asylum* was a weak album? And don't just give a negative blunt answer, either; I mean really think about it. The new dangerous album cover with the new heavy metal *Revenge* stage outfits. Doesn't changing the look of the album cover and stage setting make you hear the songs differently? Don't songs like "King of the Mountain," Any Way You Slice It," "I'm Alive,"

"Love's a Deadly Weapon," "Radar for Love," and "Uh! All Night" now make the album seem heavier?

Still not convinced? OK, let's reverse this scenario. Imagine the *Revenge* album comes out in 1992. It has the same music and balls to the wall rock songs. But it's released with the *Asylum* album cover. Also, on the tour, they're wearing the *Asylum* outfits. Yes, Gene is singing "Unholy" in his *Asylum* outfit and big wig. Now with this in mind, with the *Asylum* album cover and *Asylum* stage set in 1992, does *Revenge* still seem like a heavy album? No, it doesn't. Why? Because as fans, we would be so turned off by the bright Skittles colors of the band that it would undermine the music as well. Like *Revenge*, *Asylum* is a heavy album, just packaged differently. And of course I'm not saying that *Asylum* is as heavy as *Revenge,* but it's still heavy. Because of Bruce and Carr's performances this is my second favorite Kiss album of all time.

## THE SONGS

## KING OF THE MOUNTAIN

With the exception of *Unmasked*, and the tempo of "Is That You?" being a little slower, in the '80s, Kiss would follow the same pattern of Paul opening up the albums with an up-tempo fast song. "King of the Mountain" was the last great album opener of the '80s. I don't include "Crazy Nights" since that was actually the title track single.

I love to sing along to it. Eric's drumming and Bruce's leads, forget about it. Tight as hell!

## ANY WAY YOU SLICE IT

Back then, this was my favorite song off the album and to sing along to. The way Eric is beating the drums on the breakdown is the shit. I used to also love the ending, "Any mooooorrreee aahoo." Another great lead guitar solo. I love all of Gene's songs on *Asylum*.

## WHO WANTS TO BE LONELY

Definitely one of my favorite Bruce Kulick guitar solos of the '80s. This song is flawless. Way underrated and unappreciated. Why it's never been on a greatest hits, I don't know. Not only should it have been a major rock hit in the '80s, it should have been a major '80s hit, period.

## TRIAL BY FIRE

My favorite song on the album. I think it represents a calm, cool, collected Gene. It makes me think of the business side of Gene. I just love the feel of this song. I used to play it a lot in the early '90s.

## I'M ALIVE

It's fun to sing along to.

## LOVE'S A DEADLY WEAPON

I want to take a moment to thank Kiss for making this song. I LOVE IT! This song definitely has the demon stamp on it. Because of the way Gene sings it, with growling and straining his voice and that high note he hits at the end, he definitely took his vocal delivery back to the '70s. His delivery here is a cross between "Almost Human," "Burning Up with Fever," and "Rockin' in the USA." The only thing missing was Donna Summer's vocals. Everything about this song is tight, and Eric is getting busy. The lead, bass guitar, and drumming on the solo is the shit! I love that bass guitar. Also, the way Eric is hitting the ride cymbal on the solo. When the song ends, I would always try to see if I could hold that high note with Gene. Sometimes I could, and sometimes I couldn't. But now, in my early forties, I don't even attempt it. I get winded just walking up stairs.

## TEARS ARE FALLING

I appreciate this song so much more as an adult. As a kid, I would usually skip past it, but loved to watch the video. This song is an underrated '80s

Kiss single. I love Eric's drumming on the chorus. Is that Eric singing with Paul after the lead guitar solo?

## SECRETLY CRUEL

Another Gene song I love to sing along to. I get really comical, and I also make the big Gene *Dynasty* eyes when I sing to it. I love it to death.

## RADAR FOR LOVE

This song did absolutely nothing for me when I was a kid. Now I love it. I especially like the rhythm guitar on the breakdown, where Paul is saying "Get down!" That guitar part reminds me of the rhythm guitar breakdown on the Winger song "Seventeen."

## UH! ALL NIGHT

This is my shit! I love the rhythm guitar on the breakdown after the lead guitar solo.

## ALBUM COVER

I never had a problem with the album cover. It was what it was. I could take it or leave it. To me, it was just another boring Kiss album cover of just their faces—again. And of course, Gene and Paul are on top and the two new guys are on the bottom. That image made for a cool T-shirt, but that was about it for me. If I had to choose one or the other, I think that the picture on the back of the album would have made a better cover. In the end, it was a typical '80s album cover, but by the time Kiss did it, the concept was already a few years dated.

I like the title, but if you're going to give the album a title like *Asylum*, at least have a theme to go with it.

## THE OUTFITS

I liked the way they looked during the *Asylum* era, except for Gene, of course. But the rest of them looked good. Some outfits were better than others. I could be wrong, but I can't think of any other group who looked like that during that time. To me, it was an '80s version of *Dynasty*. I loved looking at the cool magazine pictures of *Asylum* Paul and all of the different outfits he was wearing. His outfits looked really good to me. There was one pink outfit Eric had that was really horrible, but other than that, I just saw *Asylum* as a fun era.

A lot of fans put down the *Asylum* outfits. But I believe it's because they don't like the way Gene looks, with his ridiculous colorful outfits and big wigs, so they put the *Asylum* outfits down as a whole. Gene actually had an *Asylum* outfit that I thought was good. I was trying to find a picture of it as I'm typing this chapter, but can't find it on Google images. It was a live shot of him. I remember the outfit was dark and I believe it had open holes in the upper side of the leg. It looked decent and not as cheesy as his other *Asylum* outfits. But the worst thing he wore onstage during that era was that big red sweater like thing that was really shiny. Aside from that, Gene's other *Asylum* outfits didn't bother me, at least not as much.

## THE VIDEOS

## WHO WANTS TO BE LONELY

I didn't get to actually see this video in full until *Kiss eXposed* came out. I never saw it on MTV or other video channels. The visuals for this video are perfect for this song. I love Paul's walking intro. It's weird because Gene's *Asylum* outfits could sometimes look ridiculous and silly onstage but in the three *Asylum* videos, he doesn't look that bad. He looks like Gene. In this video, he manages to look a little menacing. I also like the way they utilized the women. Instead of just being props, they were actually involved in the action of the video. All four members looked good. I like Eric's drum setup. A much-underrated Kiss video. It's my favorite Kiss video of all time.

## TEARS ARE FALLING

When this video first came out, I used to think that the woman in the video, the part where she's surrounded by fog/smoke, was Tanya Roberts from the movie *Beastmaster*. She also plays Donna's mother on *That '70s Show*. I remember seeing this video on MTV all the time. I remember just being happy that they were playing something from Kiss. I really liked Gene's bass in the video and wanted one of my own. I was trying to save up money because there was one just like it at a guitar shop a few blocks from my house. Then the shop went out of business so I gave up on that. It's another great video from Kiss.

## UH! ALL NIGHT

This video always seemed too dark. The women in the wigs were stupid. I never saw this on any music video channels either. *Kiss eXposed* is the first time I saw it. In the end, it's not a great video, but it's fun to watch.

FAVORITE SONG: "Trial by Fire"
FAVORITE RHYTHM GUITAR: "Radar for Love"
FAVORITE LEAD GUITAR: "Who Wants to Be Lonely"
FAVORITE BASS: "Love's a Deadly Weapon"
FAVORITE DRUMS: "Any Way You Slice It"

THROWAWAY: "Radar for Love"

MESSING UP THE LYRICS:

"Secretly Cruel," first verse: "Thigh-high Gene Simmons's boots!"

# Chapter 29

## CRAZY NIGHTS

One day in '87, while at home, I was in my room playing the radio on my stereo. While turning the dial, I stopped on a particular song for no reason. While listening to it, I thought to myself, *That sounds like Paul.* Then I realized that it was a new Kiss song. Anxious and excited, I grabbed a tape, put it in, and pushed record. When the song was over, I played the tape back and the recording sucked, but I still had half the song. I was pretty sure, but I had to make certain it really was Kiss. Whoever it was kept saying "Crazy nights" over and over again. I knew right then it was Kiss. Wow! A new Kiss song, which meant a new Kiss album, had to be out there as well.

My friend Jamie and I were at the mall a few days later, and I quickly walked to the record store to see if there was a new Kiss album. While walking to the Kiss section, I saw big posters of the *Crazy Nights* album cover on the walls and a row of *Crazy Nights* albums in an area all by themselves. I grabbed one and just stared at it. The broken pieces of glass on the cover had my attention, and I had that excited shaking feeling I get whenever I hold a brand new Kiss album. *Crazy Nights* was here, and it looked amazing. The only problem was I didn't have any money to buy it.

My mom said that she would give me the money when she got paid in a few weeks, so I had to play the waiting game. Talk about marking the calendar. Each day I woke up would be one day closer to my mom's payday and one day closer to *Crazy Nights*. Finally, payday came, and she gave me ten dollars, but she wouldn't let me go to the record store that night. She said I could go buy it after school the next day.

When I woke up, I was the most excited and happiest kid in junior high school. That day, I was gonna get my very own *Crazy Nights* album. From the time I walked into the school I was counting the minutes on the clock. I had already bought a magazine with Kiss in their new *Crazy Nights* outfits and would look at it whenever the teacher wasn't looking. I just had *Crazy Nights* on the brain that day. Even when my boys were playing the dozens and snappin' on each other in the hallway, I didn't join in; my mind was somewhere else. My boy Jimmy came up to my locker and reminded me that there was a dance after school and they were going to be playing all the latest rap groups of the time, MC Shan, The Skinny Boys, Kool Moe Dee, Heavy D, BDP, etc. This was an all-black junior high school. He said this was our chance to get up onstage and perform our rap songs that we'd been practicing every day at his house. Our rap group at that time was just us lip syncing to the popular rap songs of that era. But we loved doing that at the local talent shows. And this was our chance to get up in front of the girls at our school and rock the mic. I had to make a decision. Damn, I really wanted to get up on that stage in front of those girls, but what if I finally get to the record store later and they're sold out of the *Crazy Nights* album? What if the record store catches fire or if there's a hostage situation? Or what if they sell out of every copy and don't order any more? There I go again, trippin'. I made my decision and told Jimmy I had something else important that I had to do. "Come on, nigga, this is our chance!" he said. Again, I said I couldn't. In this particular situation, I chose *Crazy Nights* over rockin' the mic and mackin' to girls.

I had already grabbed everything from my locker from the class before so when the school bell rang I could haul ass out of the school and onto the city bus. I didn't even stop to say, "What's up" to my homies. While on the bus, all I could think of was *Crazy Nights*. I would get so mad every time the bus had to stop to pick somebody up or let somebody off. And of course we hit every red light. The bus ride was way too long, at least for me. I got off a block from the record store, and I ran that block in ten seconds. The track coach would have been proud. I ran in the door of the record store out of breath and asked excitedly, "Do you have the new Kiss record *Crazy Nights*?" At that very moment, some big white guy who worked there came out of the back room and yelled out "Kiss sucks!" for no reason at all. Then he turned around and walked back in the door he'd come out of. It happened so quickly and out of the blue that I was temporarily stuck and confused. It was like somebody walked into the room, slapped me in the face, and just walked away. My blood was boiling. I was biting my bottom lip, pissed off. I was gonna fuck this mutha fucka up for dissin' Kiss like that. Sure, he was twice my age, three times my size, and he looked like The Thing from the *Fantastic Four*. I'm pretty sure I could've taken him and beat that ass. But he was lucky, I had to get home so my mom didn't worry about me or I would've fucked his punk ass up. OK, the truth is I punked down, LOL. But if you would've seen the size of this white boy, you would've, too. Where's a grape Slurpee when you need one? Moving on.

The other cashier walked me to the Kiss records and pulled it out for me. He handed me my first *Crazy Nights* album. I never let go of it, not even for him to put it in a bag. I proudly walked home with it in my hands.

When I got the treasure chest home, I showed it to my mom, all excited. To me, buying a Kiss album in those days gave me the same feeling as when I accomplished something big, and I wanted to show off my trophy. My mother looked at it and was happy for me. She looked at the back, pointed to Paul, and said, "That's my boyfriend."

## WHY WASN'T *CRAZY NIGHTS* A BIGGER SUCCESS?

To me, this should have been a bigger comeback album for the band. Yes, "Reason to Live" got a lot of rotation on MTV, but unlike the other hair bands of that era, *Crazy Nights* didn't awe the audiences. The singles had the right amount of pop rock element and were catchy. The videos were big and bright, coming off the TV screen, but they just didn't have the impact in a major way. I think this album should have easily sold at least four or five million copies in its first run. The singles were there, but I guess the buying public wasn't. The *Crazy Nights* era had a lot of mystery and magic to me. Back then, there was something about seeing Kiss in those rock magazines and videos wearing their *Crazy Nights* outfits that would leave me in wonder.

## WHY DO FANS HATE THIS ALBUM?

It's funny, because to me, *Crazy Nights* has more of a Kiss makeup feel to it than any other non-makeup album. It might have something to with the party anthems on the album. It's definitely the sister album to *Dynasty* and *Unmasked*. Gene's songs and the way he sings them on this album also have the same feel as songs like "Charisma" and "X-Ray Eyes," and I think that's cool. And the chorus on "I'll Fight Hell to Hold You" is reminiscent of "Sure Know Something." To me, the whole vibe of this album is makeup Kiss. But every Kiss fan is different and hears Kiss music differently. Then there's the fact that the finished product has so much treble. I realized that when I was young, and it was confirmed when Ron Nevison spoke on that in a recent interview and said it's something on the album that he would have done differently. But that was never an issue for me. It still sounds great! *Dressed to Kill* has a lot of treble on it, but fans never complain about that. I guess that's because it's a '70s Kiss album with the original members and we associate that album with a particular period in our lives, so we give the treble on that album a free pass.

## BON JOVI?

Something else I don't get is why fans keep calling this the Bon Jovi album. I do know that in the '80s, with the success of *Slippery When Wet,* Paul was saying that they wanted to look and have that Bon Jovi sound. I don't think *Crazy Nights* sounds anything like Bon Jovi at all, nor do they have the look. But then again, a real Bon Jovi fan might see the similarities that I don't. I can't say that I've followed or paid that much attention to Bon Jovi. I'm just saying from what I've seen in his videos and the sound of his songs on the radio, I don't see the comparison.

## I THINK *TOP OF THE POPS*

The only time I saw any TV promotion for *Crazy Nights* was when Kiss performed on a TV show hosted by Nia Peeples. I think it was called *Top of the Pops*. I watched it when it aired for the first time. I thought it was so funny when Paul kept opening the dressing room doors thinking that it was going to be a certain celebrity and it would still be Kiss. Then when he gets to the last door it says Kiss on the door, and when he walks in, it's Nia Peeples. Then when they performed "Crazy Crazy Nights," I was glued to the TV set.

## THE SONGS

### CRAZY CRAZY NIGHTS

This song should have been an instant party pop rock anthem. A much bigger hit. In the '80s, it should have been up there with Poison's "Nothin' But A Good Time." Companies should be using it in their TV commercials to sell their products. But for some reason, it doesn't get its due credit for being such a great anthem.

### I'LL FIGHT HELL TO HOLD YOU

As a teen, I would think, *How can you hold somebody by your side?* Today, it's my second favorite song on the album. I like Eric's drumming on it and Paul's vocals. The lead guitar solo is tight, too.

### BANG BANG YOU

It was my second favorite song on the album when I was a teen. I like the rhythm and lead guitar solo. When I was younger, I thought it was so cool that he said "love gun" in the song.

ANTHONY X

## NO, NO, NO

To me, this song is the sister song to "Burn Bitch Burn." Same feel and all. Of course, I like Bruce's intro solo. I always imitate it with my mouth. I love singing along to it.

## HELL OR HIGH WATER

I love it! My favorite song on the album.

## MY WAY

As a teen, I would skip past this. But Mark, who was living in Kansas at the time, would always tell me how much he liked the song and played it all the time. So I gave it a second chance, and it started to grow on me. I played it a lot just to see if I could sing and match Paul's vocals. I never liked the way the song ended. Paul is singing loud and proud, then at the end, his voice drops and so does the music. I always thought they should have ended the song on a high note. Great song!

## WHEN YOUR WALLS COME DOWN

One afternoon, a week after I bought the album, I was watching a soap opera with my mom. There was a scene that I believe had some punk teenagers hanging out or something like that, and they were playing "When Your Walls Come Down" in the background. I said to my mom, "That's a song from the new Kiss album." I thought it was so cool that an afternoon soap opera was playing it.

## REASON TO LIVE

Every time I turned on MTV, "Reason to Live" was on. That was a good thing. Still, it just didn't go on to be the '80s classic it should have been. I think it should have been as big a hit as Whitesnake's "Is this Love." And today, it should be rotated on soft rock radio with groups like the Eagles, Chicago, and Tears for Fears. Again, the '80s were the real Kiss radio classics for me. What a waste of a powerful song. Retro stations just don't know what they're missing.

## GOOD GIRL GONE BAD

This was my first favorite song on the album as a teen. I liked it when Paul said "c'mon" in the chorus. I just like the feel of it.

## TURN ON THE NIGHT

I always thought this song would have been good in a Pepsi commercial. Without the band, of course. The song would be playing in the background. There would be people outside in the city, and every time they took a sip of their Pepsi, streetlights and building lights would turn on. Then at the end of the commercial, the narrator would say, "Turn on the night with a Pepsi!"

Why such a great song like this is so unappreciated is too bad. I think it's a great and powerful pop rock song.

## THIEF IN THE NIGHT

I can appreciate it now that I'm older. It's not a song that I make a point to play, but I enjoy singing along to it when it comes on. The lead guitar solo is on point.

## THE ALBUM COVER

Again, another album cover with just their boring faces that have nothing to do with the title. The title is *Crazy Nights*, which is a great title but it also suggests partying and wild times. Yet the expressions on their faces look stern and bored. Remember that *Revenge* photo shoot where they were being crazy, silly, and more heavy metal with their mouths open? That would have been a better concept photo for the cover and title than four sad faces. Also, it's kind of a dark cover and that doesn't go with the party theme. The broken pieces of glass make it too much to look at. I don't think it's bad, but it's not great. Funny how Bruce and Eric make it to the top of the album this time, but their heads are turned upside down. Poor guys. Well at least Eric made it to the top on *Creatures*.

I do like the back. I like the way Bruce and Gene are holding their guitars.

## KISS ROCKS JAPAN??

I had a bootleg copy of the *Crazy Nights* tour in Japan in the mid '90s. When I received it in the mail, I had to go to work shortly afterward and couldn't wait to get home to watch it. When I played it that night, I said "What the fuck?" The concert was horrible. It was way toned down and didn't even have a Kiss logo or fireworks. The stage looked like they were at a high school auditorium. And the way Gene, Paul, and Bruce were jumping around to "Cold Gin" was embarrassing. It was such a horrible performance that they edited some old '77 footage of Kiss into the show at the end, I guess to make up for it being so bad. I felt bad for those Tokyo fans who I'm sure expected so much more.

## THE VIDEOS

## CRAZY CRAZY NIGHTS

I still have my VHS copy with the three videos on it. I love this video. It should have gone over well on MTV and pulled the pop rock fans in more. To me, this video was a celebration of the band. Great audience shots, and Paul walking into the crowd was a good touch. A lot of excitement. Again, this should have been a big comeback album for them.

## REASON TO LIVE

I saw this on MTV all the time. I didn't like the idea of it being shot on a stage. They should have gone somewhere else with the location or background. Something like the location in the "Forever" video or outside, like the Cinderella video "Don't Know What You Got (Till It's Gone)." Also, I wouldn't have used the woman in the video. Her scenes didn't make sense, playing with a gun and setting his car on fire. It was corny and vindictive. The song pulls at the heartstrings and has a lot of feel to it so they should have taken the plot in a warm, melting direction instead. Recently, on Yahoo! news, they were showing the women who played on the ZZ Top video "Legs" and what they look like today. I was reading some of the comments below and someone asked, "Why don't you show what the woman from Kiss' 'Reason to Live' video looks like today?" If I'm correct, I believe she's married to the creator/owner of Paul Mitchell hair products. I'm not a hundred percent sure though.

## TURN ON THE NIGHT

The video is perfect for this song. No flaws. Mark used to imitate Paul when he was bent down and walking up the ramp. I used to piss on myself laughing when he would do that. It's my favorite video of the three.

FAVORITE SONG: "Hell or High Water"
FAVORITE RHYTHM GUITAR: "Bang Bang You"
FAVORITE LEAD GUITAR: "I'll Fight Hell to Hold You"
FAVORITE BASS: "No, No, No"
FAVORITE DRUMS: "I'll Fight Hell to Hold You"

THROWAWAY: "Thief in the Night"

## Chapter 30

## SMASHES, THRASHES & HITS

My introduction to this album was the "Let's Put the X in Sex" video. Initially, I had no idea what was on the album or that it was a greatest hits. All I knew was that MTV played this video a lot. I remember always keeping MTV on just so I could catch it. At fourteen, I was still in the mindset that if it was Kiss, then it was all good. At this point in my life, as a Kiss fan, there was still little Kiss could do to turn me off from them.

I was living in Junction City, Kansas, at that time. I was dating a girl who had a job. I wasn't working then, so money was funny for me. But I told her when she got paid that she had to by me the *Smashes, Thrashes & Hits* tape. She kept telling me she would, but every time she was paid, something would always come up and she never bought me the tape. As a result, I broke up with her. You could break a promise but not a Kiss promise. It wouldn't be until a year later, when I came back to Alaska, that I would actually own a copy.

Now, I don't necessarily think it was the right direction for Kiss to go in, considering all the other bands out at that time who were having hit records. *Appetite for Destruction* was still popular, the *Hysteria* album was also dominating, the Bon Jovi *New Jersey* album, and *Open Up and Say... Ahh!* were still getting major rotation. "One" was beginning to make its mark on MTV, sending Metallica to the next level. And let's not forget that the *Dr. Feelgood* album was just about to stick its head out from under the dirt. Yes, the "X in Sex" video did get a lot of major airplay on MTV, but

I don't think it did anything to help the band's reputation or place in the commercial hard rock world, at least to hard rock non-Kiss fans of that era.

## THE SONGS

It's a greatest hits package, so I won't cover every song because there's no need to.

## LET'S PUT THE X IN SEX

Let me say right off the top, I love "Let's Put the X in Sex"! I like the groove, keyboards, rhythm guitar, and Bruce's solo. I especially like the way Paul's voice gets higher during the chorus. Yes, it's very poppy, a pinch of corny and cheesy, but whenever Kiss tries to experiment with a different sound, country, disco, opera, etc., whether you like that different sound or not, they always execute it well. To me, this is an awesome Kiss pop song.

## (YOU MAKE ME) ROCK HARD

I like it a lot, especially the cowbell. Probably played off a keyboard. It's a good Kiss pop song. I like the prelude to the chorus.

## DETROIT ROCK CITY

I hated it when the classic rock station The Fox in Anchorage, Alaska, would play this version of "Detroit Rock City." It sounds hollow, dull, and flat. It doesn't complement Peter's drumming at all. I cringe at this version.

## I LOVE IT LOUD

Again, hollow, dull, and flat. What were they thinking? Where are the loud thunderous drums? Where's the depth? Fox radio plays this version too. I can't stand it.

## DEUCE

Let's be clear. Greatest hits aren't for Kiss fans. They're for turning on a new generation and potential fans around the world. So why on earth would Kiss or the label put the studio version of "Deuce" on a greatest hits package? I love the *Alive!* version of "Deuce," but I wouldn't want it on a greatest hits album. I'm not saying that just because the studio version sounds awful to me, but there were a number of songs that could have easily been put on there to turn people on to classic Kiss: "Take Me," "All Hell's Breakin' Loose," "Shandi," "Room Service," etc. Like any Kiss fan, I could go on all day, but that's just my opinion.

## BETH

I guess I can understand what made them do it at that time, but again, just because you can do it, doesn't mean you should. Let me say that I think vocally, Eric did a great job, but the bottom line is when it comes to "Beth," Peter's raspy voice plays a major part in making that song what it is. Personally, I'm OK with Singer doing it live, but I don't think Kiss should have ever attempted to re-record and package this song on an album. Paul has a lot of negative things to say about "X in Sex" and "Rock Hard;" I wonder how he feels about the decision to redo "Beth"?

Now that I think about, I always think of "Little Caesar" as being the first time Eric did lead vocals on a Kiss album. I always forget about "Beth." Ain't that peculiar?

## ALBUM COVER

I don't think that the picture itself is bad; it's actually kind of cool. My only problem with it is it's too dark. It should have been a brighter picture.

## THE VIDEOS

## LET'S PUT THE X IN SEX

I love this video. Again, poppy with a pinch of corny and cheesy, but I love it. Why does Gene's face look like it was dipped in flour? It's probably the worst Gene's ever looked in a Kiss video. And that kick he does toward the camera is a little cringe worthy. But to recap, I love it.

In the '90s, I was dating a sista who really didn't care for my Kiss obsession. She didn't mind that I liked Kiss as long as I didn't bore her with it. But one day while she was over, I was playing the "X in Sex" video that I had recorded on VHS. All through the video, she kept talking about how sexy Paul was. "He's a really good-looking man," she kept saying. Because of that video and her newfound attraction for Paul, she tolerated my Kiss obsession a little more.

## YOU MAKE ME ROCK HARD

I think some songs aren't meant to be videos, and this might be proof of that. The song itself doesn't set it up to be a cool video. It wasn't as competitive with "X in Sex" or with the other rock videos of the day. The contortionist and acrobats were OK, I guess. It's not a video that I care for or make a point to watch when I'm surfing for Kiss videos on YouTube. I don't like it or hate it, it's more of a question mark for me. I'd rather just listen to the song.

## MESSING UP THE LYRICS:

"Let's Put the X in Sex," "You're begging for an apple but you'll only get a pea."

## Chapter 31

# HOT IN THE SHADE

I believe it was Mark who saw the "Hide Your Heart" video first, then the next day, I went over to his apartment and we watched it again together on MTV. My first thought was the song and video were different from anything else they'd done before. I didn't think it was going to be a big hit, but I loved the new concept of them looking somewhat normal in a video.

Maybe a few days afterward, while driving around with Mark's fiancée, Eileene, we stopped at the Sears mall and bought our first copy of *Hot in the Shade* on cassette. While leaving the parking lot, we popped the tape in and prepared ourselves to be sucked into a world of new Kiss music. The acoustic guitar intro began; it was weird and different but cool at the same time. Then the song began, "Rise to It." OK, so far so good. It doesn't sound quite as good as "King of the Mountain" but not bad. We continued to listen to the verse, still OK. Then, the unthinkable happened—the chorus came on. When they started singing that chorus, Mark and I gave each other a look and an embarrassing smile that said, "What the fuck is this?" It sounded horrible. Paul is going to "Rise to It," OK...

As the songs went on, it didn't get that much better. "Betrayed" was OK, I guess. We already knew "Hide Your Heart." But by the time we got to "Read My Body," on first listen, I said, "That sounds like 'Pour Some Sugar On Me'." We were disgusted by "Love's a Slap in the Face," especially when Gene started singing "Nah, nah, nah, nah." I'll never forget looking at Mark and my exact words were, "A lot of these songs sound like a bunch of extras that they had lying around the studio and they just made a record out of them." Later, I would learn that I was halfway right. We just stopped the tape midway through and finished listening to it later that night. No need to make Eileene suffer through it.

After that first listen and about a week had past, I began playing *HITS* every single day. I fell in love with the album. In '89-'90, I played *HITS* more than any other non-makeup album ever. As a prep cook, in that same era, I played it twice a night at work. I just loved those songs. I think part of the appeal was that there was a new Kiss album with a lot of songs on it, and I loved new Kiss songs.

As I'm writing this, I still love this album to death, and I played it in its entirety twice last week.

## I HATE THE SNARE ON THIS ALBUM

My biggest complaint about this album is the snare drum. It's too loud in the mix, and it has too much of a *bam, bam, bam* sound to it. I find it annoying after a while. It's really loud on "You Love Me to Hate You." It doesn't take away from anything, I just think they should have gone with a different snare or brought it back a little in the mix.

## LAYOFFS

Fans love to put this album down. But I'm willing to bet if some of the songs off of *Revenge* like "Take it Off," "Spit," "Domino," "Heart of Chrome," and "Paralyzed" would have appeared on this album, fans would have said those songs suck too. But you take those same songs and package them on the *Revenge* album and it's all good? Also, you could've taken some of the songs off *HITS* like "Prisoner of Love," "Silver Spoon," "Cadillac Dreams," "Street Giveth," "Love Me to Hate You," and "Boomerang" and packaged some of them with *Revenge* and fans would've said those songs are great! I can hear some of you now, "Not me; those *HITS* songs suck!"

## THE SONGS

### RISE TO IT

I think it's the weakest Kiss opener of all the non-makeup albums. It's a long way from "Exciter" and "I've Had Enough (Into the Fire)." Still, I enjoy listening and singing to it; it's just a fun song, especially when it's played loud.

### BETRAYED

For the first ten years, I would usually skip past this song when I could. It was too much of a downer to me. And that redundant banging snare drum annoyed the hell out of me. These days, I really like it. I'll usually sing it to myself when I'm out in public.

### HIDE YOUR HEART

How come whenever there's a story in a rock song, the character's name always has to be Johnny? It's a great song and single.

### PRISONER OF LOVE

I love this song. It's my favorite song on the album. I love the feel of it and the way Gene sings it. I also like that part where he goes "Hey, eh, eh, eh!" That's a nice touch. I like the solo, where Eric and Bruce are jammin' together. I don't know why, but this song reminds me of "Got Love for Sale."

### READ MY BODY

Just like "Get All You Can Take" was a spinoff of "Keep Me Comin'," and "Bang Bang You" was a spinoff of "Love Gun," "Read My Body" was a spinoff of "X in Sex." Just heavier. Along with "Pour Some Sugar On Me," it also reminds me of "Radar For Love." They just seem similar in a way.

This is a great song! All of you haters can get that look off your faces; I'll break it down. Back in the day, when the intro beat of this song came on, it sounded really tight! I mean it was hittin'. I always wanted to sample it for one of my rap songs, but I never got around to doing it. Also, the intro rhythm guitar and lead solo were tight, but when the chorus came on, that's when the song went downhill for me. I always thought it was the words itself that made the chorus stupid, but as the years went on, having analyzed it more, I realized it was the voices saying, "Read my body" that made it sound stupid. So I began to try to hear in my head what it would sound like if Paul were just saying it by himself without the background effects or help. It was actually a lot better. It wasn't the words but the tone that made it sound stupid. Another reason I love this song is because Paul's vocals on "Read My Body" have a *Dynasty* feel and tone. This song is even better when you play it loud. I give it two thumbs up.

## LOVE'S A SLAP IN THE FACE

After I got used to it, this became my favorite song on the album back in the day. I think it was because the drumming on it reminded me of Bobby Brown's song "Prerogative." I remember reading in a rock magazine back then that they were going to make this a single off the album. I guess they came to their senses. I love it, but not as a single.

## FOREVER

During the time this single was out and being played all over the radio, everybody loved it. My mom's coworker gave her a ride home one day and "Forever" came on the radio. Her coworker said, "I can't stand Kiss, but I love this song."

One night, while leaving the club, I was in a car with two of my homies and two girls we picked up. "Forever" came on the radio. I started singing along to it really loud, and I was doing my best Paul Stanley. I was being funny but sincere. When the song ended, one of the girls, Angie, thought I was so adorable singing that song, she ended up giving me her phone number and we dated for almost a year. She also went out and bought the cassette single. She said, like my mom's coworker, "I don't like white boy music, but I love this song."

Again, the snare drum is too loud and heavy in the mix. Why isn't it rotated on retro radio stations?

## SILVER SPOON

I like the tone Paul sings it in. I love the female vocals. I used to hate the part where Paul talks in the end, but now it's all good. Back then, I used to say, "Where I'm from, everybody can do the Paul Stanley!" Love this song.

## CADILLAC DREAMS

Initially, I probably played this song the most. It was Gene being humorous in a socially educational way. I like the drumming, and that scratching noise with the guitar is tight. The horns caught me off guard the first time I heard them, but it's a nice touch. It almost seems like a throwaway from *Asylum*. I love this song.

## KING OF HEARTS

Sometimes I like it, and other times, I skip past it. I think the title is what probably annoys me the most. Overall, I like it more than I hate it. Bottom line is I always have to sing along to it when it's on.

## THE STREET GIVETH AND THE STREET TAKETH AWAY

I always find it funny when Gene and Paul try to talk about the streets or street life in their songs. It always reeks of effort. Neither of them has any street credentials or experience.

I like singing along to this song and the acoustic guitar on it. One of the winners on the album.

## YOU LOVE ME TO HATE YOU

What an awesome Paul song. I like the way he sings in that high voice on the chorus. I always thought this song would have been good for a romantic movie. One day, one of my partners who's a rapper and wouldn't listen to rock if you paid him came over. This song was playing and when it was over, he said, "That's a really good song; I like that." At first, I thought he was being funny, but he was serious. The next time he came over, he asked me to play it for him again. I love this song.

## SOMEWHERE BETWEEN HEAVEN AND HELL

This is my favorite song to sing along to on the album. I like the chorus. I believe I favor Gene's songs a little more on this album than Paul's. My favorite part to sing along to is the third verse.

## LITTLE CAESAR

It's sad that they finally gave Eric a song on an album and it becomes the second to the last song. Personally, I think it's the best song on the album. The rhythm guitar is funky as hell. I don't know why I never thought to sample it. I like the way Eric sounds on the chorus. Who knows what else we could have gotten from Eric before or after this album if given the chance or if he hadn't died. And with so many songs on the album, why couldn't they let Bruce get one in?

## BOOMERANG

I love this song to death. But it would be years after its release before I would realize how great it is. One day while it was playing, the lead guitar solo and drums came on and it just clicked. I said aloud, "That's the shit right there!" So I played that solo back about five times and wondered how come I never keyed in on that part before because Bruce's solo mixed with the drumming is tight. Also the double bass and ride cymbal. After that, I've always loved this song. Go listen to Bruce's solo with the drums on that song if you don't remember. For me, it's up there with my love for "Love's a Deadly Weapon."

## ALBUM COVER

I don't think of the album cover or title as being bad. To me, it's just more confusing in the sense of what was on their minds when they came up with them. I'm all for trying something different and unique, and it probably is one of the most unique Kiss album covers. But neither cover nor title have any spice, flair to pull you in, or get you excited. I think if maybe they would have written *Hot in the Shade* in big red letters or made it pop more on the cover, that could have made the difference. It still wouldn't have been great, but it would have given it more flair. I don't know. Bottom line is the album cover is stupid to me, but a good kind of stupid. Then again, I guess it's better than just another boring photo of their four faces. But because it's so unique, that's what makes this album cover great and special.

## THE VIDEOS

## HIDE YOUR HEART

The first time I saw this, I thought it was so cool when Gene spit on the ground. Also, when he closed the back of the ambulance door, I thought he was so mysterious and tough. Now both those scenes look cheesy as hell to me, but I mean that in a fun way. When I watch it now, it's still a great video. Good casting. I love the band performing on the roof. The gang members could have had a better, more modern car, though. And I never understood why the guy and the girl were on the roof at the end. I guess it's nothing to read into. Great video.

## FOREVER

I think it's one of their most flawless videos. Great location, great scenes, camera shots/angles, and great color. The visual complements the music. I love watching Eric play in this video and also watching Bruce play that solo. They all look good.

## RISE TO IT

The first time I saw this video, I remember thinking *Please don't put the makeup back on.* Not that I actually thought they were going to do it, but I just didn't want to see it, especially at that time. Of course the rumors, or should I say the hopefulness, was in the air for most fans. I just concluded that they were just doing this for the video and not to read too much or buy into it. Mark and I used to talk about how funny and weird Gene looked in the video with his makeup on, but we couldn't figure out why. We recently realized it was because his hairline didn't go back like it did originally. I guess he was wearing a wig or hair plugs.

I love the video and think its fun to watch. It's one of those scenes where you think as a fan, it would've been great to have been there and participated. The crowd and Kiss themselves looked like they were having a good time. The video makes the song seem not so corny.

FAVORITE SONG: "Prisoner of Love"
FAVORITE RHYTHM GUITAR: "The Street Giveth and the Street Taketh Away"
FAVORITE LEAD GUITAR: "Boomerang"
FAVORITE BASS GUITAR: "Somewhere Between Heaven and Hell"
FAVORITE DRUMS: "Boomerang"

THROWAWAY: "King of Hearts"

## Chapter 32

# MARK'S FIRST KISS CONCERT

I'll never forget the afternoon when Mark called me at home in Alaska from Arizona and said he'd just bought tickets for him and his wife to see Kiss during the *Hot in the Shade* tour in Phoenix. This was his first Kiss concert. For some reason, I had felt we would see our first Kiss concert together. Before the show, he called me from a pay phone at the arena to tell me about the hype, the excitement, the fans, and the energy surrounding the show. In addition, after the show, he called me again, telling me how dope and surreal it was.

To this day, I have never known that kind of jealousy.

## Chapter 33

## ERIC'S PASSING

From the time he joined, I never looked at Eric Carr as a new member. I have always looked at Eric as an original member who joined later on. To this day, I can still remember, as a kid, my sister Lorraine waking me up early in the morning and telling me that the new Kiss drummer was going to be on *Kids Are People Too*. I was so excited to see who he was and what he was going to look like. I remember seeing him come out from backstage for the very first time and how cool he looked. I couldn't stop staring at his face. It almost seems like yesterday. What's even weirder is only a decade later, I was watching MTV when they announced he had passed away. I was lying in bed relaxing when MTV news came on and announced it. My jaw just dropped as I stared at the TV screen without blinking. I didn't even know he was sick. But Mark did say that during the *Hot in the Shade* show he'd attended, Eric looked sick, tired, and like he was out of breath. After I heard the news, I picked myself up and put in my *Asylum* tape, lay back down, and just listened as tears rolled down my cheeks.

RIP Eric the Fox!

# Chapter 34

## SINGER'S ARRIVAL

Again, it always came down to finding out in a magazine. I was at a convenience store one night, flipping through a rock magazine, when I saw the new Kiss drummer for the first time. *A blond guy?* No, I wasn't shocked, surprised, or caught off guard because he was blond. In fact, at that moment, I thought it was cool that they were mixing it up a little. *I doubt he's as good as Eric Carr, but we'll see.* I had no clue about Eric Singer or his musical history. I just wanted to see what he was going to bring to Kiss.

ERIC SINGER IS A NICE, GREAT GUY, BUT TO BE HONEST…

I have to be honest. Initially, I didn't like his drumming style at all, and it remained a style that I never became a fan of. Singer just slowed things down, and to me, his playing wasn't special or did anything for me. Yes, he did a good job on the *Revenge* album, but in many ways when performing live, I found his drumming style to be a little choppy and slow. His style with Kiss wasn't consistent, and he didn't have that octopus effect like Eric Carr did, especially the way Eric played from 1980–85. He didn't complement the past Kiss songs like Carr did when he joined.

When I watch Eric Carr perform on the *Unmasked, Creatures,* and *Animalize* tours, my eyes and ears tell me that not only is he a far superior drummer than Peter or Singer, but he can run circles around them. So when it comes to people who say that Singer is better than Carr, I try to keep an open mind to what they're hearing. Still, I don't see or hear it. I believe when it comes to Kiss, Singer is the weakest drummer in terms of what he brings to Kiss. Both Peter and Carr brought a sound to the band that was needed and probably couldn't have been easily duplicated. But to me, Singer's sound was a dime a dozen, nothing unique. I'm not saying that Singer isn't a great drummer, but again, I'm saying his style doesn't work that much for me. But at this point in Kiss' career, it doesn't matter because now it's really just about the show/spectacle. For the record, I think personality wise, they couldn't have picked a better replacement after Carr's passing and Peter's second departure from the band. I love Singer's personality, attitude, and singing voice.

# Chapter 35

## *REVENGE*

One evening in '92, I was in my bedroom writing rhymes and going over a new beat my producer gave me. My TV was on and tuned to the local video channel but the volume was low. I looked up at the screen for a moment and saw what appeared to be Paul. I jumped up, ran to the TV set, and turned it up. It was a new Kiss video that I had never seen before, "Unholy." I caught it during the first chorus.

I didn't know what to think about the song or the video as I watched; I just stared at the tube. And when it ended, my mindset was "OK..." I didn't like it. Nothing about it excited me. I thought *Kiss has a new record and I need to call Musicland and find out if it's already out or coming out,* but I just sat back down and kept writing my rhymes.

I think my problem with the "Unholy" video when I first saw and heard it was the song wasn't the "Kiss sound" or image at all to me. I felt like "OK, now this year, you guys are trying to be hard core/metal?" Last album, we were "Rising to It;" before that, we were "Putting the X in Sex;" the record before that, we were "Turning on the Night;" but on this new song, we're so "Unholy." I wasn't buying it.

The next morning, I called Musicland and they told me that the new Kiss tape would be available the following Tuesday. When that day came, I was at the Sears mall at 9:30 a.m., Musicland opened at 10:00 a.m. I sat in my car in the parking lot anxiously awaiting the new tape. I didn't care for the way "Unholy" sounded on my cheap bedroom TV or the new direction they were going in musically, but it was still exciting knowing that Kiss was doing something different, and that made me curious as hell. *What is this new tape gonna sound like?* I wondered.

I paid the $10.99, I believe it cost, and was unwrapping the shrink-wrap as I walked to my car. I popped the tape in and just waited to see what would happen next. "Unholy" started and I listened to it on my good car speakers. By the time I got to the second verse, I thought to myself, *I was wrong; this song is off the fuckin' chain!*

## IT SOUNDS SO GREAT BUT I STILL HAVE A PROBLEM WITH IT

*Revenge* is awesome and powerful! They definitely should have stuck with this sound throughout the '90s. But as great as I think it is, it's not an album I care to listen to that much. I'll play it every once in a while. It's Kiss trying too hard to do the metal thing. That doesn't mean I don't love or appreciate the songs when I hear them, I'm just saying it doesn't do that much for me. When I listen to it, I know that Kiss is purposely trying to sound hard and metal, and that's kind of the subconscious turn off. I understand that when they recorded *Unmasked,* they were purposely trying to sound pop. But the difference to me is *Unmasked* sounds more like the "Kiss sound" than *Revenge* does because I can associate the *Unmasked* songs with the songs off of Gene and Paul's solo records, *Dynasty,* and in some ways, *Destroyer.* But it's easier for me to swallow the *Unmasked* pop phase than it is for me to swallow the *Revenge* metal phase because *Revenge* just reeks of effort to me.

## TOO MUCH TREBLE AND HIGHS ON *REVENGE*

Of the two metal albums, *Creatures* and *Revenge,* I like *Creatures* more. Not only do I think the songs are better, but *Creatures* has more bass in the mix. *Revenge* has too much treble for me. Sometimes, listening to *Revenge* is like nails on a chalkboard. Domino's lead guitar solo is a perfect example; it shrieks.

## THE SONGS

### UNHOLY

Kiss' answer to "Enter Sandman." At least I always thought so. It was obvious that with the success of Metallica's *Black* album, Kiss was trying to follow in that direction. Even the lead guitar solo on "Unholy" sounds like the solo on "Enter Sandman," not the same melody, but the same sound/tone or whatever the terminology is for it. Even in the beginning of the third verse, Gene's quoting the line the little boy says in "Sandman's" breakdown.

This is another song that could easily be on classic rock stations. The intro is tough as hell. One of the greatest Kiss songs ever recorded.

### TAKE IT OFF

To me this sounds closer to the "Kiss sound," and I love it, but at the same time, I don't think it should have been on *Revenge*. It doesn't fit with the rest of the songs; it's too plain and simple, with no edge. And from the album rotation, it's a weak follow-up for "Unholy." To me, it's equivalent to the follow-up that "Saint and Sinner" is on *Creatures*. Remember how I said I didn't think it fit or belonged on *Creatures* for the same reason.

"Take It Off" is Kiss' late answer to "Girls, Girls, Girls." But I love this song, its basic rhythm guitar, and the cowbell is jammin'.

### TOUGH LOVE

It's my favorite song on *Revenge*. The rhythm guitar on the intro and chorus are what do it for me. I also love Eric's playing on it as well as Gene's voice on the chorus.

### SPIT

I don't know why, but whenever I hear "Spit" it always reminds me of the *Hotter Than Hell* era. I can't put my finger on it. I remember this being one of my favorite songs on *Revenge* when I first got it. I liked the way Gene and Paul are going back and forth and the way the music stops and picks back up. One of Bruce's best solos on *Revenge*. This song just has so much character, and it's fun. I used to think that it was so cool the way Gene mentioned Bruce's name in the song. Bruce's leads on the end are tight, too.

## GOD GAVE ROCK & ROLL TO YOU

When I was younger, I would play it a lot because I liked the video. Now I just skip past it. It slows the party down for me. I always thought it was so out of place for it to be the fifth song on side one. To me, it should've definitely been last. I think it's a great song. Alaska rock stations would play it all the time, and that was the only time I would turn it up and really get into it.

## DOMINO

Years ago, I had a coworker who hated Kiss but loved the hell out of "Domino" when it came on the radio. He liked the line where Gene talks about the woman bending over. He would always sing along to that part.

OK, by now, you've noticed for the most part that I'm not actually quoting the lyrics of these Kiss songs I'm talking about. That's for copyright reasons. Even when I do "Messing Up the Lyrics," I'm just giving you the altered versions of those lyrics the way I used to personally say them. So that's why when I talk about my friend liking the part in "Domino," I say, "He liked the line where Gene talks about the woman bending over" instead of the actual lyrics. Long story short, I don't want Gene to sue me.

Initially, I hated this song and always skipped past it. I would think, *Why did they put this stupid song on here?* But when I saw Eric Singer play it live and the way he was kickin' it on the *Revenge* tour, I began loving it. For a long time afterward, I would watch the live version on bootleg just to watch Eric play it. Well also because it was a great concert, of course. But for me, it's Eric's drumming that makes the song good.

## HEART OF CHROME

This title is kind of cheesy to me. But I like this song, including the rhythm guitar intro. Eric's drumming is tight, too. It's pretty much the same rhythm guitar from "Tough Love," but shorter.

## THOU SHALT NOT

This was my favorite song on *Revenge* when I first got it. Something about that chorus just sucked me in. I loved the way he said "Thou shalt not!" I always thought this song should have been the second song, coming after "Unholy" on *Revenge*. It would have flowed better. A very powerful, underrated Kiss song.

## EVERY TIME I LOOK AT YOU

It seemed like the band was in a mindset of "OK, we're trying to be hard core and metal this year, but before we go all out, let's see if we can cash in on the success of 'Forever' one more time." I believe they failed. What I mean is "Forever" was more sincere and really pulled at the heartstrings. It had a lot of feel to it; it made you think of the woman you wanted to be with. "Every Time I Look at You" just seemed pushed and plotted. It's also very cheesy. It always reminds me of that Mr. Big song "To Be With You." Not that I think that's a bad song.

But to me, this song doesn't fit or belong on the album at all. I think if they were going to do a ballad, it should have had more of a metal feel and maybe not even been about a girl. I think since they were already jumping on the Metallica bandwagon, it would have been better if they had made a few slow songs like "The Unforgiven" or "Nothing Else Matters." But even though I think it's cheesy, it's still a great song to listen to.

I was at a performance by one of the Kiss tribute bands, Gods of Thunder, here in Las Vegas not too long ago, and their Paul Stanley dedicated and performed this song for his wife in the audience. He played it on his electric guitar without the band. It sounded pretty good.

## PARALYZED

Initially, what I loved about this song was the breakdown, where Eric was kickin' it on the drums and Gene was speaking over it. I loved that part then and still do. Even though it's recorded with a lot of treble/highs, it's still a great song to sing along to and imitate Gene's voice. One of the winners on the album. Now that I think about it, I think Gene's songs are more dominant than Paul's on *Revenge*.

I still don't know what Gene is saying on the breakdown. Something about the *Village Voice*?

## I JUST WANNA

Another song that should be played on classic rock radio but isn't. I listened to it a lot back then, but now, I usually skip past it.

It often annoys me that I have to get up and turn this song down whenever it comes on. It's so damned loud in the mix. That was usually a trick record labels used in the past, making certain songs on tapes/albums louder than others, so when you were driving down the street playing it, other people would hear. Another trick they would use was to turn the vocals down in the mix, because naturally, when people couldn't hear the vocals, they would turn the volume up. *Appetite for Destruction* is a perfect example. Have you ever noticed how low the vocals are on that record? Listen to how low the vocals are on "Paradise City." I'm sure the label and producer saw the potential in that song being a major hit single. That's probably why the vocals were lowered so listeners would have to turn it up. Just speculating. I know of a lot of R&B records that are recorded like that. Personally, I don't think they should ever alter the integrity of a song just to sell records.

## CARR JAM 1981

I don't like this solo, and that's coming from an Eric Carr fan. Not that it's bad, but it just doesn't show how raw and talented Eric Carr really was as a drummer. I would rather they had taken a solo from one of his live *Creatures* or *Animalize* performances and put that on *Revenge* than some light no balls drum solo they had lying around the studio. It just doesn't complement him at all. They shouldn't have put it on *Revenge*. My opinion.

## ALBUM COVER

To me, the cover is cool, but it doesn't do anything special for me. It's simple and basic but in a good way. I like the title. I love that picture on the inside sleeve with the brownish gold color behind them. That's actually my favorite picture from the *Revenge* era. If I had that as a big poster, I would frame it. What I never understood is why Kiss doesn't take great pictures like that and sell them as big wall posters. There are so many awesome photos of them in makeup and non-makeup that would make great posters. Why they don't sell or capitalize on them, I don't know.

I also never understood why they had "Carr Jam 1981" on *Revenge* but not his picture anywhere on the inside. A nice memorial picture of Eric would have been great.

## THE VIDEOS

## GOD GAVE ROCK & ROLL TO YOU

Mark saw the video first and he excitedly told me all about it. He said the video had old Kiss footage in it, and it was really cool. I finally got to see it a few days later, and he was right, the old-school clips and footage were cool. Initially, I thought it was so cool that Gene's hair was flat and liked how different he looked.

## UNHOLY

To me, like the song "Unholy," the video was also a rip-off of "Enter Sandman." Scenes flashing in and out, and even the close-ups are the same. It was as if Kiss went up to the director and showed him the "Enter Sandman" video and said "Make ours look exactly like this!" Go online and watch both videos back to back and you'll see the obvious comparison. "Unholy" is not a video I like to watch because to me, it's just not visually exciting. Too dark.

## DOMINO

Have you ever seen the original video for "Pour Some Sugar On Me," where they're performing it inside a house? It was horrible! I couldn't believe Def Leppard or their label would allow that video to even be made, let alone released. It's a good thing they made a second video for it with live shots and an audience or that song would probably never have taken off. If you haven't seen the original video, go online and check it out; it's pretty bad and beneath them. The point I'm making is the way I see the original video of "Pour Some Sugar On Me" in all of its suckiness is the way I've always seen the "Domino" video. I think it's Kiss' worst video ever. It doesn't complement the song at all. I think Paul, Bruce, and Eric looked really good performing the song but the idea of Gene driving around in that ugly ass car while singing the song was just stupid. I don't know who thought that would be a good idea. Maybe all the popular gangsta rap videos from that era, with rappers driving around in their cars, is what inspired Gene or the director to do it, I don't know. But it's cringe worthy.

## EVERY TIME I LOOK AT YOU

True confession time. I didn't even know until 2011 that there was a video for this song. I just happened to catch it on YouTube one night while watching Kiss videos. You would think as a die-hard, this is something I would have known about from the beginning, but I never saw it on TV or heard anyone, especially fans, talk about it. As I said, I was just on YouTube one night and there it was. I called Mark to tell him, and he was just as surprised as I was. "How could we have missed that?" he said.

Not only do I think it's the best of all the videos from the album but I also think it's flawless. The imaging, directing, and editing just complement the song so well. Watching it also makes me hear the song differently and appreciate it more. All the members look good and sincere.

## I JUST WANNA

I only saw it on TV maybe twice. I can't remember if it was MTV or a local video channel. It looks like they used the same director from "Unholy" on this one. Some of the shots even look like leftovers from "Unholy." I think this should have easily been a big hit on MTV. The video just seemed cool and current for its time, plus it had the catchy controversial line of "Fuh." I thought it would have caught on, and this video would have been the turning point for this album in terms of popularity and sales. But it just didn't happen.

When my rap group was meeting about shooting a video for one of our songs, I showed this video to the director and told him I wanted our video to look like this. I loved the white background with the shots coming in and out. He looked at me and said, "You guys are rappers, you want your video to look like a rock video?" I told him no, I just wanted the same white background and to be shot the way they did it. He didn't get it.

## OUTFITS

I always thought they looked ridiculous when they wore the black leather outfits, like the tall photo of them inside the record sleeve. Also when Paul wore the shirt that said "Fuck" on it, I thought that was really stupid. When I would watch *Kiss X-treme Close Up* in the past, I would cringe at what Gene was wearing. I can appreciate that they were trying to look more edgy and badass than the recent past, but it wasn't Kiss to me. To me, it represented Kiss trying to be something they weren't. But what they wore onstage on that tour looked good and more natural, especially Bruce.

FAVORITE SONG: "Tough Love"

FAVORITE RHYTHM GUITAR: "Tough Love"

FAVORITE LEAD GUITAR: "Spit"

FAVORITE BASS GUITAR: "Take It Off"

FAVORITE DRUMS: "Take It Off"

THROWAWAY: "Every Time I Look at You." I would say "Carr Jam 1981," but I never considered that an actual music track.

# Chapter 36

# MY FIRST KISS CONCERT, REVENGE TOUR!

In September of '92, I moved to Flagstaff, Arizona, and lived there for a year. But one afternoon in the month of December, while watching TV, Mark said, "I wonder if Kiss is coming to Phoenix anytime soon." He picked up the phone and called the ticket counter at the mall to see if they had any info on an upcoming Kiss tour, and that's when the woman on the other end told him that Kiss was performing in Phoenix at the America West Arena in three days! He looked at me bug-eyed. He didn't even ask if they still had tickets left, he just hung up and said, "We gotta get to the mall!" We couldn't believe that a Kiss concert was only three days away, and we were just now finding out about it. After he hung up, we jumped in the truck and raced to the mall, running every red light, plowing over pedestrians, and leading the police on a high-speed chase that ended in a shootout with bullets and guns blazing! It was like that chase scene at the end of *The Blues Brothers*.

The whole ride there we kept saying, "I hope they haven't sold out; please, let there be some tickets left!" But I knew deep down they were going to say it was sold out. Why? Because it would be my chance to finally see a Kiss concert. Of course the fates wouldn't be on my side. They wouldn't let me see my first Kiss concert knowing how much joy and pleasure it would bring me. After all, the fates hadn't even let us know there was a Kiss concert until three days before the show. Everything is a conspiracy against me. Why me? You have to remember, I'm from Anchorage, Alaska; sure, bands come through there, but not as much as they do in the States.

After we outran a hundred police cars and got away from the helicopters, we finally made it to the mall. We jumped out of the truck and ran toward the ticket booth. In my mind, I could already visualize thousands of people and Kiss fans standing in line waiting to buy tickets. But regardless, I knew we still had to try, even if it meant camping out for the night.

When we finally made it to the ticket counter, I was in for a surprise. Nobody was there standing in line or waiting to buy tickets. There was one woman working behind the counter who smiled at us and said, "How can I help you?" Mark said anxiously, "We need to buy three Kiss tickets!" After looking in her computer, she said that there were plenty of tickets left on the floor. Mark gave me a look of approval. At eighteen, I was new to the concert going experience, so when she said there were plenty of tickets left on the floor, I didn't see that as a bad thing or that it meant Kiss tickets weren't selling. I just thought it was awesome that we were going to be on the floor and up close. We got our Kiss tickets and drove back home.

The next few days were a nightmare for me. I was so worried about something going wrong that I checked to make sure the tickets were in their safe hiding place every half hour. In my head, I was expecting the worst. My whole life had been building up to this day, and I believed that something was going to ruin it for me.

On the day of the show, I woke up with a surreal feeling. Was I really going to actually see a Kiss concert that night for the first time? Was this really happening? I continued my attitude of "Something's going to ruin this for me." If Mark didn't get to go, it was no big deal because he got to see them on the *Hot in the Shade* tour. But in my head, this was the only show Kiss was ever going to play again, their last concert. After this show, Kiss would cease to exist. I was so paranoid.

Our friend Adam would drive us there in his truck and use the third ticket. As we started our drive, I thought to myself *This is it; I know now what's going to happen. Adam's truck is going to break down on the way there and we'll miss the concert.*" But the truck didn't break down. On the way there, we repeatedly listened to the new Dr. Dre tape, *The Chronic*, and we made it to Phoenix with no problems or incidents. Actually, there was one incident. I have a phobia of dead animals and dead things in general. When Adam pulled the truck over so I could take a piss, I walked a little deep into the woods, out of view from traffic. As I was going, I smelled something that reeked like an outhouse. The smell was horrific! When I looked over my shoulder, I saw a dead deer or whatever it was that was totally eaten away by maggots and insects. I screamed like a bitch and ran back to the truck as fast as I could with piss running all down my leg. And as usual, Mark was there to show his support by laughing at me.

## MY FIRST STANDING IN LINE EXPERIENCE

I can't begin to tell you what I was thinking when we were standing in line at the America West Arena. I couldn't believe I was surrounded by all of these Kiss fans. They had makeup on and wore Kiss shirts. To me, just being outside surrounded by all of these fans was an experience in itself. I was having my first real Kiss concert experience, and I loved it. At one point, I looked at Mark and said, "We're the only black people here."

But while we were standing in line, it hit me. I thought to myself, *Kiss is inside this very building I'm standing next to.* It was as if they were only a few feet away from me! It was surreal to me knowing that the only thing between Kiss and me was a wall. All I could think about was what was it going to be like once Kiss hit the stage. How was I going to handle it? Would I be calm, or would I go out of my mind and have a panic attack right there in the audience? Then the doubts began to come back again. Even though I was really close, I still felt like something was going to ruin this concert for me. There was a security guard who came from out of nowhere and stood inside the front door, and I thought *That's it; he's standing there waiting for confirmation that the concert has been canceled, and he's going to open the door and tell everybody to leave.* But he never told us to leave.

I'll never forget the overweight woman who was standing in line wearing a Kiss shirt. She was probably in her late twenties and was continuously talking about Kiss and making no sense at all. You ever meet a Kiss fan who acts like they know what they're talking about and they just sound so stupid? Like even they really don't believe what they're saying? Not only did she sound stupid, but when other fans challenged her, she spoke as if her words were fact and not opinion. She said things like, "Ace and Paul are the ones who hired Gene in '73. Kiss did five concerts without makeup in '77. Peter's wife wrote 'King of the Night Time World,'" and so on. Her voice and ignorance annoyed everyone there. Probably me more than everyone else because I was just anxious about getting inside.

## ALMOST THERE

Finally, they opened the door and security waved us forward to be frisked and patted down. Even though I didn't carry a weapon, I just knew that fate was going to plant a gun on me, and not only wouldn't they let me in, but I'd be banned from all future Kiss concerts. I was so paranoid about something going wrong that I was creating obscure scenarios and outcomes in my head. While the line was moving forward, Mark kept reminding me to run straight for the front of the stage as soon as we got inside. The way he talked about the struggle of getting to the front of the stage made me think it was going to be like battling in the Thunderdome. Kiss fans with chainsaws and long sticks with sharp blades at the end of them going at it for the privilege of being close and up front.

When we finally got in, we ran through the hallway, and I remember seeing a bunch of fans lining up at the merchandise counters to buy shirts and whatever else. I thought to myself, *Are they nuts? Don't they know that it's important to get to the front of the stage to be as close to Kiss as possible? Why are they wasting time buying T-shirts?*

When we got on the arena floor, we hauled ass to the front of the stage. I'll never forget the feeling of grabbing onto that railing and holding on for dear life. I thought, "Here I am, finally, a few feet away from a stage that Kiss is supposed to be playing on anytime now."

Because it was my first concert, I didn't know anything about opening bands. I thought when you went to a Kiss concert, you saw Kiss and then went home. I believe Trixter was the first opening band, and I'm not saying they were bad, but it was definitely something I would never want to see again. I guess in retrospect, they were pretty lame. I remember this chubby girl standing next to me wearing a Trixter T-shirt, holding up a big picture of them and screaming her head off. Mark looked at me and said, "Is she serious?"

Great White came on next. I will say that musically, I thought they were good and had good songs. The problem was I wanted to see Kiss, and it seemed like their set just went on forever. Every time I thought their set was done, they would start another song. It was frustrating for me. The more songs they sang meant more time for something to go wrong and for Kiss not to hit the stage. Then the lead singer did something that was majorly annoying. You know how Paul does his vocal thing at the end of "I Want You" or like he did during the break of "I Still Love You" on *Unplugged*? Their lead singer did something similar; he just kept going on with this vocal exercise, yelling into the mic like the audience was supposed to be impressed by his vocal pitch or something. All I kept thinking was *Get the fuck off the stage, you dumb mutha fucka, you!* Finally, Great White's set was over, and it was time for the main attraction!

While the roadies were setting up for the Kiss show, I was still in a mindset that this wasn't real. I was still waiting for something to go wrong and for someone to grab the mic and say that the Kiss concert was canceled. Then something happened. A fight broke out onstage. Two roadies began exchanging fists right there onstage in front of all of us. At the moment, I thought, *This is it! This is how the concert is going to get ruined and canceled, two dumbasses fighting onstage.* One of them grabbed a hand full of what looked like speaker cords that were wrapped in a circle and hit the other roadie in the face with them. The impact was so loud, I felt it. The other roadies came and broke it up. Once the fight was broken up, they all went back to work like it never happened. *That was some weird shit*, I thought. But it didn't stop the concert from going forward. I do remember at one point looking back into the audience and thinking, *Where's everybody at? Kiss is about to go on, and the arena is not even half full!* It was actually pretty empty. Then that magical moment came. The house lights went down, my eyes widened, my heart raced, and I began to shake. It was the moment

I had waited fourteen years for! Then it happened. Kiss was standing in front of me.

## UNREAL IS MORE LIKE IT

When Kiss finally hit the stage, time for me just stood still. Seriously, I was just frozen in place. I couldn't move. I wasn't pumping my fist, I wasn't singing along or nodding my head like everybody else, I was motionless and expressionless. I guess the only way to describe it is like being on a ledge on the seventieth floor of a skyscraper and being afraid to look down. That's how I was.

It just didn't seem real to me; it didn't really feel like I was at a Kiss concert. It seemed too easy to be there, like I had gotten there without effort. My whole life, I always thought the only people who actually got to go to Kiss concerts were fans who were really blessed or lucky as hell. I just couldn't believe it was actually happening to me or that it was my time as a fan to be there, but there I was. All I did was stare at each member and try to take it all in. I remember at one point, Gene and I made eye contact and he grinned at me, and instead of indulging him, all I thought was *Did Gene just grin at me?* To me, it was like it wasn't really Gene Simmons but someone else. My eighteen-year-old mind couldn't process that this was really happening, that Kiss was really in front of me, not on a poster or an album cover, but live in the flesh. After about the fifth song, I began to loosen up and came out of my surreal type of trip, focusing on where I was and that, yes, this was really happening, I was actually at a real Kiss concert, and that was really them playing right before my eyes.

I couldn't believe how good the set list was. I'll never forget, when they began playing "Parasite," Mark and I just looked at each other and said "Yeah!" I remember being so jealous when everybody else was catching the guitar picks and they kept flying over my hands. I didn't want to leave without a personal souvenir from my first Kiss concert. At one point, Paul flung a white pick out and a bunch of fans grabbed for it, knocking it in front of the railing. I motioned a woman photographer to pick it up for me and she did. To me, it was like finding a piece of gold in the street, I was actually holding a guitar pick that Paul himself had played with! Then Gene kept throwing them in my direction and they kept going over my head. I was so close to getting a Gene pick, but I guess it just wasn't in the cards. Or was it?

As the show continued, I noticed a short guy standing behind some other fans and me. He was struggling to see. He kept standing on his tippy toes trying his best to see over us taller guys. After a while, I started feeling really bad for him. He was just a fan trying to enjoy the show, and he couldn't. Plus, he had a really cool *Creatures of the Night* shirt on. So what good is the Kiss Army if we can't be there for each other and help each other out, huh? I was already in one of the best places in the whole arena, holding onto the railing and standing right in front of Kiss, but I had to do something for this guy. I reached back through the crowd, grabbed him by the front of his shirt, and pulled him up front to where I was. I told him to hold onto the railing and not let go. That guy looked at me with the most grateful smile on his face and he got to enjoy the rest of the show without having to look over us taller people. As a result, I ended up losing my place and got pushed back into the crowd some, but I didn't mind; I got to help a fellow Kiss fan in the process.

After the concert was over and the house lights came up, I was so disappointed that it all had come to an end. Even though it was a pretty long show, I still wanted more. As we were walking through the parking lot, a fan walked up to me and said, "You got something on your forehead." When I pulled it off, I realized it was one of the guitar picks Gene kept throwing that went over my head. It turned out that the grease in my hair was melting and dripping down my head from all of the heat during the concert. So when Gene flung his guitar pick in my direction, it hit my forehead and stayed stuck there throughout the show. Since '92, I've kept both Gene and Paul's picks in a glass frame with my ticket stub from that concert. And that *Revenge* show will always go down as my favorite Kiss concert ever!

# Chapter 37

# ALIVE III

I hate the recording of this album. There's too much treble and highs and not enough bass. Even Gene's bass sounds like a guitar sometimes. The recording makes Eric's drums sound horrible.

I liked the sound of the songs when I was live at the concert in Phoenix and when watching the concert on DVD, but the album itself is just awful to me.

The audience cues are horrible and sometimes they're placed in awkward moments of the songs. The audience doesn't sound as natural as *Alive* or *Alive II*. Well, maybe just *Alive!* And Paul's voice sounds strained.

This album is so awful to me, that I remember owning it when it came out, but I don't remember buying it. It's that forgettable to me. Mark plays this album a lot, but I have no connection to it, so it'll be kind of tough to review it, but I'll try.

THE SONGS

CREATURES OF THE NIGHT

It's the worst version of *Creatures of the Night* I've ever heard.

## DEUCE

When you play this version of "Deuce" on the house speakers, Eric's drumming sounds pretty cool. If they were going to put throwback songs on here, personally, I would have preferred "Parasite" or "She."

## I JUST WANNA

Paul's vocals sound strange. Like he has a cold.

## UNHOLY

To me "Unholy" has never sounded good live. It always comes off as too weak and soft and like it doesn't have enough balls like the studio version. Also, Gene sounds weird when he sings it live.

## HEAVEN'S ON FIRE

The only time this song ever sounded good to me live was on the *Animalize* tour. Don't like this version.

## I WAS MADE FOR LOVIN' YOU

The only time this song ever sounded good to me live was on the *Unmasked* tour with Eric Carr's drumming. Don't like this version.

## WATCHIN' YOU

I guess the scratching noise on the guitar is cool, but the *Alive!* version will always be the best.

## DOMINO

Cringe.

## I STILL LOVE YOU

A waste of six minutes, especially on a live release. Why does Paul keep trying to shove this song down our throats? It's on *Creatures*, just leave it at that. Not that I want to hear it live, but they should have put "War Machine" in its place. To me that would make more sense.

## ROCK AND ROLL ALL NITE

It's OK I guess. Kind of up-tempo and cool.

## LICK IT UP

I like the way this version sounds. Not as good as the *Animalize* tour version, but it's cool. They play this version a lot on the rock radio stations in Vegas.

## FOREVER

It sounds pretty good on this album. But I can take it or leave it.

## I LOVE IT LOUD

The only time I liked this song live was on the '83 Rio/Brazil tour, where it was more up-tempo. Other than that, I don't care for it live. Especially this slow, draggin' version.

## DETROIT ROCK CITY

Gene's bass sounds weird.

## GOD GAVE ROCK & ROLL TO YOU II

Sounds pretty cool.

## THE STAR SPANGLED BANNER

Tight!

## ALBUM COVER

Nothing visually exciting about it at all. Maybe it would have been cooler if they used the actual picture itself for the cover instead of putting the picture inside of the Kiss logo, where it's hard to see.

The pictures of the band's history on the inside are very boring, redundant, and too basic. They could have a least put some exciting pics in there. And the chart or the family tree is kind of cool in a historic sense. Overall, I would have preferred something else more visually exciting. I'm trying to keep an open mind, but this album does nothing for me.

## I LOVE IT LOUD VIDEO

The song version sucks, but the video has a lot of cool visuals of the band, stage, and camera shots of the crowd.

FAVORITE SONG: "Lick It Up"
FAVORITE RHYTHM GUITAR: "Watchin' You"
FAVORITE LEAD GUITAR: "Rock and Roll All Nite"
FAVORITE BASS GUITAR: "Lick It Up"
FAVORITE DRUMS: "Deuce"

THROWAWAY: "I Still Love You"

## Chapter 38

# CARNIVAL OF SOULS

I was at a grocery store one afternoon in '94, and as usual, I stood in the magazine aisle looking at all of the new releases of rock and metal magazines, hoping, of course that there would be some cool Kiss pictures and articles in them. I can't remember what magazine it was, I want to say *Metal Edge* or *Hit Parader*, but as I flipped through the pages to the back, I saw ads where people were selling rock items and advertising their guitar, bass, and drum services. But what really caught my eye was an ad where some guy was claiming to have a bunch of '70s and '80s Kiss concerts and interviews on VHS for sale. The ad said to write him for a free catalogue.

Remember, this was way before YouTube. Also, it sounded way too good to be true. *This guy is actually claiming to have Kiss concerts from the '70s on VHS. It's a scam!* You have to understand I was raised in Anchorage, Alaska, so for the most part, all we had was new, current Kiss merchandise. By '90 to '95, older items were very rare to come by, especially concerts on VHS. Yes, every once in a while, you might come across a collectable, but it was rare. Plus, I wasn't hip to the idea that fans with items like this were pretty common in the States. I was just one of those naïve Kiss fans who thought if it sounded too good to be true then it must be.

Still, I was curious, and when I got home, I wrote this con artist for one of his Kiss catalogues. If memory serves me, at the time, he lived in Indiana.

Two weeks later, I received his catalogue in the mail. When I opened it up, I was pretty impressed by his collection of old Kiss concerts. He even had a rating system of how good each recording was from good, to great, to excellent! Yes, what he claimed to have was very impressive, but I still believed it was a scam to get my money. I just couldn't believe that anybody could have this many classic Kiss concerts and interviews in their possession. And if he did, then he was the luckiest son of a bitch in the entire world!

Wanting to believe that all of this was true, I went along with it, knowing that I was being scammed for my money but at the same time, hoping maybe he was legit and I was just trippin'.

To test the waters, I only picked two tapes. The 1974 compilation tape that included the *Mike Douglas Show* and the 1979 compilation tape that included the Famous *Tom Snyder Show*. Why I specifically chose those at that time, I don't know. I think they were just random picks, and besides, what difference did it make, I was never going to receive them anyway. He charged $20.00 per tape, so I put $40.00 in the envelope, dropped it in the mailbox, and kissed my money good-bye. Two weeks had gone by and nothing had come in the mail for me. I checked it every day faithfully. *I knew it was a scam. Mutha fucka got my money!*

One day almost three weeks after I sent him the money, I was getting off work and had to rush because my rap group had a show that night. My partner in my group had his girlfriend pick me up, and she was waiting for me out in the parking lot. I had to change clothes in the back seat while she broke all the traffic laws to get me to the show on time. That night, we had the audience bumpin' and screamin' from beginning to end. We spit those lyrics like we were performing at the Grammy's. There was something about rapping onstage that was just a magical feeling to me, plus seeing the crowd's reaction. As a group, we felt good about our performance and took pictures with "at the moment" fans.

While at the after party, of all the things I could have been thinking about, I actually started to think about my Kiss VHS tapes that had never come in the mail. It was bringing me down even though I was surrounded by beautiful women wearing the sexiest hip-hop style of the day and giving me rhythm. After the party, my boys wanted to go to another after-hours nightclub but I told them that I was done for the night and was going home. I gave a few pounds, shoulder hugs, and bounced.

After stopping at a twenty-four hour Wendy's and convenience store, I finally made it home. When I turned my headlights off, I noticed something leaning up against my front door. It was a brown package. Instantly, my heart began to race. Could that actually be my Kiss tapes? Leaving my food, I leaped out of the car and ran to the door. I opened the package right there and I couldn't believe it, it was two VHS tapes. I quickly ran into the house and put one in the VCR. I waited anxiously to see what would come on the screen. My joy quickly turned to anger when I saw a square looking guy on the screen talking about nothing. It was Tom Snyder. At that time, I didn't know who he was or anything about his show. I just thought that it was some crap that was on the tape. "I knew this mutha fucka was fake!" I yelled out. At that moment, it didn't occur to me to just wait to see if something else would happen or if Kiss would come on the screen. I just stood there cursing. Already having given up, I fast forwarded it a little to see what would happen. When I pushed play, the most amazing thing came on the screen. It was Kiss in their *Dynasty* outfits sitting down in a studio being interviewed by this square guy. It was like my whole life as a Kiss fan just flashed before my eyes. It was incredible! Keep in mind that growing up, I didn't see makeup Kiss on TV a lot. I missed most of the important TV appearances, and up until that point, I had never heard of Kiss being on the *Tom Snyder Show* or even the show itself. I think at that point, the only time I saw makeup Kiss on TV was *Kiss Meets the Phantom, Kids Are People Too, Hot Hero Sandwich, 321 Contact*, and *Fridays*. There could be one or two appearances that I might be forgetting about. Now I was in a position to buy and see all of the great Kiss TV appearances that I never got to see as a child. Each tape was about two hours long, and for the next week, I watched them over and over again. I counted the days until my next paycheck and kept my eyes glued on that catalogue. To me, owning that catalogue was like owning the goose that laid the golden egg. I couldn't wait until more tapes came in the mail. And when they did, I would load up on snacks and soda, stay in my room, and have Kiss marathons.

For the first time, I saw Kiss on the *Mike Douglas Show*, and by the way, I didn't even know it existed until then. I also had the entire '74 San Francisco show and an *Alive!* era show where Paul knocks his mic down during "Strutter" and Gene had to temporarily take over the lyrics. Old news today, but in my mind, back in '94, I was the luckiest guy in the world to have these in my possession! After the smoke cleared, I spent about two grand with this guy on Kiss VHS tapes. I was hooked.

## MY FIRST LISTEN TO *COS*

One day in '95 or '96, not too sure of the year, he sent me a letter saying that he had a copy of a new unreleased Kiss tape. I didn't know anything about Kiss having new music or a new tape that was supposed to come out, but he said it was cool and I could hear it before the other fans did. I believe I paid him $20.00 for the tape. It was *Carnival of Souls*. But at that time, the tape he sent me had no album title.

The first time I played it, I had no clue what I was listening to. It didn't sound like Kiss at all to me, and nothing about the songs jumped out at me as being anything special. I just sat on the floor and listened. Between the recording and weird style, it sounded like a bunch of demos, some incomplete and some were just strange. And that's what I thought I had paid for, a tape full of unreleased demos, not an actual new unreleased Kiss tape. Don't misunderstand me, having Kiss demos was tight, but at the same time, I felt he'd misled me. But because he supplied me with classic Kiss on VHS tapes, I let the demo cassette incident slide and didn't call him on it. I didn't want to bite the hand that was giving me my classic Kiss fix. In retrospect, I would have felt the fool if I had called him on it because it really was *COS*. When the tape was over, I just took it out and placed it back in the cassette case and that was it. I actually remember thinking *Imagine if they would have released those songs to the public!* To me, those songs just weren't as good as the songs on *Revenge*.

## I THINK I'M ACTUALLY STARTING TO LIKE IT.

As the weeks went by, I continued to play it just to see if it would start to grow on me, and it did. I found myself really liking the songs "Hate,"

"Rain," "Childhood's End," "I Will Be There," "In My Head," and "I Confess." And my appreciation for the other songs just fell into place. Before I knew it, I was playing it every day. I grew to love the different sound and direction the band went on this record. At that time, I didn't interpret it as a wink toward the grunge era. I didn't listen to grunge and knew nothing about it, so the concept of Kiss going through a grunge phase was lost on me. I just thought that, like with all of their other albums, Kiss was trying a new sound, and I liked it. I don't know why Kiss is criticized for this being a grunge album when practically every Kiss album is an experimental album in some form or another.

## COULD THIS POSSIBLY BE THE BEST KISS STUDIO ALBUM EVER?

Now, don't get your panties in a bunch over what I just said. I understand that the idea of *COS* being the best Kiss studio album would make a million Kiss fans charge the castle with their pitchforks and torches. And if a Kiss fan had asked me that question ten years ago, I would have looked at him like he was stupid. And no, I'm not saying that it is their best studio album. But I will say this, for review of this book, I recently played *COS* from beginning to end, something I haven't done in almost a decade. Usually, there are just a few select songs that I listen to, maybe five or six. But having actually sat down to absorb it in its entirety, I gotta say even I didn't realize how brilliant and underrated this album really is. I'm gonna go out on a limb here and say that if the recording was different, mixed down with the sound of *Creatures* or *Revenge,* I think it could have possibly been their best studio album since *Destroyer.* My opinion. No, it wouldn't have been my favorite but it could have been a classic Kiss album. And before you reject the idea, lock yourself in your room, put your headphones on, turn it up loud, and absorb the music. Listening to it years after its release, I now hear it in a different way. Not only do I think it's a potentially phenomenal album, but musically, I can appreciate how they evolved and started singing about mature issues and less of the cock rock clichés. I think as a whole, the songs on *COS* are better than the ones on *Revenge.*

## WHERE'S VINNIE?

This album was also missing Vinnie's songwriting. Some of the writing on this album is pretty basic, but Vinnie's lyrics could have been the icing on the cake to complement the songs even more.

## MY BIGGEST COMPLAINT ABOUT THIS ALBUM

The tone of Eric's drums. Especially the snare drum.

## THE SONGS

### HATE

This is such an awesome unique heavy Kiss song. Hard rock stations should be rotating this song every hour. I love Eric's drumming on it. Way underrated. To me, Gene's songs don't sound grunge at all. They just sound like the demon. But then again, what do I know about grunge?

### RAIN

This was the first song I liked off the album. It was the rhythm guitar with Eric's drumming that sucked me in. I could have seen this song and video being rotated on radio and MTV in '95.

### MASTER & SLAVE

It's just a cool song. Love the bass line.

### CHILDHOOD'S END

Another song that should have easily been a hit for the band. I don't know why, but this song always reminded me of "Why Can't We Be Friends?" I can never listen to one without thinking about the other. I love the way Gene sings it, especially the chorus.

## I WILL BE THERE

Such a brilliant and unique ideal for a ballad. I love the western feel to it. It's one of those songs where you could turn the vocals down and just listen to the music. I think it would have been much better if Kiss had performed this during *Unplugged* instead of "Every Time I Look at You." Since "Every Time I Look at You" failed to be a big single for *Unplugged*, I think "I Will Be There" probably would have gotten more consideration. But then again, who knows what politics was going on behind the scenes with MTV and the label.

## JUNGLE

Mark has loved this song from day one. It never really did anything for me. I guess what I find to be so annoying about it is, again, Paul is singing about the streets. I'm sure Paul has sung about a lot of things that he's never experienced firsthand, but him singing about the things that go on in the streets is like "OK, come on Paul, really?" I guess I don't need to receive a lesson about the streets from someone who didn't grow up in the streets. At least when he was singing "All Hell's Breakin' Loose," he was being a little humorous and upbeat, and that made it OK. And yes, I know it's not that serious. I'm probably just reading into it more than I need to and in the end, it's just a song.

## IN MY HEAD

This is one of those songs that make me wonder why this album isn't more loved by fans. I think "In My Head" is the shit! Gene's vocals are on point here. I love the way the rhythm guitar comes in during the middle of the verse, like the same guitar melody from the verses of, "I Was Made for Lovin' You." Definitely a highlight from this album.

## IT NEVER GOES AWAY

I didn't learn to appreciate this song until years later. Now I think it's brilliant. I love Paul's vocals on the chorus. You can't help but sing along to it.

## SEDUCTION OF THE INNOCENT

This song always had a *Creatures/Lick It Up* feel to me, like it was originally recorded in that era. It's softer but still heavy.

## I CONFESS

Great song. I love the rhythm guitars as the song is ending.

## IN THE MIRROR

I like it, but at the same time, I don't think it fits on the album and is a throwaway. I hate it when Paul says the word "deny" in a song. I guess I always think of that word as one of those safety words that Paul writes when he needs something to add to a sentence. I guess it's not that serious. But yes, I like listening to it. It just should have never made the album because it throws off the whole vibe.

## I WALK ALONE

I think this song could have been phenomenal if they arranged it a little differently. I love the intro even though the melody is a little bit of a rip-off of "Fractured Mirror." First, I think Bruce should have made more of an effort to actually sing the lyrics as opposed to just talking through them. The producer could have worked with him a little on that. That breakdown with the reverse recording beat going through it was dated even for its time. Take out Gene's vocals at the end and keep the song arrangement basic, and I believe you have an MTV hit. If I were the producer or calling the shots at the label, I would have pushed for this song to be the first or second single. I think it's pretty strong. Unfortunately, like Eric Carr, Bruce finally gets a song on an album and it's pushed toward the end of it. I would have made it the third song on the album. I wonder what Gene or Paul would have thought if Bruce's song did go on to become a big hit for this album. Would they have been jealous or would they have pushed him to sing more songs? We'll never know.

## ALBUM COVER

Who knows what it would have looked like if they released it when it was originally supposed to come out. But most will agree that the cover it got was horrible and didn't do the music or the sound justice. Personally, I thought that if anything, the picture on the back of them sitting down looking into the camera would have been a better picture for the album cover.

I understand at this point that the band had already moved on with the whole reunion thing and maybe they didn't have any control over releasing the album at this point and the label was responsible for the release. But it seems to me that they could have made more of an effort to package it a little better. Even the inside of the jacket was pretty generic, with that cheap black and white print. Too bad they couldn't just utilize that picture of the flaming head with his hand around his throat. That would have been tight!

FAVORITE SONG: Used to be "Rain," but now it's "Hate."
FAVORITE RHYTHM GUITAR: "Rain"
FAVORITE LEAD GUITAR: "Master & Slave"
FAVORITE BASS GUITAR: "Jungle"
FAVORITE DRUMS: "Hate"

THROWAWAY: "Look in the Mirror"

# Chapter 39

## *UNPLUGGED*

I remember the night this aired on MTV. My boy Jimmy wanted me to go to the club with him, but I wasn't going anywhere. Not only was Kiss coming on TV, but Ace and Peter were going to be performing with them for the first time in years. I planned my whole month around this event.

When it finally aired that night, I sat on the floor in front of the TV like I was a kid who was getting ready to watch *Kiss Meets the Phantom* for the first time. There was something pretty cool and magical knowing that the original Kiss would be performing onstage again and knowing that there were other Kiss fans around the world who were also witnessing this at the same time I was.

I was excited when it finally aired. I wasn't all that big on unplugged music and didn't know how much I would like it until I saw Kiss perform their classics in an acoustic set. They sounded tight, and the acoustic guitars added another dimension to the songs. I was actually impressed. I instantly loved the way Bruce sounded, and it made me appreciate Eric's drumming more. I thought it was so cool that they were performing songs like "Comin Home," "Plaster Caster," and "Goin' Blind." I was jammin' through each song, air guitaring and drumming like I was actually in the audience.

Seconds before Ace and Peter came out onstage, I remember my heart started beating really fast. I was having a small anxiety attack, if you can believe it, and when they walked on the stage, I could feel myself getting a little emotional and teary eyed. All of the old-school thoughts and feelings came back to me again, and it humbled me as a fan. I could feel the excitement and the energy in the room like I was actually there. And while they played, I remember thinking to myself *Why did you guys wait so long to perform together again?* Again, timing is everything. Ace's guitar playing was so good on "2000 Man" and Peter just looked so happy, like a little kid, when he performed "Beth." It was so magical to me to witness this historic event in Kisstory. I knew at that moment, watching the original Kiss playing together, that Kiss as an entity would never be the same again. I knew this would be the beginning of something, but what exactly, I didn't know.

Even though Bruce and Eric played great, in retrospect, for nostalgic reasons, I think it would have been better if they could have done the entire *Unplugged* set with just the original four performing the original songs. I don't know if it would have sounded as good, but it would have been pretty cool.

## GET YOUR COPY TODAY!

The day it came out, I bought my first copy on cassette at a Borders Bookstore. I remember reading the song list and being excited about some songs that were on it and disappointed about others that weren't. One thing I found odd was for the first time, I noticed a lot of rock fans who weren't Kiss fans were playing *Unplugged* a lot or had it in their collection. I mean, I would walk into a pizza place and the cashier would be playing it or some car would pull up next to me blasting it. One day about a month after its release, I went to a guitar store to rent some mics for an upcoming show, and there were six rockers sitting in chairs with acoustic guitars, playing along to the *Unplugged* version of "Sure Know Something." And they were focused! It seemed to me that a lot of these so-called "rockers" were all of a sudden interested in Kiss' music or taking it more seriously because now it was Kiss music done on acoustic guitars. At least that's the way I saw it.

## THE SONGS

## COMIN HOME

They definitely brought new life to this song. It's always been an underrated song to me, but now they put it back on the map. Awesome version! I wish they had added "Got to Choose" on this album.

## PLASTER CASTER

Bruce's lead solo. Nuff said.

## GOIN' BLIND

Again, Bruce's lead solo. Nuff said.

## DO YOU LOVE ME

It doesn't do that much for me, but it's cool.

## DOMINO

I like this version better than the *Revenge* version. I love watching Eric play to this song on the *Unplugged* DVD.

## SURE KNOW SOMETHING

The end of the song, where Bruce is playing lead, is something I must have played a million times.

## A WORLD WITHOUT HEROES

Don't like it at all. If they were going to do something off *The Elder*, I would have preferred "Under the Rose."

## ROCK BOTTOM

The acoustic intro is tight and flawless. Like the *Alive!* version, Gene's bass is loud and thick. I love that!

## SEE YOU TONIGHT

I love the album version, but it doesn't work for me on *Unplugged*. I would have preferred "Mr. Make Believe."

## I STILL LOVE YOU

Way better than the *Alive III* version, but still wasted space. Would have preferred something else for this slot.

## EVERY TIME I LOOK AT YOU

I usually skip past it. It sounds pretty close to the album version though.

## 2000 MAN

My second favorite song on *Unplugged*. I love watching Ace's fingers playing the solo on the DVD. The intro guitar is tight, too.

## BETH

This is my favorite live version of "Beth." It must be the acoustic guitars. The solo is tight. Could you imagine how stupid it would have sounded if they would have let Peter play those stupid bongo type drums or whatever they were?

## NOTHIN' TO LOSE

I like this version. Eric's voice is perfect for this song.

## ROCK AND ROLL ALL NITE

Tired as hell of this song, but it's a good acoustic version.

## ALBUM COVER

I don't think it's bad, but it doesn't leave that much of an impression. I think something like the *Revenge* album cover would have been a little better. Just the Kiss logo with the word "unplugged" beneath it. And the MTV logo, if necessary. Truth be told, I don't remember what the inside of the jacket looks like or what was in it. I own the CD itself, but not the jacket.

FAVORITE SONG: "Comin Home"
FAVORITE RHYTHM GUITAR: "Goin' Blind"
FAVORITE LEAD: "2000 Man"
FAVORITE BASS: "Rock Bottom"
FAVORITE DRUMS: "Domino"

THROWAWAY: "A World Without Heroes"

## Chapter 40

# THE REUNION

I remember the day that Tupac introduced Kiss onstage. I really didn't know what to think about it. What was Kiss gonna look like, would they still look good in the makeup and outfits, was it gonna be cool, what was gonna be the next chapter in the book of Kiss? I had no clue. What I did know was that at any moment, the '70s version of the band was going to emerge onstage in full attire.

When Tupac said, "Let's shock the people" and Kiss came out, I have to say I felt absolutely nothing. I wasn't shocked, anxious, happy, or even excited. I just looked at the screen and thought, "Well, there they are; it's official, they're back together again." And that was it.

I can't explain it, but even to this day, Kiss reuniting in makeup has never made me excited or even seemed magical to me. When they reunited and did *Unplugged* together on an acoustic set that almost brought tears to my eyes. But that was different because it wasn't supposed to be permanent, or at least that was my understanding at the time. They were also stripped down to a fun, relaxed acoustic set and environment. But something about putting the makeup and outfits back on seemed a little unappealing to me. As a fan at that time, I didn't know if it was something I really wanted. Again, I don't know why. Maybe a small part of me felt betrayed for Bruce Kulick and Eric Carr, who had already passed away, and all the hard work they had contributed. What about Eric Singer? I know he's the new guy, but what's he going to do now? I had created a strong bond and connection to the non-makeup era, and now I was being told that it wasn't going to be anymore.

Not once as a fan have I ever said, "I wish they would bring Ace and Peter back." Yes, I loved Ace and Peter for what they contributed to the band in the '70s, but to me, that was the past, and good or bad, it had nothing to do with where Kiss was at in the mid '90s. I had a lot of uncertainties. I wasn't stupid; I knew that Kiss records and tickets weren't selling in the '90s, and financially, this was the smartest move they could have made at that time. Yes, the reunion would be successful and what really mattered to the Kiss camp was the millions of people around the world who weren't real Kiss fans but wanted to come to the shows for the magic and legendary stories they heard about Kiss. Regardless of my personal doubts, there were hundreds of thousands of die-hard Kiss fans around the world who were pissin' on themselves and rejoicing that it had finally happened. It was also cool to see everyone taking an interest in and talking about Kiss again, something that hadn't happened in many years.

In '96, every time I would walk into a store, there would be Kiss posters or merchandise for sale. All of a sudden, retailers wanted to sell Kiss again. One day during this era, I went into a Sam Goody's and they had a big life-size Kiss cut out of the *Love Gun* album cover. I spoke to the manager, and she agreed to give it to me when they were done using it. I wanted it so badly that I would stop in there twice a week and make small talk with her. I even bought her lunch a few times. She probably thought I was flirting with her and wanted to ask her out, but in all actuality, I was just trying to secure my Kiss cut out. A month and a half later, it was mine. But even though it seemed like the Kiss reunion was something I should want as a fan, I just wasn't sure. As a fan, I went along with it because I obviously had no choice, and I kept an open mind as to what could be.

# Chapter 41

# *MY BIGGEST REGRET AS A KISS FAN*

I was in Anchorage, Alaska, when Mark called me from Flagstaff, Arizona, saying, "Negro, I just bought both of our tickets for the reunion Kiss concert in Phoenix. It's oooonnnn!" Mark actually had our reunion tickets in his hand. And because I was short on funds at that time, my mom said without hesitation that she would pay for my plane ticket, no problem. I didn't have to pay for a concert or plane ticket. Everything that I needed to see the original Kiss onstage for the first time was being handed to me on a silver platter. So why was I sitting on my bed trying to talk myself out of it? *Anthony, you've been emotionally invested in Kiss since you were four years old. Kiss has been the center of your world. So why are you even entertaining the possibility of not going?* To be totally honest with you, Kiss Army, I was deathly afraid of flying. And my thinking at that time was *This is the biggest thing in the history of Kiss; the fates won't let me witness this because I'm unworthy. The fates will make sure that my plane crashed before they would let me witness this historic event.* I actually convinced myself that my plane would crash before I made it to Phoenix.

It was the hardest decision I had ever made in my life at that time, and even though everything was being handed to me on a silver platter, I made the decision not to go to the reunion concert in Phoenix, Arizona. All because of my fear of flying. I let fear stop me from doing something that would have given me a memory I could hold onto for the rest of my life and take to the grave when it was all over.

I made up some excuse to Mark about why I wouldn't be able to make the concert, but no excuse I gave him was good enough. "Are you fuckin' kiddin' me? Get yo' ass on that plane!" But I wouldn't budge. How could I make him understand that the fates would have me die in a flaming plane crash before they would let me witness this historical event? He wouldn't understand. Up until the last few days before the concert, Mark kept trying to get me to reconsider. I could hear the disappointment and sense of betrayal in his voice. In his mind, as Kiss fans, we had waited our whole lives to witness and be a part of something like this, and now I was walking away from it. Even my mom seemed confused and annoyed about my decision not to go. Even though I was an adult, I felt like a little kid who didn't know how to explain his bike getting stolen. But the plane crashing with me in it was my logic, not theirs. Finally, I just had to tell my mom that I was afraid to get on that plane because I knew that it would crash. My mom began to sympathize with me and gave me a lecture about how safe it is to fly and how hundreds of planes fly every day and don't crash. Bless her heart, it still didn't matter. I never got on that plane. The Phoenix concert went on as scheduled, and CNN never reported any plane crashing.

Mark called me after the concert and was talking a hundred miles an hour. He told me how magical and great it was. He said the atmosphere of Kiss fans was like nothing he had ever seen before and it was something you could never understand unless you were actually there. In a way, he was trying to rub it in to make me feel bad, but in this case, he probably had a right to.

I went into a depression for the next few months. I tried to overcompensate by spending a bunch of money and trying to buy and order everything with the Kiss logo on it. But no matter how much money I spent, it still didn't make up for the fact that I missed the reunion tour for no reason other than the fear of flying. Fear had won that battle.

# Chapter 42

## PSYCHO CIRCUS

"What are Kiss' new outfits gonna look like?" is what fans all over the world and myself wondered. Like many fans, I had what I thought was a lot of great ideas for new Kiss outfits. I was so excited to see what the outcome was gonna be. And I was so disappointed when I opened up a rock magazine to see them wearing their *Destroyer* outfits. It was a major letdown. I felt like they were going backward. What's funny is I actually sarcastically said to myself, *What're the next outfits gonna be, the* Alive! *era?* And that's exactly what happened. In retrospect, I think the *Destroyer* outfits were pretty cool during the *Psycho Circus* era, especially Paul's. Ace's looked cool, too. There are a lot of cool pictures from those photo shoots. It was just my initial reaction at that time.

But the bigger issue at hand was the new Kiss record. When was it going to come out and what was it going to sound like? I was hoping for a continuation of *Revenge* and my bootleg copy of *COS*. I just automatically assumed that they were going to make a heavy hard rock album. I guess, in all actuality, *Love Gun* was the last studio album they all played on together because on *Dynasty*, "Dirty Livin'" is the only song that Peter played on, depending on what source you listen to. But I really didn't want another *Love Gun*.

All of these thoughts went through my mind about what the new album was gonna sound like. But when the new album title, *Psycho Circus*, was revealed, I began to have my doubts. Then in interviews, Gene and Paul started talking about how this album was gonna take the listeners on a journey and they were using *Destroyer* as a model for the new album. I began to have more serious doubts. Between the record title and Gene and Paul's usual interview rhetoric, this album was sounding more and more cheesy. But I could be wrong because, after all, they just came off *Revenge* and *COS*, so this album can only be better, right?

## OH WELL

The day it came out, I brought it home, put it on the boom box, sat on my bed, and just listened. I had already heard the song "Psycho Circus" on the radio a few times, so there was no surprise there. When "Within" came on, I thought it was really cool and had the demon's stamp on it. But after that, the album went downhill for me. It was just one soft song after another, with no backbone. *Psycho Circus* was quickly becoming a major disappointment and was not living up to my expectations of what a Kiss reunion album should sound like. When the tape finished, I just took it out, rolled my eyes, and shook my head. I thought, *Not only did I not like it, but there's only one song each from Ace and Peter.* I wanted to hear at least two songs from each of them. Not only that, but the demon only had one hard song and his other two are "We Are One" and "Journey of 1,000 Years." I wanted to hear more "Almost Human," "War Machine," and "Paralyzed." To me *Psycho Circus* was unbalanced, tame, and confused.

## GIVE IT A LITTLE TIME

After a while, it began to grow on me. That same year, I would listen to it going to and from work, and I began appreciating *Psycho Circus* on its own level. No, it wasn't *Revenge* or *COS,* but it had some pretty cool, fun songs on it. It sounds like a mixture of *Dynasty* and *Unmasked* to me. To this day, I call it Kiss' attempt to make a *Sergeant Pepper*'s album. "Welcome to the show!"

THE SONGS

## PSYCHO CIRCUS

Sometimes I like it, and other times, it annoys me. I don't like it when they throw it in the set list at a show. I'd rather hear another Kiss classic. I can go either way on it.

## WITHIN

Initially, I thought "Within" was the only song on the album that was really worth listening to. It has balls and backbone. I love the breakdown.

## I PLEDGE ALLEGIANCE TO THE STATE OF ROCK & ROLL

This is a song that they should do live more. I love the feel of it.

## INTO THE VOID

Ace may have only gotten one song on the record, but it's tight and has his signature all over it. It has an *Unmasked* feel to it.

## WE ARE ONE

Definitely not a song that I wanted on a Kiss reunion record, but it's a great song, and to point out the obvious, it belongs in a Pepsi commercial.

## YOU WANTED THE BEST

Such a horrible song. I think it's the most generic song to ever appear on a Kiss record. I always wondered what they were thinking when they gave this the green light to be on the album. It's corny as hell, but it's still fun to listen and sing along to.

## RAISE YOUR GLASSES

My favorite song on the album. I love the chorus.

## I FINALLY FOUND MY WAY

This is an absolutely beautiful song. It could have easily been a big radio hit for this album, especially on the country stations. But at the same time, it's such a cliché to have Peter sing a ballad. As a fan, I don't need to hear "Beth" part 2. We haven't heard Peter's voice on a Kiss album since '79, and when he finally gets another song, it's a ballad? Maybe it wouldn't have been so bad if he'd had one or two more songs on the record that were heavy, but it proved to me that Gene and Paul didn't know or care about what the fans really wanted at that time.

## DREAMIN'

The first time I heard this song, I felt it could have easily been a throwaway from one of their '80s records. Because of the way it sounds, I'm gonna say it belonged on *Asylum*. But I like it.

## JOURNEY OF 1,000 YEARS

Even though we don't get to hear much of the demon on this record, it's still a very good song. I didn't really appreciate it until years later.

## ALBUM COVER

I think it would have been cooler if their faces weren't on it, just the weird clown face, and if they made it a darker picture, more of a heavy metal thing. I don't own a copy of the CD, and I forgot what the back and the inside looked like. I guess it wasn't that memorable.

## PSYCHO CIRCUS VIDEO

I've only seen the video maybe three or four times. I don't really care for it all that much. Why it was recorded on video instead of film at that time, I don't know. Probably to save money. But personally, I don't like that effect. It looks cheap to me. It worked well for the "I Love It Loud" video but not for "Psycho Circus."

FAVORITE SONG: "Raise Your Glasses"

FAVORITE RHYTHM GUITAR: "I Pledge Allegiance to the State of Rock & Roll"

FAVORITE LEAD GUITAR: "You Wanted the Best"

FAVORITE BASS GUITAR: "Within"

FAVORITE DRUMS: "I Pledge Allegiance to the State of Rock & Roll"

THROWAWAY: "You Wanted the Best"

## Chapter 43

# "WORST KISS CONCERT EVER!" KISS COMES BACK TO ALASKA, JANUARY 3, 2000

I woke up early one morning to start my car for work. It must have been fifteen below zero. I had a four-door Honda Accord, and usually, it would start under any conditions, but on that morning, it was struggling. Finally, after cussing at it for a few minutes, it started. It's *ALIVE!* All my car needed was "Something to Bring It Up."

The first thing I noticed was that "Love Gun" was playing on the classic rock radio station The Fox. When I wasn't listening to rap or R&B CDs in my car, my radio was set to four different stations, and The Fox was one of them. I had it tuned to The Fox because I liked checking to see if they were going to play a Kiss song. Not because I needed to hear a Kiss song on the radio, I just liked that they were showing support for the band when other stations weren't. But to be honest, sometimes, I thought The Fox only had two CDs in their collection, Ozzy Ozbourne's greatest hits, and AC/DC's greatest hits because they got the most airplay of all. Even more than Zeppelin. Moving on.

I didn't think anything of "Love Gun" being on the air. I just thought "cool" and went back in the house. When I came back out twenty minutes later and opened my car door, I heard "Black Diamond" was playing. I thought, "Wow, two Kiss songs in the same hour; that's cool." But it didn't stop there. All the way to work, The Fox kept playing one Kiss song after another. I knew something was wrong then, because I've never heard any radio station in Alaska rotating so many Kiss songs, especially that early in the morning. But I couldn't figure it out. I pulled into the parking lot of my job, got out of the car, and decided to let it go. *Maybe playing all of those Kiss songs was just a fluke*, I thought. I went inside the building, clocked in, and headed to the Pepsi machine. As I was plunking in quarters, my coworker Steve came up to me and said "Hey, Anthony, are you excited?" "Excited about what?" I asked. "About Kiss coming to Anchorage." As soon as he finished his sentence, it hit me. "That's why The Fox was playing Kiss songs all morning!" I shouted. Still, I had to be sure.

I ran to the phone, called information to get The Fox's number, called the station, and yes, they confirmed that Kiss was coming to Anchorage, Alaska, on January 3, 2000. From the moment it was confirmed, I was a nervous wreck. I couldn't relax or get a good night's sleep. I was too excited.

## YOU'VE NEVER SEEN ANYTHING LIKE THIS AND YOU NEVER WILL

I was friends with some guys at work who were in a band, Mike, Nate, and Ace. Nate and Ace were brothers. They played metal, hard rock, and sometimes mixed in a little funk. They were awesome musicians and should have easily gotten a record deal, but it never turned out that way for them. Anyway, they were going to go to the show, too. I bragged to them every day how a Kiss concert was the most exciting thing in the world and how they'd never seen anything like it. I boasted about how they were all going to be blown away by the experience. After all, this was the original Kiss with their full show and everything else that comes with it. They were really excited and pumped up. Ace, the older brother and the drummer of the band, said he couldn't wait to see Peter's drum kit.

## IT'S GONNA BE A LONG NIGHT

At that point, I had only been to one Kiss concert, and that was *Revenge*. This would actually be my second Kiss concert, but my first time seeing them with makeup and my only time seeing them perform with Ace and Peter. But there was still one problem; the tickets hadn't gone on sale yet, and I was nervous that they would sell out before I got mine. After all, Kiss coming to Alaska was a big deal. I'd have to check my copy of *Kiss Alive Forever*, but I believe the Sullivan Arena only holds eight to ten thousand people, maybe less. I was afraid that with all of the hype surrounding the concert, it would sell out fast. In all of my years living in Alaska, this was the first time that the whole state was talking about Kiss at one time.

I decided to do what any logical Kiss fan would do. I would go to the Carrs grocery store on Northern Lights Street twelve hours before the ticket counter opened and just sit and wait. By the way, this was the same store where I used to go admire the *Asylum* album.

I was in for a little surprise, because when I arrived, there were at least a hundred people already there who had the same idea. *Why is everyone so excited about Kiss all of a sudden?* I thought. *I've been a Kiss fan all my life in this city, and I was mocked and ridiculed for it. But now, all of a sudden, you same people who used to put me down for liking Kiss are standing in line to buy Kiss tickets?* I was one of those Kiss fans who had a sense of entitlement because I had paid more dues than those casual fans. But what could I do about it? So I stood in line for twelve hours with all of the fair-weather fans.

I made a temporary friend with a fat guy; I forget his name. He was actually a cool guy, and he talked about how big of a Kiss fan he had been since '75. He said Kiss was his world. What was also funny about him was he had no idea what the fuck he was talking about. Like the ignorant annoying heavyset woman who was standing in line at the *Revenge* show, whose Kiss facts were unreal, this so-called Kiss fan was just as delusional. He would say things like "Eric Carr was in Ace's solo band before he joined Kiss. Ace and Gene were roommates in college. The song 'Beth' was really about Paul's first girlfriend," and so on. He wasn't even drunk or high, but he spoke as if what he was saying was fact. He sounded so stupid to me, I didn't even bother to correct or challenge what he was saying. In fact, I found it entertaining and was curious to see what bullshit he was going to say next or what part of Kisstory he was going to fuck up. Yes, he was a dumb fuck, but he kept things interesting while we waited in line.

Finally, the ticket counter opened. Everybody stood up anxiously. As the first person tried to purchase their ticket, a problem developed. The store's computers were frozen. The manager tried for the next fifteen minutes to get them to work, but wasn't having any luck. I began to panic in my mind. I was already imagining the other ticket counters all over the city whose computers weren't frozen, and all of the people buying up all of the tickets and it being sold out. *This can't be happening!* I thought. Then the dumbest Kiss fan in the world came up with an idea. He called Alaska's most popular bar Chilkoot Charlie's, which was only a few blocks away, and asked if they were selling Kiss tickets. He hung up his phone and said, "They only have a few tickets left, we have to go now!" We ran to my car like Bo and Luke, where he jumped and slid his fat ass over my hood, we climbed through my windows because my doors were welded shut, and Roscoe, (James Best, RIP) chased us to Chilkoot Charlie's. OK, now I'm just being stupid, LOL. But long story short, we got our tickets, and I was that much closer to seeing the original Kiss.

I hid that ticket at my mother's house. I would show up every other day to make sure it was still in its hiding place.

## YOU WANTED THE BEST. YOU GOT THE BEST? (Notice the question mark.)

The morning of the day of the concert, I went to work full of excitement. I went to find Mike, Nate, and Ace. I had a surprise for them. I pulled out three Kiss shirts from my personal collection to give to them to wear to the concert to commemorate this awesome occasion. It was like Apollo Creed giving Rocky his American flag shorts before he got in the ring. They thought the shirts were really cool and were anticipating the show to be awesome!

That night, I had a pretty good seat in the thirteenth row. While the arena was filling up, I began to study the stage and everything inside the building. While observing, I began to realize a few things. I didn't see any attachments to help Paul fly or a platform for him to fly out to. I didn't see a rig for Gene to fly above the stage either. I could see Peter's drum riser was pretty basic and didn't see any way for it to be levitated. The stage was pretty small. No big screen in the back. And I didn't see much lighting effects either. That's when it hit me—*This is going to be a very toned down show. Nothing spectacular at all.* Don't get me wrong, as a Kiss fan, Kiss could've come out and played on stools, and I would have been happy just to see them. However, there were a lot of people who went there expecting to be mesmerized and blown out of their seats. But can that happen with a C show? I understand that sometimes Kiss has to change things up according to the codes, restrictions, and size of the buildings they're performing in. But as a Kiss fan who had been bragging about the band for years, I expected them to come to Alaska and prove me right and make all of the haters swallow their words and turn them into believers. I had to admit, I was getting nervous that wasn't going to happen and I might be embarrassed. Maybe I was more concerned with my own ego being validated than the audience actually enjoying themselves.

## WELCOME TO THE SHOW!

The moment of truth had finally come. The house lights went down, people rushed back from the bathrooms and concession counters, and all eyes were glued to the stage. Everybody braced themselves for the choreographed assault. Alaska was finally going to get the Kiss experience. The pyro went off, Kiss appeared onstage, the audience went wild, and then everything went downhill from there.

## THIS IS REALLY EMBARRASSING

As a die-hard Kiss fan, it's sad for me to think that I only saw the original band in concert one time, and it was the worst concert I've ever been to. That includes all other acts. I saw Carrot Top live in Vegas and even that was more entertaining than this concert was. Sad but true.

Forget the fact that special effects wise, it was a very toned down show. That's understandable and couldn't have been helped. But the biggest problem the show had was that Peter's playing was extremely slow. Throughout the show, I kept thinking to myself *Why can't Peter just pick it up and play a little faster?* There was no real up-tempo beat for the audience to get into.

Almost midway through the show, the audience was getting bored. It was as if everybody was waiting for something big to happen and it wasn't. Also, it seemed that this Alaska audience really didn't know any of the obscure songs, especially when they did a song like "100,000 Years." The novelty of Kiss live in Alaska was diminishing quickly because the decisive moment was here, and it wasn't looking too impressive. I know that people in the States have an image of Alaska as being a third-world country or that we live in the wilderness or in snow huts out in the bush areas because that's the stereotypical way TV portrays us. But no, Anchorage is a city like any other city in America. Moreover, Alaskan rock fans are serious about their rock music and the rock bands that come through there. A lot of big name rock acts had played in that particular arena, including Aerosmith, Metallica, Mötley Crüe, Journey, Lynyrd Skynyrd, Elton John, and Def Leppard, just to name a few. It's the Cobo Hall of Alaska. But word was those acts blew the roof off that place. Unfortunately, Kiss wasn't having the same effect. The audience wanted to be blown away, they wanted to see the legends they had heard about for so many years, but Kiss wasn't delivering.

Another problem I personally had was that Ace was motionless. He didn't move around much, and for the most part, he just stood in one place and stared at the audience with a dull blank look on his face. *Why doesn't Ace smile, move his head, make some kind of facial expressions?* I thought. He could've even walked to the other side of the stage just to get out of that spot or something, but don't just stand there.

Again, people were becoming bored with the show. At this point, a lot weren't even paying attention. I noticed that the stairways were becoming full of people going to the bathroom, getting more drinks, or just going out to get high. In Ace's defense, he was actually a major highlight of the show. When I would see Ace do his smoking guitar on the TV screen, it never really looked very cool or impressive to me. Usually, I would skip past his solo to the next song. However, on that night, seeing it live for the first and only time, it was amazing! And the audience went wild. I could have never imagined that seeing his solo live would've been that cool. Ace's smoking guitar solo got the audience back into it a little more.

Paul did some talking with the audience. He said, "I saw something that I never saw before in my life. While riding in my limo, I saw mooses walking in the middle of the street." Then he asked the audience, "Wait a minute, is it pronounced moose or mooses?" Everybody began to yell "MOOOOOSSE!" Paul couldn't understand what the audience was saying and laughed it off. He probably Googled it after the show.

Gene was spitting blood and there was no screen for the people in the crowd to see what he was doing. I remember thinking, *These people have no idea what Gene is doing. They probably think he's just up there making weird sounds with his bass.* I think a lot of stuff was lost on the audience that night.

The only time the crowd really got into it was when they started "Rock and Roll All Nite" and all of the confetti blew over their heads. After Paul did his "We love you, Alaska" rap, it was all over. The worst Kiss show I had ever seen. Not that I'm picking on Peter, but if he would have been able to play a little faster, to a degree, I think it could have helped save the show.

## FORGET ABOUT IT

The next morning as I drove to work, I listened to The Fox morning show. The host talked about last night's performance and said, "Not only did the show not blow me away like I expected it to, but it was the worst concert that I've ever seen." *Ouch!* I thought. People were calling in expressing their opinions and views about the show and they were, for the most part, negative.

I had pulled into the parking lot of my job. You know in the mafia movies when they say if you get a call and are sent for it more than likely means you're going to get whacked? Well that's how I felt that morning going into work. Like I had been sent for and I had to face the music. I had to face my work buddies who were hard rockers. I held my head low when I walked in. The first person I saw was Nate, the bass player. He walked toward me, shaking his head and said, "Don't feel bad, Anthony. This is not the '70s anymore. You can't expect them to still be good." About twenty minutes later, I ran into his brother Ace, the drummer, who said, "What the fuck was up with Peter's drumming? If he played any slower, they were going to have to roll him out in a wheelchair." *Ouch!* again. I never asked the lead guitar player, Mike, his opinion of the show, but the fact that he never brought it up when he saw me spoke volumes.

# Chapter 44

## *ALIVE! 4*

When it came out, I listened to it from beginning to end. It sounded like crap. I never played it again.

# Chapter 45

# WILL THE REAL SPACEMAN AND CAT MAN PLEASE STAND UP?

## CAT MAN

The first time I saw Eric in the cat makeup, I actually thought it was pretty cool. I did wonder what happened to Peter, but that thought was short lived. I guess I figured that I was used to members coming and going and really wasn't that surprised by the switch. By that point, I felt Peter was just too slow, so it was refreshing and a joy for me to see Eric back in the band, playing drums at the level that he could play. But not once, as a die-hard Kiss fan, did I have a problem with Eric wearing the cat makeup. I welcomed Eric as the new cat man with open arms. However, it wouldn't be until years later that I would see him live onstage as the cat.

But with Eric, it was easy for me to accept and move on because, after all, he was already family. I was happy he was back in the band, and the fact that he was wearing the cat makeup just made things more interesting to me.

## SPACEMAN

I don't think I even knew who Tommy was or the work he did for the band until I saw him in the spaceman makeup. I just remember seeing a Kiss picture in a magazine and some guy I didn't recognize wearing Ace's makeup. I do know that it didn't have an effect on me one way or the other.

I didn't know if Ace quit or was fired. I didn't even bother to try to find out. In other words, I just didn't care if Ace was in the band or not. I just figured if Ace wasn't in the band anymore, then there must be a reason for it. Next! I didn't have faith in either Ace or Peter as band members.

Do you know what my only complaint about Tommy being the new spaceman was? The makeup at the bottom that curved to point to his lips was too thick and wasn't as sharp or as thin as Ace's was. It was something he later corrected. But that was it. That was my only complaint. I didn't care that he was wearing Ace's makeup or outfit. I really didn't. I felt like "If this new guy can step in and work hard and do the job that needs to get done, then welcome aboard, stranger!" It always seems like the fans don't have as much of a problem with Eric in the cat makeup as much as they do with Tommy in the spaceman makeup.

## TOMMY! TOMMY! TOMMY!

My loyalty was never to the original members, but to whoever came into the band and was willing to work hard, sacrifice, give a hundred percent, and go above and beyond the cause as a member in the band. Can it be fair to say that aside from maybe Paul, no other member of the band has worked harder for Kiss than Tommy Thayer as the spaceman and also behind the scenes? Maybe even more than Gene in some areas. Can anyone disagree that when it comes to giving hard work, sweat, and passion for Kiss, Ace can't even compare to Tommy? Ace was lazy and showed no passion for being in the band. Let's be real, the only thing Ace had to do was show up and play his guitar, that's it, and he managed to turn that into a chore for the band. Tommy was a hard worker, period. No nonsense, handled business, dependable, and gave himself a hundred percent to Kiss on and off stage. Even I was surprised when I learned of all the business and arrangements he did for the band behind the scenes. I wouldn't want his job, but he does it day after day and night after night.

## SERIOUSLY, DOES IT EVEN MATTER?

I like watching reruns of *Two and a Half Men,* but I can only watch the episodes when Charlie was still on the show. The episodes after Charlie left the show are hard to sit through, so I just turn the channel. For me, it's no Charlie, no show. But I don't share that mindset when it comes to Tommy and Eric in the spaceman and cat man makeup. I don't even think it matters because as a band and business, Kiss is in a different place right now than they were twenty to twenty-five years ago. I see Kiss now as more of an attraction than ever before. Sure, in a perfect world, if I had my way, I would love for Kiss to put out a balls to the wall album every year that wasn't produced by Paul. I would love it if they would stop putting on the same tired, predictable, redundant, outdated special effects live show that they do every tour with the same tired set list. But whether I like it or not, that's the place and comfort zone they're in right now. Having said that, does it really matter that in the new place for the band, two other guys are wearing the spaceman and cat man makeup? Not to me.

## "BUT WHY CAN'T TOMMY AND ERIC COME UP WITH THEIR OWN MAKEUP DESIGNS?"

Sometimes when I hear Kiss fans ask this question, I can't help but wonder how old these fans are. Do they not understand how a business works? It's business. Tommy and Eric have no control over that. And let's be real, that only matters to a handful of die-hard Kiss fans. Or Ace and Peter fans. Kiss is in a place right now where they do not have to appeal to the small percentage of fans who make an issue of this. And the thousands of people who are buying their concert tickets don't share the same view as this small percentage of fans. If I were the same age I am today back in '80–'83 and they tried to do the same thing with Eric Carr and Vinnie by putting them in the spaceman and cat man makeup, then maybe I would've had a problem with that. I probably wouldn't have accepted it because back then, Kiss was in a different place with the way the fans and the public looked at them. In this day and age, with forty plus years behind them, the public has a totally different view and perspective about Kiss. To them, Kiss is a spectacle. They don't care about the personalities behind the makeup. When Kiss played in Vegas in 2012 and Paul asked the audience "How many of you have never seen us live?" at least 70 percent of the hands in the arena went up in the air. Even I was surprised by the number of people there who had never seen Kiss live. Bottom line is the audience was there to have a good time. They didn't care about the beefs that were circulating among the original members. They didn't care if that was Tommy singing "Shock Me" instead of Ace. They didn't care if Singer didn't sing "Black Diamond" the way Peter does. They didn't care that Gene and Paul were wearing wigs or hair plugs, depending on who you ask. And they didn't care what song Gene was going to sing after spitting blood. They just wanted to have fun and see a great show, and that's what they got.

Now, as a die-hard Kiss fan, I picked the show apart. I complained about what songs they didn't sing, how the drum solo could have been better, how the show wasn't long enough, why Gene was singing this song instead of that song after spitting blood, and so on. But no matter what problems I found with the show, I was still in the minority group. Everybody else was blown away, and not only did they not care about my personal issues with the show, they also loved Tommy and Eric, who gave a 110 percent while at the same time wearing the spaceman and cat man personas.

At this point, I don't agree that Tommy and Eric should come up with their own designs. Yes, maybe when they first started wearing makeup, it would have been cool to see Singer in the hawk makeup or see what they came up with for Tommy. Who knows, maybe they did have their own makeup ideas. But as of right now, I prefer them to leave things just the way they are. I think Tommy looks really cool as the spaceman and sometimes I even have to do a double take to see if the cat in the picture is Eric or Peter. Not that I want Eric to look like Peter, but that's just how good Eric looks to me in the cat man persona. They're also in good shape and take really good care of themselves.

## I NEVER WANT THEM BACK

Truth be told, I never want Peter and Ace to come back to the band. Ever! I would never pay to see Peter and Ace perform with the band again. Even if I was given a free ticket to see the band perform with Ace and Peter, I would just sell my ticket. I will never support that lineup in the future. I'm not one of those fans who has blind loyalty to any member of Kiss. I'm not one of those fans who tries to give Peter and Ace more significance than is needed because they're original members and were there during the "magical years." A fuck-up is a fuck-up, and a dumb ass is a dumb ass. I'm a grown man, and as a grown man, I'm not going to sit around making excuses and defending the self-destructive behaviors of other grown men.

Kiss is not only something that's been a major part of my life for almost four decades, it's also something that I love! And anybody who does something destructive, sabotages, or does anything else to hurt the band I love can go away and stay away for good, including certain band members. And if someone else is in a better place mentally, emotionally, and physically than they are and that person wants to be there onstage every night giving a hundred percent instead of off stage getting loaded and high, then I'm all for it.

Look, I'm not saying just because I have absolutely no problem with Tommy and Eric wearing the makeup that you should feel the same way I do. This argument has been going on for years, and there are thousands of Kiss fans who have different perspectives and opinions on this matter. And everything I've said above is just that, my opinion and perspective. But it's not the only one, and I'm open to hearing other perspectives as long as they can give it without arguing and show some sense and intelligence. And for the Kiss fans out there who have a problem with Tommy and Eric wearing the spaceman and cat man makeup, I understand where you're coming from and I don't fault you for feeling the way you do. All I'm saying is stop trying to convince everybody else to feel the same way you do. Stop trying to convince everyone that your way of thinking and perspective on this matter is the right one, written in stone, or that because you don't like Tommy and Eric wearing the spaceman and cat man makeup, it makes you more of a real fan. It doesn't.

# Chapter 46

# SONIC BOOM

When it was announced that Kiss was going to release a brand new studio album after *Psycho Circus,* I can't say that I was too excited. By that point, I'd been used to Kiss disappointing me, not just with albums but also with other Kiss related items, projects, and decisions in general. Yes, I wanted to believe that this album was going to be great because as a Kiss fan, you always want to believe that eventually they're going to get it right or outdo themselves the next time around. But at the same time, I didn't want to get my hopes up.

When I heard the news that Paul was going to be producing the new album, I was immediately disappointed. Sure, I loved the work he did on *Animalize* and *Asylum,* but that was a long time ago. By this point, they had a lot more money than they did in the early '80s, had already been put in legendary status by the rock community, and had nothing else to prove, so bottom line, at least in my mind, neither Paul or Kiss as a band were hungry anymore. Think of it in terms of a pack of lions. If they've already gotten their meal/kill for the day, later that evening, when herds of wildebeest roam by, even if they were to attack them, they still wouldn't do it with the same hunger, drive, or direction they would if they hadn't eaten in a week. So I was afraid that because of Kiss not being hungry anymore, this album would sound like an album produced by Paul with no hunger, drive, direction, and most importantly, no balls. Even though I was trying to be open-minded about the album, I still had little faith in the idea of a

Paul Stanley produced Kiss album. My mindset was just because you can doesn't mean you should.

Paul said during an interview that the album was going to be, to paraphrase him, a '70s throwback album. Only the band would write and perform on the album. Also, there would be no keyboards or special effects on the album, just straight guitars and drums. I have to say, as a die-hard Kiss fan, I don't need a '70s throwback Kiss album. I don't care if Kiss writes the songs or if they bring in ghostwriters. I don't care if Kiss themselves play all of the instruments or if they bring in ghost musicians to perform on some of the material. Bottom line, all I want is a great, awesome Kiss album. An album that'll not only make me smile and send a shiver down my spine the first time I hear it, but an album that'll also knock me on my ass!

When I finally saw the artwork for the album cover, I knew I didn't need to listen to the album to know it was gonna suck.

## THE BIG DAY

On the day of its release, I went to Walmart to buy my copy. Afterward, I sat in my car in the parking lot so I could listen to it in peace. When I opened it up and saw another CD inside of re-recorded Kiss Klassics, my curiosity was sparked. I guess in a way, I wanted to prolong listening to *Sonic Boom* to build up the anticipation. So I put in the other CD with the re-recorded Kiss Klassics first. I went through each track and listened to these Kiss Klassics being butchered. Not only did the re-recorded songs sound horrible to my ears, but I also wondered why on earth Paul thought it was acceptable to release this to the record buying public, especially those who weren't longtime Kiss fans. If Paul was trying to attract new fans to Kiss classics, this was definitely not the way to do it. I actually said aloud, "I never need to listen to this again!" I took that bullshit out of my CD player and flung it out of my window like a Frisbee. I didn't even bother to see where it landed.

Then the moment of truth came. I put in *Sonic Boom*. I was going to finally get to hear the new Kiss CD. People of the press, Kiss Army, your holiness, thank you all for being here on this joyous occasion. Let us all now listen to *Sonic Boom*!

When the CD finished, I sat in the Walmart parking lot and said in a calm voice, "That was horrible!" I didn't think it was going to be great, but I expected it to be a lot better than that. To me, *Sonic Boom* was like a slip and fall in the grocery store that could have easily been prevented. With the right songwriters and producer, this could have easily been something great. I mean, this was the same band who delivered *Destroyer*, *Creatures*, *Lick It Up*, *Revenge,* and *Carnival of Souls.* Instead, this new album was delivered with what sounded like a bunch of throwaways and half-assed concepts. Whenever I eat Papa John's pizza, it always tastes undercooked to me. Whenever I eat Subway sandwiches, I can barely taste the meat, all I taste is bread and lettuce. And that's exactly how I describe *Sonic Boom*, an album that's undercooked with barely any meat or substance to it. My ears didn't tell me that this sounded like a '70s throwback album; my ears told me this was a generic record of generic songs with zero backbone or substance.

I'm just speculating, but I couldn't imagine for a minute that deep down, Tommy and Eric were really happy with the outcome of this record. Then again, Eric probably didn't care as long as he got his check. Gene probably didn't care and had other business ventures on his mind. But I always wondered if Tommy really didn't like the direction the album was going in but was too afraid to tell Paul's sensitive ass, "Hey, Paul, these new songs don't really sound all that great. Let's scrap 'em and start fresh from the beginning and push out some real balls to the wall rock. Oh, yeah, let's also get a real producer in here." The reason I say Tommy speaking to Paul is that when it comes to the business side of Kiss, I know Gene and Paul have a heavy hand in that. But when it comes to the creative side of Kiss, I always imagine that Tommy and Paul handle and take care of that side of the band. Or maybe they all do equally; I'm just speculating.

I called Mark in Arizona; he was planning to buy his copy later that day. I told him not to waste his money and since I was mailing some stuff to him later that week, I would throw in the *Sonic Boom* CD and he could keep it.

If I were a younger Kiss fan, I probably would have loved it and played it three times a day for six months straight. But as an older Kiss fan, listening to *Sonic Boom,* I was offended. But I totally get why the newer and younger fans like it. And just because I'm an old-school Kiss fan who doesn't think it's a good album, that doesn't mean other old-school Kiss fans feel the same way I do.

## GIVE IT SOME TIME

In 2011, I wanted to give it another chance and see if I heard it differently. After buying it the second time around, I learned to appreciate it on its level. I also found I enjoy listening to it more. *Sonic Boom* is still a very poor effort to me, and I think it's beneath the band, but like Steven Seagal movies from the '80s and early '90s, even though they're generic, with bad acting and writing, they're still fun to watch. And despite all of its flaws, *Sonic Boom* is still fun to listen to from time to time. But I still say it stinks!

## THE SONGS

## MODERN DAY DELILAH

I love it! If all of the other songs on this record had the same feel as this song, the record would have been great! At least to me.

## RUSSIAN ROULETTE

Again, love it! It's my favorite song on the record.

## NEVER ENOUGH

"Don't need nothing but a good time!" At least that's what I thought the first time I heard it. Stupid, dated, but I like it.

## YES I KNOW (NOBODY'S PERFECT)

This song is a long way away from "Rock and Roll Hell" and "Almost Human." I'm not asking Gene to be "perfect," just use some better judgment when submitting material for a new Kiss album. Still, I like to listen to it.

## STAND

I cringe when I hear this song. Especially when Paul says to "look over your shoulder!"

## HOT AND COLD

Gene didn't just drop the ball here, he deflated it. I like to listen to it though. You know the saying, "It hurts so good"? Well, this song sucks so good.

## ALL FOR THE GLORY

This song sounds like a bad '80s montage from one of those awful '80s *Cannon* movies. I think it would have been great if they would have given Eric a heavier song to sing. I've always liked his voice a lot. This song is really stupid to me.

## DANGER US

To me, this is the only song that sounds like it could have been on a '70s album. In the chorus, where Paul says "Danger us," I always say "Danger Mouse!" from the old cartoon. I'm not even trying to be funny, but that's what always seems to come out when I hear it. This song is horrible.

## ANIMAL

I didn't think much of this song until I saw them perform it on the *Sonic Boom* tour. After I heard it live, I really liked it a lot.

## WHEN LIGHTNING STRIKES

The first time I heard it, I liked this song and thought Tommy's voice sounded really good. I think it's cheesy that he had to sing a song that had to do with lightning, but I think it's one of the better songs on the album.

## SAY YEAH

I guess it's not a bad song when they perform it live. Mark likes it.

## ALBUM COVER

From day one, it has always reminded me of an energy drink. And again we see their boring faces on the cover. Also, as usual, Gene and Paul are on the top and Tommy and Eric are on the bottom. I don't need to beat this into the ground. It's probably the dumbest album cover in the history of the band. It just tells me that at the time, Paul was really out of touch with the fans to think they would find that album cover acceptable or appealing. It's really annoying on the eyes to look at. But I'm sure Paul would tell you it's the greatest album cover they've had since *Destroyer*.

FAVORITE SONG: "Russian Roulette"
FAVORITE RHYTHM GUITAR: "Modern Day Delilah"
FAVORITE LEAD GUITAR: "Modern Day Delilah"
FAVORITE BASS GUITAR: "Russian Roulette"
FAVORITE DRUMS: "Hot and Cold"

THROWAWAY: The majority of the record.

# Chapter 47

# SONIC BOOM TOUR

This was without a doubt the best makeup show I've ever seen from Kiss. Remember, I've never been to a '70s or early '80s show. On this tour, I saw them in Phoenix, Arizona. I was living in Vegas at that time and took a bus down to Flagstaff, then Mark and I drove to Phoenix.

The lights, the energy, and the sound were really tight, and the band was refreshed and up-tempo. Coming off my last show with Ace and Peter, I didn't expect much of a difference, but I'm glad that I was wrong, because from beginning to end, this was just an awesome performance. By this point, playing with Tommy and Eric had made such a big difference and the sound and songs were more up-tempo and had more life to them. After this performance, I couldn't wait to see them again.

# Chapter 48

## MONSTER

Off the top, let me say that I won't critique *Monster* or the songs. The reason is because I don't have much of a connection to it. At least not yet.

Again, like *Sonic Boom*, I bought it at a Walmart and sat in my car listening to it in peace. After hearing it the first time, I smiled a little and thought, *This is pretty good! I like this.* I began driving and started the CD over from the beginning. When I heard it the second time, I realized I liked it a little less. Then, while still driving, I played it a third time and realized I didn't like it at all. I know it sounds strange to say "I liked it at first, but less than three hours later, I didn't like it at all." But that was the case. I guess the first time I heard it, I wanted to believe that Kiss was going to make up for *Sonic Boom* by making a kick-ass album. So I hyped myself up with preconceived expectations. But when the smoke cleared from the first listen and I heard it a second and third time, things began sounding a little clearer to me. This album didn't necessarily suck, but it wasn't great, in my opinion.

My problem with *Monster* is that Kiss was trying too hard to make a heavy album. But the real problem was that Paul was steering the ship. And for me personally, it just didn't work. It was like Paul was in the mindset of believing that in order to make a good hard rock album, all you have to do is play faster and louder. Duh…Paul's production on this album reeked of effort, and to me, the end result was a generic cheesy hard rock Kiss album.

There's a reason why hard rock albums like *Creatures, Lick It Up,* and *Revenge* sound so good, and that reason is Michael James Jackson and Bob Ezrin, and Paul is neither of them. I don't fault him for trying, but for me, it just didn't work or come together. And really, who was there who would tell Paul that it's not great. Paul is gonna do what he wants to do. His mind is made up that he's going in the right direction and what he's producing is great. Or to quote, "The best album we've done in thirty years." Now don't misunderstand me. Yes, I do think that *Monster* has at least four songs that are decent/good, but in the end, I give this album a C minus.

I understand from a business perspective that it's cheaper to let Paul produce new Kiss albums and have the band write the material than to pay for outside writers and producers, but as I'm writing this, I hope if there is going to be a next Kiss album, Paul does not produce it.

But to wrap this up, I took my copy of *Monster* to a used record/CD store in Vegas called ZIA Records. They gave me $4.00 credit for it. I used that $4.00 credit to purchase an Ohio Players CD. I figured I'd give it a few years and purchase *Monster* again. Then I would see if I heard it differently. So far, I haven't been that motivated to go out and buy it, but I will.

## Chapter 49

# OUT OF CONTROL, TROUBLE WALKIN', ASSHOLE, LIVE TO WIN, OH MY

It's funny, because as a Kiss fan, I never really had a desire to go out and buy any of the solo albums the members recorded outside of Kiss. I never thought *Oh, Peter, Ace, or Bruce has a new solo album coming out. I'd better get to the store or go online and buy it.* I guess to me, they weren't Kiss albums, so the interest wasn't there. Why do I love the original '78 solo albums? Because even though they're not Kiss (the band) albums, meaning the band didn't play on each album, they were still Kiss projects. The members were still in makeup, they were in their prime, mysterious, and last but not least, the '78 solo albums were a big part of my childhood.

### PETER

I love the cat man, but what Peter Criss (the man) wants to do or record outside of Kiss doesn't appeal to me. I don't really consider Peter to be a great songwriter or producer. To me, he was only magical and great when he was associated with Kiss. I will say this, though, I always thought if Peter's voice was being guided and directed by the right producer, he could have been the next Don Henley. I could easily hear Peter's voice doing the same type of pop rock songs that Don was doing in the '80s. And in some cases, Rod Stewart; again, with the right producer, I could hear Peter doing a song like "Forever Young." I have never heard any of Peter's solo stuff outside of Kiss and have no desire to. His solo albums might actually be really good with great productions and songs. I just don't care enough to find out.

## LIVE TO WIN

Why is it that whenever Paul does a solo album, it automatically has to be so damned sappy, watered down, cheesy, with no spine to it, and full of clichés? I already said what I had to about his '78 solo album, but when I bought *Live to Win*, I didn't know what to expect.

I put the CD in, sat down, and listened to it from beginning to end. When it was over, I thought it was horrible. It wasn't a CD I would want to play over and over again. I put it away in my CD case. Two years later, I wanted to see if my opinion about it would change, so I played it again, this time really loud to get a better feel for it. After I listened to it, I realized I was right the first time, it was horrible to me.

## ASSHOLE

I actually thought *ASSHOLE* wasn't a bad album. OK, as a whole, it wasn't great, but I thought it had some cool songs on it. I thought "Weapons of Mass Destruction" would have been cool on a new Kiss album and it'd be extra cool if a new Kiss album opened up with "Firestarter." Something different sounding. I also thought the song "Asshole" itself would have been a cool song on a new Kiss album, of course mixed in with other heavier songs. I like the song "Beautiful," the feel of it and the background instruments. I no longer own it and can't remember what I did with my copy. I guess it's not memorable enough to motivate me into running out and buying or ordering it again. But I definitely choose it over *Live to Win*.

## VINNIE

From what I can remember the only time that I ever heard a Vinnie Vincent Invasion song was when I saw the video to the Freddy Krueger movie soundtrack, and at the end, Vinnie was wearing the glove. Growing up, I was already not that much into rock as it was, and not only did the song not do anything for me, it didn't have a Kiss feel to it whatsoever. So I had no reason to want to buy one of his albums or listen to it. Musically, Vinnie was only valid to me when he was in Kiss. Outside of that arena, there was no interest or appeal.

## BRUCE

I don't know anything about Bruce's solo material. I don't know if he sings or doesn't or what other instruments he plays on the songs or who the members are or were. I'm just totally in the dark about his solo projects. I feel guilty about not supporting Bruce's solo projects because I'm such a big fan of his. One of these days, as a Kiss fan, I'm just going to have to buy the solo albums I don't own and listen to them. I might end up loving them.

## *FREHLEY'S COMET*

To me, there's a reason why Ace's '78 solo album was the best of the four. And there's also a reason why I feel like no matter how many solo albums the other members release, they'll never be as good as Ace's.

The only Ace (after Kiss) solo album I have ever owned and repeatedly listened to in its entirety was the first one from 1987, *Frehley's Comet*. I have never heard any of his other solo albums after that one. But I love this one to death. I love the intro to "Love Me Right." I always play it loud. "Breakout," forget about it, it's just fuckin' tight! It's just a good feeling album. You'd think that would be reason enough for me to go out and buy his other albums, like *Second Sighting*, *Trouble Walkin'*, and so on, but again, I guess I don't care to. Wait a minute, as I'm writing this, I'm remembering that I did listen to *Anomaly*. I thought maybe there were three good songs on there but the rest of it was booty.

I remember telling Mark that my problem with *Anomaly* was there wasn't enough unique rhythm guitar and leads like he had on his '78 solo album and on *Frehley's Comet*. I never listened to *Anomaly* again.

I used to wonder what if Ace were still in Kiss in '87 and some of the songs from *Frehley's Comet* were on *Crazy Nights* because they were released the same year. What would it sound like and how would the record flow if songs like "Dolls," "Into the Night," "We Got Your Rock," and so on appeared on the album? I always thought that Ace still had a cool look in the '80s that would have fit in the band. But maybe not the guitar sounds of the times. Not that I had a problem with the way he sounded, but I'm sure that aside from his self-destructive ways, his sound wasn't what Paul wanted at that time. But still I think there would have been some cool songs from him.

I heard three songs from his album *Space Invader*. After hearing them, I rolled my eyes and said, "OK, I'm done." Seriously, Ace, "The Joker"? Again, I want to hear Ace play some unique and original rhythm guitar and leads. I don't want to hear some plain, simply produced Ace song about a problem he's having with some girl.

But no matter what, for me, *Frehley's Comet* will always be the best post-Kiss solo album there ever was or will be.

## Chapter 50

# HOW COULD GENE AND KISS BE SO DISRESPECTFUL TO A LOYAL FAN?

I read online that Kiss was going to be appearing at the opening of the Kiss Mini Golf course in Las Vegas. The entry fee was $500.00. When I called to get more information, the woman on the phone told me that what I would get for my $500.00 was I'd be sitting in during the press conference for the Q&A as well as being in attendance when Kiss and other celebrities were doing their walk on the red carpet. Also, my favorite tribute band, Mr. Speed, was going to be performing there. I was really looking forward to hearing what their set list would be. Last but not least, afterward, Kiss would be inside the golf course meeting, signing autographs, and taking pictures with fans. At this point, I had been living in Las Vegas for only a couple of years. Being raised in Anchorage, Alaska, Kiss fans like me didn't get opportunities like this. To my knowledge, Kiss had only been through Alaska twice, once in '74, and the time I saw them live in 2000. I'm sure Kiss fans who grew up in the States saw and got to meet Kiss or the members all of the time, but for me, I saw this as a once-in-a-lifetime opportunity. Not only could I meet my childhood heroes, but it was only a fifteen-minute drive from my house. I'd waited for this opportunity since 1978. No way in hell would I pass this up. To meet Kiss, I would have paid a thousand dollars easily. I paid with a credit card over the phone and was told that I could pick up my pass at the mini golf course on the day of the event.

The day of the event, I woke up feeling funny and tingly inside. It was a weird thought knowing that on that day, after so many years, I was finally going to get to meet Kiss, shake their hands, get a picture taken with them, and exchange a few words. To me, it was like I was finally going to meet a long lost brother or sister I had only seen pictures of in person. That's what Kiss was to me, my other family and my childhood heroes. On that day, I was really soft-spoken. I felt humbled knowing that later in the day, Kiss and I were going to meet one on one.

## KISS TONIGHT! KISS TONIGHT! KISS TONIGHT!

My girlfriend drove me there, and we were a few blocks away from the building when I noticed three limos pull up next to us at the light. I instantly felt excited. I yelled to my girlfriend, "I bet Kiss is in those limos!" As a Kiss fan, you can just feel it when you're right. As we followed behind, the limos pulled up into the back entrance of the parking lot. But we couldn't go where they were going. I saw that the parking lot was full of Kiss fans. Never had I seen so many people in one place at one time wearing Kiss T-shirts and hats. Not even at a Kiss concert. There was the electricity of Kiss mania in the atmosphere. It was really exciting to see all of this as it was happening. But I had to get focused, I still didn't have my pass in my hand that I'd paid $500.00 for, and without that, I didn't feel secure. When I had that pass in my hand and saw Kiss, then I'd feel secure.

I found the table where they were handing out the VIP passes and gave the lady my ID. She gave me my pass and told me to wear it around my neck at all times. I looked up and saw the masses of other Kiss fans behind the secured area of the parking lot. They watched as the Kiss fans who could afford it collected their VIP passes. I have to admit, I felt kind of guilty. They were Kiss fans like me, but I was going to meet the band and they couldn't. They could only be spectators on the sidelines. I guess I shouldn't have felt bad about that, I would have liked to have bought all of them a VIP pass so they too could meet the band, but that's not reality. I decided that I would enjoy my time there and not spend it feeling guilty about something I couldn't control. At that point, it was just a matter of time. I had to play the waiting game.

## KEEP IT IN THE FAMILY

While roaming outside in the parking lot, I kept my VIP pass in my pocket in case some bold desperate Kiss fan tried to snatch it from my neck. Sure, I could beat that ass, but it was more a question of what if he could outrun me or if he disappeared into the crowd and I couldn't get a clear description. I was just being paranoid and extra cautious because it was my first time meeting Kiss and I didn't want anything to go wrong. Still waiting for the big event to happen and for Kiss to make an appearance, as the crowds got bigger, I found myself behind the secured line standing next to a guy who was holding a Gene Simmons Axe bass guitar. His wife was standing next to him. I overheard their conversation. He said, "I wish I could get in there." His wife said, "Maybe next time they come through Vegas, we'll be able to afford it." He responded, "Hopefully, I can meet Gene outside and he'll sign my bass for me." After hearing that, I once again began to feel bad for those fans who couldn't afford the $500.00 VIP pass to get in and participate. So I turned around and said to the guy, "I'll tell you what. When everything starts happening, Imma go inside, meet Kiss, get an autograph and picture, and when I'm done, I'll come out and give you my pass so you can get inside." Kiss Army, I'm not lying to you. He seemed so happy and touched that I thought he was going to start crying right there in front of me. But I was happy to do it. "Just make sure you stay in this area so I can find you when I come out. Be looking out for me," I said.

## SHOWTIME

Then the big moment came. They opened up the doors to the golf course to begin the press conference. Fans with VIP passes around their necks poured inside and I prepared myself to see Kiss. Forgetting that my pass was in my pocket, I got stopped at the door by security, like I was some kind of threat. "Hey, do you have a pass?" one of the security men asked me arrogantly and with an attitude. I was too excited about meeting Kiss to focus on the security's rudeness, and I couldn't risk getting thrown out by being verbally aggressive with him, so I just calmly took out my pass and placed it around my neck. I held it up and arrogantly said "See!" Like

I said before, I'm sure Kiss fans in the States are used to going to events and meet and greets like this and know the protocol, procedure, and how things work. But this was my first time doing something like this, so I was just a rookie who was learning.

The first thing I noticed when I walked in was there were a ton of fans gathered at the back of the store. The media were gathered at the front of it all. I began to make my way through the crowd when security stopped me. He told me I couldn't go beyond the red rope. I said that I had a VIP pass and was told that sitting in on the press conference was part of my package deal. Besides, I could clearly see that there were other Kiss fans with VIP passes in that area. He said that beyond the rope was for press only. And that those other people weren't fans. This guy was a dumbass, because they were clearly fans. But he was being firm about "doing his job" and not letting me pass. This was my first Kiss event and I was just happy to be there. But at that moment, I had to make a choice. Do I get all street on this guy and let my blackness take over and get loud and in his face? After all, I could give a damn about a cheesy press conference. My main goal is to get up front and close to the band to get a picture together. I decided not to risk getting thrown out, and let it go for the greater good. Kiss finally came out and did the press conference, and with me standing six foot one, I still couldn't see a damned thing.

When it was over, I saw Doc McGee sitting down. I approached him and asked if we could take a picture together. Not only was he nice about taking a picture with me, but we even tried different spots in the building to get better lighting. Meeting Doc was a cool experience for me. Sometimes I think Doc McGee, Sam Kinison, and Vince Neil are secretly the same person?

## OUTSIDE

Everybody gathered outside for the walk on the red carpet or whatever they called it. This situation was no different. All VIP pass holders were told that they had to stand on the outside of the waist-high gate. Only press was allowed in front of the red carpet, where the ceremony was taking place. Now it was clear to me that I wasn't going to get my $500.00 worth. I rolled my eyes and said, "This is some bullshit here." But still, I had to remember what my motive was—to meet Kiss one on one. The red carpet walk was a joke for the most part, C-list entertainers and people I never heard of, nobody relevant. But even though I was behind the small gate, it was still cool to see Kiss, especially Paul, walking down the red carpet and talking to the press. Paul just looked cool to me. But still, I was getting a little frustrated because of the money I had spent to participate in this, and not only was I not getting my money's worth, but the staff and security were rude. Regardless, I had to stay focused on my goal. But I was getting really annoyed.

## THE MOMENT OF TRUTH

When the walk on the red carpet was over, they let all the VIP pass holders back into the building for meet and greets with Kiss. When I finally made my way inside, I could see that fans were gathered around a long sales counter in the middle of the room, where Kiss was on the inside, interacting with fans, taking pictures, and signing autographs. What I didn't realize, and being new to this meet and greet thing, was how rapid this occasion was going to be. It seemed like the fans were only in there for a short time when members of the band started disappearing, one by one. *Maybe they're taking a break or something and are going to come back*, I thought. Before I knew it, Gene was the only one left. All of these fans paid $500.00. Why would Kiss just walk away like that?

## JUST CALL ME MR. HOLLYWOOD

At that point, there weren't a lot of fans left at the counter. All I can remember was some guy and I were patiently waiting for our turn to meet Gene. Gene was probably only a few feet in front of us, but we weren't crowding or being pushy, just calmly waiting for our turn while he was with another fan. I thought to myself, "So, there he is, the man whose picture has been on my walls since I was four years old. That's the guy who's on the cover of the *Alive!* album, who was in *Kiss Meets the Phantom*. There's the guy I thought was so funny and cool as I watched *Kiss eXposed* a million times. I had to say, it was a really cool moment for me. In just a few seconds, I was going to actually exchange words with Gene Simmons. I made the pilgrimage and I was finally here, and it only cost me $500.00. I'd waited for that moment since 1978. All of that hard work was going to pay off. And yes, being a die-hard Kiss fan is hard work. All of those years growing up and getting into fights just to defend the Kiss honor from other kids and teens who put them down. Being looked at differently and always having to defend my right to be a Kiss fan in general, while other people and rock fans laughed and sneered at me. Trying to earn money by doing odd jobs for my parents or for people around the neighborhood just so I could buy a Kiss album I didn't own or buy another because my first copy was damaged, or to buy the latest rock or *16 Magazine* with Kiss on the cover. And last but not least, still standing my ground as a Kiss fan although all the other fans jumped ship when Kiss released *Dynasty* through *The Elder*. I was still loyal! All of that blood, sweat, tears, and hard work was now about to pay off. But then something happened. Gene finished talking to that fan. He saw the guy and me standing there in front of him as loyal fans with our $500.00 VIP passes around our necks shining brightly for the whole world to see. And what does he do? He bypasses us and motions for a group of girls to come to him. These particular girls were part of the event. They weren't Hooters girls, but they were wearing Hooters style outfits. And to be honest, they weren't that attractive. I didn't take the diss by Gene personally. I thought it was just Gene being Gene. He was taking pictures with the girls and making his "I'm Gene Simmons; I'm the man. I get all of the girls" expressions for the camera. I expect Gene to show out to the camera. Not that big of a deal. But still, I thought it was kind of disrespectful to the two loyal fans standing directly in front of him wearing the $500.00 VIP passes. I mean, it's not like money grows on trees for fans like us. We earn an hourly wage just like everybody else in the room. That money could have gone to groceries, car payment, insurance, savings, or what have you, but we chose to spend that money to come see him, and he puts these girls before us? If I were to ask any of those girls a question like "What drummer played on the *Dynasty* and *Unmasked* albums?" "What two albums does the song 'See You in Your Dreams' appear on?" "Who does the introduction on the beginning of the *Alive!* album?" or "What sitcom mom did Gene used to date?" these girls naturally wouldn't have a clue what the hell I was talking about. And why would they? They have no emotional connection or investment in the band, and I wouldn't expect them to. But at that moment, Gene felt it was more important to acknowledge and put them before the two die-hard Kiss fans just standing there with their $500.00 VIP passes around their necks patiently waiting while he did his thing. So what could we do? We waited.

## LOVE'S A SLAP IN THE FACE

Finally, Gene was done showboating with the girls and I prepared myself to meet him. This was it! Finally, Gene and I one on one, even if only for a few seconds. Then once again, something weird happened. Some guy came and whispered in Gene's ear and Gene smiled, slowly turned around, and just walked away!

The other fan and I kind of looked at each other like, "Did that just happen? What's going on? Is he leaving, is he coming back?" Gene wouldn't just walk away from two loyal fans he clearly sees standing here patiently waiting to talk to him. Would he?

A few fans and I made our way to the side door we saw Gene go through. We didn't stand close to the door, just far enough to let Kiss know there were still fans out there who didn't get the chance to meet them yet. Then the door opened for a few seconds. You could see Kiss and the staff inside talking among themselves, some laughing, some eating and drinking. Then the door closed. A female fan started getting upset. She said, "This is so messed up. I paid all of this money and drove all the way down from Tucson to see them, and this is how they're acting toward the fans? I'll never do anything like this again!" I was mad too, because the whole thing was a bust for me, but if I could salvage the whole day just by getting one picture or even a lousy handshake with a band member, it'd be worth it. But it was looking like even that wasn't going to happen. Honestly, I can't tell you how much time Kiss actually spent with the meet and greets with the fans, but it really seemed like they were only in the building for about fifteen to twenty minutes. And I'm not saying there weren't other Kiss fans who didn't get their money's worth or who didn't get what they wanted out of that event. But I can say that for me and some of the other fans there, it was turning into an insulting experience. I mean, again, we paid $500.00 for this privilege.

Finally, we all got a glimmer of hope. The door began to open again. Maybe Kiss was going to come out after all and finish talking to the remainder of fans. And like the other fans who actually got close to Kiss that afternoon, we began to get a little excited. But the few seconds of anticipation were short lived. When the door fully opened, the room was now completely empty. Kiss and their staff must have slipped out a back door. It was all over. I never got to meet any of the members, especially Gene and Paul. What's a disappointing thought for me is that if Gene would have never taken the time to acknowledge those girls who were not even Kiss fans and who also didn't want to be around him in the first place, he would have given those two Kiss fans who were patiently waiting to meet him a memory they would have never forgotten. But in the end, he dismissed us and chose those girls.

I walked outside feeling disappointed. But for what it was worth I wanted to keep my promise to the guy with the axe bass guitar. I told him that unfortunately, the band was gone, and it didn't go well for me, but he could still have my pass and go inside and take a look around. After all, it was still a cool place to be in. He was cool and grateful that I at least gave him my pass. We gave each other a pound and parted. I called Mark who was in Arizona and told him what had happened. He was so pissed, saying, "I should go to Bookman's (a place in Flagstaff that buys and sells used rock items and instruments) and sell off all of my Kiss shit right now!" He was really mad for me. I told him I was gonna stay for the Mr. Speed show, but I'd call him later.

## MR. SPEED TO THE RESCUE

Even though I was feeling low and disappointed about the way everything turned out and what could've been my only chance to meet Kiss was now gone, I decided I was going to spend the rest of the evening enjoying watching Mr. Speed. I sang and jammed to every song. Not only did they once again deliver onstage, but they also got me out of my funk. When their show was over, I approached the stage to talk to Rich Kosak. When I stuck out my hand to shake his, he gave me a strong grip and immediately said how much he appreciated the letter I had sent to the band and how grateful he was for fans like me. Before this event, I had seen Mr. Speed perform at the Hard Rock Cafe and instantly became a fan. I wrote them a letter letting them know how much I enjoyed their performance and how great the band was in general. What really surprised me was that he even knew the letter was from me! I figured he put two and two together. And what's really strange is that not Kiss, but Mr. Speed, was the highlight of that event for me.

Later, my girlfriend picked me up and asked, "How was it?" I responded, "It was very disappointing. But do you know what the highlight of my night was? Seeing Mr. Speed and talking to Rich Kosak. He's a cool guy."

# Chapter 51

# KISS/DEF LEPPARD TOUR

## LAST NIGHT'S KISS CONCERT WAS HORRIBLE

Below is what I wrote online the next day after seeing this concert in Phoenix, Arizona.

Last night's concert in Phoenix was the second worst Kiss concert I've ever seen. They literally sounded like the bad tribute bands I usually see that come thru Vegas. And no, that's not an attack on Tommy or Eric, it was just that musically and vocally, they weren't in sync and the sound was horrible. One of the impressive things for me was that Tommy was playing the lead solos on point, almost the way they sounded on the old albums.

Kiss was boring and redundant as hell and the band just seemed to be going thru the motions. The set list was awful. It was the same boring tired ass songs they perform every tour, "Psycho Circus," "Deuce," "Shout It Out Loud," "Black Diamond," "Lick It Up," "I Love It Loud," "War Machine," "Detroit Rock City," etc. Every song was butchered and "Hide Your Heart" was irrelevant and out of place. I cringed through almost all the songs.

I did my best to try to get into the show, but couldn't do it. What was sad was the only interesting part was when Paul got temporarily stuck on the platform he flies out to. But they managed to get him back during the intro of the next song.

Toward the end of the show, I told my brother Mark we could leave early if he wanted to beat traffic because I was tired of watching this train wreck of a live performance. And I felt bad for wanting to leave early, but I just didn't want to watch it anymore. I actually thought to myself that I'd rather be at home watching reruns of *Cheers* on Netflix. I was serious.

I'm a die-hard Kiss fanatic, and the band could sit on stools and play a full concert and I'll still love it. My problem is I'm tired of going to Kiss concerts to see and hear the same boring/redundant show and songs every tour. All of this so-called "Kiss money" and yet they can't come up with something new? A new stage design and choreography. Different songs! As a fan, it's kind of insulting that Kiss takes their fans' money and keeps spoon feeding them the last tour's leftovers. It's like there's no effort on their part to dramatically change things up and do something fresh, new, and spontaneous.

Paul flying over the crowd, Gene flying up in the air, the hydraulic lifts, knowing all of the cues and exactly when and where everything is going to happen, knowing what songs they're going to play next based on Paul's raps—it's just too much of the same thing. Paul even did that tired ass thing he does when he says "People over here make some noise, people over there make some noise, animals on the floor let me hear you!"

Every tour, Kiss should make the fans wonder what they're going to do next that's new and exciting, but they don't. They just microwave and reheat what they did last time. The bottom line is if I don't like it then I don't have to go, and I won't. Having said that, last night's concert will probably be my last show unless Kiss is in my immediate city and I only have to travel maybe thirty minutes at the most to see them. It's not worth the two-hour drive and the cost of tickets just to see the same thing over and over again. Even Eric looked bored playing drums. What was sad was I was there to see Kiss. I could've cared less about Def Leppard. But in the end, Def Leppard turned out to be the highlight and I enjoyed listening and watching them more than Kiss. It shouldn't have been that way.

For me, there's no excuse that would be good enough for why they keep putting on the same show tour after tour, why they're still using effects that are thirty to forty years old. There are a lot of legendary bands and performers who continuously go out on tour and put on a new different show and performance. They don't just keep doing the same thing over again. To me, it means Gene and Paul don't care. And if they don't care, then why should I care to spend my money. And to repeat myself, their special effects are so outdated and redundant.

## ADDING TO THIS IN 2016

On the Crüe's last tour, Tommy Lee's drum set came out into and above the audience, like a roller coaster. Why isn't Kiss doing new stuff like that? Even Kanye West, who I can't stand, has a stage that flew over the audiences. Recently, I looked up a new Kiss show on YouTube from July 2016. Again, it was the same tired ass predictable performance and songs, but I guess the "major change" was now they use guitars on "Beth." What an incentive.

As for the songs, I get that Kiss has to perform the standards for the casual fans like "Detroit Rock City," "Rock and Roll All Nite," "Love Gun," "Shout It Out Loud," "Cold Gin," "Deuce," and so on. But why can't they do half a set list of standards and for the other half, go a little deeper? They don't need to play "100,000 Years," "Shock Me," "Psycho Circus," or even "Black Diamond." Not that those are bad songs but they're just too redundant and unnecessary live and the casual fans won't miss them. And I'm not saying they have to necessarily perform deep cuts like "Strange Ways," I'm just saying they need to be more spontaneous and mix it up a little more. As for the argument, "If you want to hear deeper cuts, that's what the Kiss Kruise is for," well, every Kiss fan doesn't have a few thousand dollars lying around just to go on a cruise to hear deeper cuts. My reply to that is that's what concerts are supposed to be for. And if the band isn't making the effort to do anything different, then I should just stay home and let those fans who want to make the effort to be there enjoy themselves.

I know every Kiss fan has an opinion and perspective about the redundant Kiss performance and set list; these are just my opinions and feelings.

## Chapter 52

# WHAT DO I THINK OF THE MEMBERS PERSONALLY AND AS A FAN?

I really don't know any of the members personally. I don't know them as human beings or what they're really like behind closed doors. So my opinions about the members are from me observing, watching, and reading about the band over the last thirty-eight years. Having said that, as a die-hard Kiss fan, I do have my own perspective on how I see the men who have been members of or participated in my favorite band of all time. Remember what I'm saying about each member isn't fact, it's just my opinion, me having a little fun, picking on each member and sharing my thoughts from all of my years being a fan. And no matter what I say, I love all Kiss members. They're all significant to me. But just because I love all Kiss members doesn't mean I always like what they do or say.

### GENE

At this point, as a fan, I have no desire to ever want to meet Gene. I remember watching an episode of *Family Jewels* where a Kiss fan won a radio contest to spend the day with Gene. Right there on camera, Gene was being disrespectful and impatient with this fan. Not only do you not treat a die-hard Kiss fan like that, you especially don't do it on camera and embarrass him in front of the whole world and his family. Yes, the guy was annoying, too much of a fan boy, and spending time with him would've gotten on my nerves, too. But is spending time with a fan who has invested so much into the band after so many years and giving him a memory he'll remember for the rest of his life too much to ask from Gene? Again, you just don't do that kind of stuff to a fan on camera.

I definitely see Gene as someone who's insecure and overcompensates. Sometimes I wonder why someone his age feels the need to act like that. Seriously, how many other entertainers, whether they're in movies, TV, or in music, do you see acting like that at that age? Not a lot. Why does Gene feel the need to walk around trying to stress and emphasize that he's the man, he's rich, and thinks that financial status puts him above others? I think in his mind, he feels that acting and dressing like an outdated porn producer from the '70s is appealing and makes him look cool and hip to Kiss fans and today's media audiences. And yes, there are some simpletons out there who might think that's true. But really, it just makes Gene look ridiculous and a little pathetic. Even my dad, who of course is not a Kiss fan, once saw an episode of *Family Jewels* and said to me afterward, "That guy is already a rock legend; he doesn't have to keep trying to prove himself by acting like that." I thought it was interesting that even my own dad saw how stupid his behavior was, and that he actually watched an episode of *Family Jewels*. I think that Peter described Gene the best when he said "Gene is the smartest guy I know with no common sense."

Of course it's an act for the most part, and of course Gene is just trying to find an identity that he can portray to the public. I think what Gene doesn't get is that he's interesting enough without acting like an old fool/idiot. Where he was born and raised, coming to America and learning how to speak English, becoming a schoolteacher turned rock star, the persona he created in Kiss, and so on. I remember watching an episode of *E! True Hollywood Story* on Gene. I believe that's what it was. Instead of making the focus about his real life story and interesting back ground that I mentioned above, which would have been a lot more appealing and interesting, they focused more on his ego, how "great" of a businessman he is, and that stupid "Firestarter" video where he's dressed like a pimp surrounded by girls. It was a waste of a biography on an interesting man. I remember years ago, my roommate, who was a woman, was at the movies with her boyfriend. Before the movie started, while the house lights were still up, they would show pictures of advertisements and fun celebrity facts.

A picture of Gene came on the screen and the question was "What was Gene Simmons's occupation before cofounding Kiss?" When she found out that he was a schoolteacher, she was floored. When she got home, she talked about that with me and said she never would have guessed that about him. But from an outsider, non-Kiss fan perspective, that's what she found most interesting about Gene, not his tongue, his money, his stupid dark shades, or that rose in his coat pocket, but the one thing with substance, that he was actually a schoolteacher.

I'm sure thousands of fans have met Gene and had a great time with him and found him charming, nice, down to earth, etc. But if I was meeting him today for the first time, the first thing I would think is, *What persona of Gene am I gonna get today? The real Gene, the bullshit Gene, the short answers Gene?* And so on. That's just too much thinking.

From what I observed over the years, the realest I've ever seen Gene, where he was being the most genuine and sincere, was from the *Revenge* era. He seemed so cool and down to earth, like someone you could have a real conversation with. If I could sit down with that era of Gene and interview him and have a true conversation with the real man himself, getting honest answers to my questions, then as a fan, I would want to meet him. But other than that, I find his persona, insecurities, and overcompensating to be a major turn off.

## PAUL

It's funny, because even before Paul's book came out, I always thought Paul seemed like the type of guy who was very insecure behind closed doors. I got that impression because of his humor and the way he would tell jokes or try to be funny in interviews or behind-the-scenes clips. His humor just always seemed to come from a place of insecurity, like he was trying to get validation or approval by being funny. At least that was the impression I got. I'm not saying it like it's a bad thing. It's just an observation.

The '80s were my favorite era for Paul. To this day, I like going on YouTube and watching his interviews from the '80s. Paul used to have a sincerity about him when he was being interviewed. It was like back then, you could count on Paul to be honest, tell you what was really going on, and tell it like it was, even if he was holding back a little. Like maybe because he was fighting for the band to stay afloat and compete, he spoke with a little more conviction. I loved that about him. But today's Paul I find to be a little full of shit, annoying, and way out of touch, maybe because he has so much money now. Sometimes, depending on the interview or appearance, you get pockets of the old Paul who is more sincere and real, but lately, it seems that he's becoming more and more just as full of shit as Gene is. And no, I'm not saying it's because Paul's publicly taking an active role in more business ventures.

When I hear Paul talk today, to me, he sounds like he's hiding something. He talks about Kiss related topics as if the fans are stupid and don't know any better or we can't see through his bullshit. When something they're doing or presenting is obvious crap, he tries to validate that particular thing by telling you how great it is or why you should participate in it. As a fan, I wonder when and why Paul became like that. What happened to the real Paul from the '80s? Of course, Paul's an awesome, great guy, and there's not much bad you can say about him. After all, to me, he's the spine of Kiss. I'm saying that lately, I see more of a side of him that's a turn off. For instance, when did Paul all of a sudden turn into Tony Robbins, always trying to talk like he's some kind of motivational speaker. "If you believe in yourself and don't let anyone hold you down, you can achieve anything. All you have to do is work hard like me and follow your dreams." That is so annoying to me when he talks like that. Or when he tries to use those stupid Gene analogies, "Life is like an apple pie, if you cut out one quarter, you still have three quarters left to fight with. Be like me, go for your dreams and don't let anything stop you." By the way, every time I imitate Paul's voice, I always use a lisp. The point I'm making is Paul needs to shut the fuck up with all that bullshit. All of a sudden, because he and Kiss have some money and success, hit the lottery twice, now he wants to pretend that makes him an authority on telling people about hard work, sacrifice, and determination? You know how some bands, entertainers, magicians, and even comedians spend ten to twenty years working on the road in one dive after another just to eat, in hopes that one day, they'll get their big break. Well, I'm sorry, but Paul went from living in his parents' house to getting a record contract. Paul went from starting a band to a little over a year later, if even that, getting a record contract. Now Mr. Tony Robbins with the star on his eye thinks he's an authority figure on motivating people. Paul, get the fuck out of my face with that bullshit. And even though the '80s may have been a little bit harder for Kiss and Paul in terms of ticket and album sales, there are a lot of entertainers who would have loved to have sold as many tickets and albums as Kiss did in that era. And yes, Peter was right, Paul didn't pay as many dues as he or other musicians have, and no, Paul does not have to apologize for his success. All I'm saying is just stop the motivational speaker routine because you sound ridiculous.

Now having said all that, Paul, can you loan me twenty grand? I swear I'll pay you back on the first.

I will say the thing that I think is great about Paul is when he's being interviewed, he stresses his love for his family. Or he'll bring them up in an interview in a positive way. His mindset is family first, and to me, that says a lot about him. Out of the original band, Paul is the only one I would want to meet if given a choice.

## PETER

Forget about it! Peter is definitely my least favorite of the original band. Everything about Peter's personality, behavior, and attitude is a turn off for me. I will always love the cat man, but I can't stand the guy behind the makeup.

To me, Peter seems like the kind of person who when you first meet him in a social situation, comes off as really sweet, warmhearted, and humble. But if you hang around him long enough, you'll see his insecurity, immaturity, bitterness, unaccountable, entitled side come out and take over. In other words, Peter's a great guy, but in very small doses. Peter likes to be in control, even if he doesn't know what he's doing or could even handle it. His insecurities and ego need to be validated to bring him back into his comfort zone. And what does Peter do if he doesn't get his way? Does he handle it like an adult or even a businessman? Nope, instead, he those tantrums, tries to sabotage the situation, or tries to hold the situation hostage until he gets his way or his demands are met.

One minute, this guy only has $100,000 in a bag, hiding in his apartment with the barrel of a gun in his mouth. The next minute, he's given a second chance, touring the world, and in his own words, "Making $40,000 a night in some markets." Do you know what I could do with $40,000 a night? Especially after being given a second chance and after getting himself fired from the band he cofounded thanks to his self-destructive behavior. And to top it all off, he should have really been grateful for that second chance because let's be real, his drumming skills just weren't there. Did he think that this was 1975 and he was still a great drummer? As bad as his drumming skills were from the reunion tour and afterward, he should have been grateful if they only gave him $5,000 a night. Personally, I don't think he was even worth that. At his age, he should have been grateful for anything he could get his hands on. But after all of that, he still had this attitude of entitlement. I believe the reunion tour wouldn't have been as successful without him as the fourth piece of the puzzle. But after the reunion tour was over and all of the hype had died down, the adult/businessman inside of him should have thought "Back to business as usual. I'm an employee in a band called Kiss, and I'm going to ride this thing until the wheels fall off and make as much as I can before I'm retired for whatever reason."

To me, Peter is just an idiot, a big dumb kid who's tried to convince himself he's something that he's not or has something that he doesn't. He thinks with his emotions first and his ego/pride second, but business and common sense are lost on him. Personally, I can't relate or connect with that type of mindset. I find it weird that a grown adult man at his age still can't figure out how to put himself in check. I just don't like Peter. As a fan, I have no desire to meet him, and if he were doing an autograph signing a mile away from my house, I wouldn't have any desire to go. If I did go, it would be just to be a part of the environment and be around other Kiss fans. But the only time I would want an autograph from Peter is if it were on one of his solo albums or drumheads and I could potentially sell it online. Again, he's my least favorite of the original band.

But aside from all of that, when it really counts, as a human being, I believe Peter Criss has a heart made out of pure gold, a real humanitarian who cares about other people and animals. And until the day he breathes his last breath, that can never be taken away from him.

## ACE

I can't figure him out at all. Again, love the Space Ace, don't like Ace Frehley. Ace seems like he would be an awesome guy to talk to or hang out with if he wasn't under the influence of drugs or alcohol. Who knows, maybe he's still a fucked up person even when he's sober. Unlike Peter, I don't think Ace is an idiot by any means. I think he's actually intelligent. But because of his substance abuse, we rarely get to see that side of him. I guess I can blame all of the bad stuff he did in the '70s and the '90s with Kiss on his substance abuse. But as an older fan, not only would I not trust or count on Ace anymore, I just don't care. I don't think he deserves to be in Kiss anymore. To me, he's still lazy, unpredictable, unprofessional, and I don't think he ever wanted to be in Kiss from the start of the reunion tour. As a Kiss fan, I have no desire to meet Ace or get an autograph or picture together. If Bruce Kulick and Ace were doing an autograph signing in my town at the same time and I only had time to visit one of them, I would pick Bruce over Ace in a heartbeat. I also think that because of his attitude and behavior, performers like Ace are exactly where they need to be, performing in small clubs and showing up hours late for meet and greets.

## CARR

It was strange to me when I started hearing the stories of how Eric was unhappy about being in the band in the mid to late '80s, not getting along with Paul. I guess I always had the impression that he was happy and grateful to be the drummer in Kiss. But when you're young, you always think everything is cool behind the scenes with your favorite band and they're just one big happy family.

Out of all of the members, when you hear about a member everybody loved and wanted to be around, who made people laugh and smile, it was always Eric Carr. Of all the great qualities the other members possessed, you never hear them receive accolades the way you do about Eric. They said when fans would wait outside the hotels where Kiss was staying in the cold in hopes of getting a glimpse of the band, Eric would go out and bring them food, water, and blankets. Or after a show, he would go downstairs to the bar in the hotel and have drinks and talk with fans. Or even how he would personally write them back when they sent in fan letters. Eric wasn't just all heart, he was also all character. Testimonies from fans and peers speak for themselves. Kiss was definitely better for having had him in the band.

## VINNIE

When it came to Ace and Peter, at least for the most part, you knew what their malfunctions were. But Vinnie was and still remains one big question mark. Let me say right off, I liked his makeup a lot, and in some past pictures and interviews, I think he looks really tight! To me, his makeup image fit the heavy metal/lead guitar master early '80s vibe they were going for during that era. Vinnie's character has a lot of mystique to me. He's like that quiet warrior on the battlefield. He's quiet, calm, doesn't look you in the eye, but when he unleashes, it's devastating. Now mind you, I'm talking about the character, not the person. When I hear fans bash Vinnie, I wonder if they are bashing Vinnie the person or Vinnie the character.

To me, he could have been the perfect replacement for Ace, but like Ace, who wasn't working with a full deck, Vinnie was, and he was using that deck to play Russian roulette until he shot himself in the foot.

But it seems to me that Vinnie is such a self-destructive individual and he's dealing with something inside of himself that's so dark and disturbing, you pity him for that, and you just can't pick on him, put him down, or belittle him. You just know something is wrong with this person, but you can't put your finger on it. Or maybe we're just giving him too much credit and he's not disturbed or dealing with demons at all, and he's really just stupid enough to repeatedly shoot himself in the foot.

I guess I never really looked at Vinnie as a full member of the band. To me, he was more of a seat filler, a substitute teacher, someone to hold that space until the rightful owner of that position, Bruce Kulick, claimed it.

Even now, when I look at old pictures or watch videos and live concert footage, he just never seemed to unify with the band. He always looked unhappy, like he didn't want to be there. It always seemed like he was in his own world, planning and working on his own agenda. The thing is, I always thought he had the right New York look to be in Kiss, but the will to want to connect with the band just didn't seem to be there.

As a Kiss fan, I would never want to meet him. If he wrote a tell-all book and was honest about his time in Kiss, I would definitely buy it. But I couldn't imagine Vinnie writing a book and being truthful. He would probably do what Peter did, write a book about his life, play the victim, and blame everyone else for his problems and shortcomings, including Gene and Paul.

## BRUCE KULICK

To me, Bruce is family, he's blood, a real member of and contributor to Kiss. Yet I feel that Bruce doesn't get his due or true respect from fans. Sometimes I'm amazed at the blind loyalty some fans have toward other members who were drug addicts, alcoholics, cheating the fans, giving fans the finger, walking out on the band, not giving the fans a hundred percent, etc. These fans are so loyal to these members and make up excuse after excuse for all of their bullshit. But when a Kiss member like Bruce Kulick comes into the band and gives a hundred and ten percent, plays his ass off every night, isn't abusing drugs or alcohol, doesn't show up late or not show up at all, he's quickly dismissed, put on the back burner, and isn't given the same respect by the fans. Why is that? Because he's not considered a bad boy, he's not stupid or doing idiotic things or putting himself in self-destructive situations. What is it about us as music fans that makes us want to reward stupidity, immaturity, and simple minded behavior from our musical heroes? Is it because some fans can relate to Ace's behavior more than Bruce's clean-cut attitude?

Let's be real, if Ace were your neighbor and acting the wild partying way he did, you would either beat the shit out of him or constantly call the cops on him. You would view him as an idiot loser. But you take that same person, strap a guitar around his shoulder and give him a stage to stand on, and now you want to classify him as a god. Now all of the self-destructive, self-abusive things he does to himself or others become extremely cool and entertaining.

I guess the point I was making about Bruce before I went into an Ace rant was I'm tired of some fans acting like other band members aren't as relevant because they weren't original members, including Bruce. Bruce came in and gave his blood, sweat, and tears to Kiss. He wasn't a fuck-up by any means. He didn't fuck up his brain or mind or put himself in a position where he couldn't deliver the goods to the fans each night. Instead, he did his job. He stayed focused and worked hard. You didn't have to drag him out of bed or go have a bodyguard try to figure out where he was or if he was even conscious.

What really kills me about members like Carr, Singer, Bruce, and Tommy is that they weren't even making that big Kiss money Peter and Ace were in the '70s or being appreciated as real members of the band. But they still worked/work ten times harder, busted their asses, and didn't/don't cause the same headaches or stress as Ace and Peter. Yet fans are still praising two lazy, immature, self-destructive, entitled idiot members. And for what? Because they were original members? Or is it that you want to believe their role in the band was so relevant that they were irreplaceable? To me, members like Bruce are the real members of Kiss. I praise those members like him who sweated while in the band for the fans in the name of Kiss!

## SINGER

While Mark was at the '95 Kiss convention in Phoenix, he saw Eric Singer behind one of the tables where band members were talking to fans. He said he couldn't believe that not only did Eric go out of his way to talk to him, but he wanted to make sure that he was taken care of while he waited. Eric didn't have to go out of his way to do that, but he did. He wasn't just being a rock star, but a decent human being. When I was at the Kiss Mini Golf course on opening day, I remember how Eric came out of the side door and was hanging out with fans. He talked, signed autographs, and took pictures. I didn't get my turn to meet him at that time, but I thought it was so cool that he would do that for those fans who couldn't afford a VIP pass. No better person could have replaced Carr.

## TOMMY

I'll never forget the day I became a fan of Tommy Thayer. It was during the Kiss tribute band contest at the Hard Rock Cafe. Mr. Speed won that day. Tommy was one of the judges.

After the event was over, I stood in line to meet Tommy. I decided so as not to take up too much of his time, I would shake his hand, say a few words, and move on so other fans could get their time in with him. When I finally got my turn to meet him, I did just that, shook his hand, said that I appreciated him being in the band and I looked forward to the next concert, etc. I kept it short. When I was done, I was going to walk away when he surprised me by saying, "Why don't you take a picture with me?"

I couldn't believe it, I didn't ask—he asked me to take a photo with him! I thought that was so cool. Here was a member of Kiss who was extremely busy and had a lot of other fans waiting to see him, but he still wanted to take the time to take a picture with me. I was touched by that gesture. Not only did I respect him for that, but I became a fan of his as well. I still have the picture and the autographed photo he gave me of himself. I plan on framing it. What do I think of Tommy? A class act!

# Chapter 53

# THE KISS BOOKS

I always thought it would have been cool if they wrote their books and released them at the same time. And like they did with their original solo albums, the book covers would have their solo album pictures on them. Just my thought and imagination.

The one thing that syncs and ties Ace's, Gene's, Peter's, and Paul's books together is that there are no cool classic obscure Kiss pictures in them. Was adding more never before seen pictures of the band too much to ask for?

GENE/*KISS AND MAKE-UP*

Uuuggghhh! This book was so boring to me that while reading it, I had to keep slapping myself to stay awake. Even my mom said it wasn't a good book, and she loves to read about legendary celebrity's lives.

As much as Gene claims to be such a smart businessman, loves attention and exploiting himself, plus the title, I thought for sure Gene was going to make the focus of this book about his past lovers, especially with celebrity women, like the actress Yvonne De Carlo who plays the mom on the classic TV show *The Munsters*. In other words, give the fans and the media something to talk about. Now don't get me wrong, personally, I couldn't care less about Gene's sex life or which celebrity he lay with. But that would have made a hell of a lot more interesting read than the book he put out. Even when it came to the subject of Kiss, there wasn't anything that wasn't known or shocking. It was just filled with the same stories fans had already heard a million times over. The biggest problem I have is there was no accountability for the fucked things he did to Kiss, especially during the '80s. Gene spoke a little about checking out during the '80s era, but still glosses over it. What makes me mad about Gene is when it comes to Kiss, he rarely talks about anything real. He never breaks things down and tells you how he feels or what his mindset was during certain eras or while certain things were going on in the band. Again, I'm talking about real stuff. When it comes to talking about Kiss, Gene usually gives bullshit answers like "This new album is the best album we've recorded since *Destroyer*. On the next tour, we're going all out. It'll be the best show you've ever seen." The only time you hear Gene being real about a topic is when he's talking about his mother and the hard life she had. Then you get real conversation from him. But when it comes to Kiss, he talks about the band like the fans who are reading or listening to him are stupid and don't know anything, especially about the band. Again, when it comes to Kiss, he never talks about anything real, and that's why this book fails in my eyes. As a whole, for me, this book is not motivating, is uninspiring, and just a boring, confusing read with no real direction.

I always wondered what mindset he was in while writing this book. To me, his book was the worst. He didn't just drop the ball, he deflated it.

1 out of 10 rating, I give it a 3.

## ACE/*NO REGRETS*

Out of the four original members, Ace's book is my second least favorite. I was really hoping that Ace was going to step up and take accountability. Most celebrities, especially rock legends, use their autobiographies as a way to cleanse themselves and let go of old demons and the monkeys on their backs by letting it all out in their memoirs. I really wanted to appreciate this book, find a new respect for Ace, and see him in a totally different light. But again, for me to do that as a Kiss fan, Ace would have had to lay all of his cards on the table and come clean and take accountability for all of his negative, self-destructive behavior and actions in Kiss. That is the only way I could respect him as a member of Kiss and as a fan. Of course, I'm not saying that Ace is asking for or needs my respect personally as a human being. I'm only speaking from a fan perspective. Then again, maybe I'm giving him too much credit and because of being loaded and drunk most of the time, he really doesn't remember most of the things he's said or done from his past years with Kiss or is delusional about them. I bought this book with the preconceived notion that was what I was getting, accountability. I was disappointed to find out I was wrong. The small doses of accountability he does give in this book are usually minor, watered down, or glossed over.

Keep in mind that before I read his book, I first read the book *Kiss & Tell* by Bob McAdams and Gordon Gebert. Then I read the book *Into the Void* written by his ex-girlfriend Wendy Moore. Her book really blew me away. I will say that both of those books knocked me on my ass. Even I didn't know how fucked up and far gone Ace really was most of the time in the '70s. After he rejoined the band for the reunion tour, I thought Ace was sober and loving his new success in the rebirth of Kiss. In Ace's book, he barely spoke about his time after rejoining Kiss, but Wendy Moore had more than enough to say about it. I thought after her book was released, Ace would have no choice but to explain himself or at least tell his side of the story. Again, I was wrong. He either doesn't or just barely mentions how fucked up he was after rejoining the band, but he doesn't fail to mention that he punched Tommy Thayer. Let's be honest. At that time, Ace was an out of shape, alcoholic drug user. Tommy was always in shape, working out, and is pretty cut for a guy his age. He could've easily beaten the shit out of Ace and put Ace's old tired overly abused body in the hospital if he wanted to. But guess what? Tommy knows he works for Kiss and can't risk getting fired for beating up or altering the face of one of its stars. So like any other hard worker who pays his dues, sometimes you have to roll with the punches. But these two books written by his ex friend and girlfriend really blew me away. Let me just say I always liked to read books about Kiss that weren't written by them because you usually get a version of the truth and insight that you don't get from the members themselves. And who better to tell these stories than the people who were actually closest to them for a long period of time. I don't believe at all that these individuals are lying about Ace just to sell books. They're just telling stories about the time they spent with him for however many years. And you'll never hear any more shocking stories about a member of Kiss than you do in those two books.

One thing I do like about Ace and this book is that he doesn't waste too much time playing the blame game toward Gene or Paul. That, I can respect. But for me, it was a forgettable read.

1 out of 10 rating, I give it a 4.

## PETER/*MAKEUP TO BREAKUP*

When I started reading Peter's book, I had a hard time putting it down. It's a page turner. Even when I got tired and put the book down to rest, twenty minutes later, I would have to pick it up again and keep reading. As a Kiss fan who can't stand Peter, let me say that Peter wrote a damned good book about his life in Kiss. I appreciated his honesty and how he told a lot of insightful stories about the band. Some were things fans already knew, but there were a lot of new revelations he shared about the past. Does that mean I believe everything he wrote was true, a fact, or that there aren't holes in some of his stories? Not exactly. But I do believe that for the most part, he told the story to the best of his ability and what he remembers. I'm sure he has a lot of blackout moments from the '70s. Sometimes it's hard to tell who was more messed up, Ace or Peter.

## LIKE THE HOLIDAY FESTIVUS, IT'S TIME FOR PETER TO DO THE AIRING OF GRIEVANCES

I also have mixed emotions about the book in the sense that I can appreciate how Peter purposely threw himself under the bus numerous times throughout the chapters, but on the other side of that coin, he doesn't take accountability for his behavior, either. How can you admit the things you did but not take accountability for what you did at the same time? It was as if his attitude said, "Yeah, I did a lot of drugs, acted like a baby, and by 1979, my drumming had diminished some. But if it weren't for Gene and Paul, those things wouldn't have happened to me." When Peter plays the blame game for his life and choices, that's where the book comes up short for me. His book would have been perfect if it had not been for that.

What really bothered me the most was how he acted like an immature, entitled, and "if you have anything to say to me, say it to my wife!" idiot after the reunion tour. And again, like Ace's book, he doesn't take accountability for his negative behavior when given a second chance in Kiss during that era. "It's all Gene and Paul's fault! They're out to get me, cheat me, steal my money, take advantage, and use me for my great drumming skills because they know I'm the real star of the band and the band wouldn't last without me." OK, Peter, we get it. Your life is fucked up because of Gene and Paul. If you had never met those guys, you would have gone on as a solo artist, you would have won seven Grammys by now, sold over seventy million albums, and be living in a twenty-bedroom mansion in Beverly Hills, rubbing shoulders with the who's who. Gene and Paul robbed you of all your success and greatness. You're the real reason Kiss is what it is today. Duuuhhhhh!

Aside from all that, it is a good book. At least it must seem so to me because I've read it three times.

1 out of 10 rating. If it weren't for the blame game, I'd give it a 9. But for that reason, I give it an 8.

## PAUL/*FACE THE MUSIC: A LIFE EXPOSED*

Paul pretty much nailed it! This is, to me, by far the best book of the four. Honest and sincere, he wasn't trying to make himself look good. He just told it. This book also had a good balance of his personal life and his life in Kiss. He went into so many details about so many things without rehashing stories we've heard a million times over. I loved how Paul talked about the failing of the *Creatures of the Night* tour and how he was so depressed that he would sometimes fall asleep while applying his makeup. To me, that's real shit! How Gene's nonexistent presence in the band was affecting him and how he finally had enough and had to confront Gene, even if it meant the end of the band. When it came to ragging on each other, how he could dish it out but couldn't take it when the joke was on him. He finally talked openly about his sister, after all of these years, who fans knew existed but heard so little about until the book's release. He spoke about his strained relationship with Eric Carr and how he and Gene were seen as the bad guys at his funeral. That's what I mean when I say "Real shit!" The kind of real, honest, from the heart stories that Gene never talks about.

There are a couple of things that annoy me about his story, though, and that's how Paul tries to sell and paint the picture that he grew up having such a hard and dysfunctional home life. Paul, eat a Snickers. I guess I can speak for myself when I say that as a black man growing up in black neighborhoods in the late '70s and early '80s, I've seen some real horrible shit and I've experienced a hell of a lot worse than that. I also know lots of brothas and sistas who not only would've gladly traded places with his home life in a second, but grew up in some seriously dysfunctional environments that would make Paul's family look like *The Brady Bunch*. So Paul's so-called rough upbringing was lost on me. I was waiting for the bad part to come, but it never did. His worst story was that he had to lock himself behind a door to get away from his sister. OK, that's heavy stuff there. But just because I don't consider it rough doesn't mean that it wasn't rough for him. We all see things differently.

The second thing I didn't like about his book was all of the Peter bashing he was doing. Now, again, this is coming from someone who doesn't like Peter, but it was too much. It was like Paul never missed a chance and went out of his way to demean Peter. He would say things like, "In the '70s, Peter couldn't play certain drum parts, he couldn't play on beat or keep time, he couldn't carry a note, he couldn't write a good song or with structure. Blah blah blah." And I'm sure a lot of it was true. It wasn't that Paul was saying these things about Peter that made it so bad, but it was more of the place it was coming from, anger. It's obvious from his book that Paul still has a lot of anger toward Peter. My point is the way Paul carries on about Peter just makes him come off as a little petty and bitter. I mean, after all, you're Paul Stanley from Kiss; you're supposed to be better than that. He should have kept some of that anger to himself. And if he had to say those things about Peter, he should have said them in a different way and tone. None of us fans thought Peter or any member of Kiss was or is perfect, but Paul didn't have to spell it out in blood. I also noticed when it came to Ace's mistakes and fuck ups, he wasn't as petty, bitter, or mad. When he spoke of Ace's mistakes, he spoke in a manner of "Well, that's just Ace being Ace; we were used to that. But Peter?! That's an entirely different story!"

I don't like how Paul has put me in this awkward position to have to defend Peter. But in this case, I take Peter's side. Paul was wrong. And if Paul wants to point fingers about who made mistakes in the '70s, as much as I love the song, I'm sure it wasn't Peter's idea to release a disco song called "I Was Made for Lovin' You" to Kiss fans all over the world. But then again, in 1979, Paul didn't record that for the fans; instead, he was trying to impress the wrong audience and people. He wasn't thinking of Kiss fans when he made that song. And he might not have made as many bad mistakes and choices as Peter did, but Paul made some and was not perfect either.

Speaking of mistakes made by Paul, the cover of the book itself. Cringe! All of the other members' covers look awesome! Using old photos for their covers was the smart thing to do. Paul's cover is just weird; from some angles, it doesn't even look like him. It looks like the kind of photo that would be on the package of a workout/exercise abs device. I can't explain it, but when I see it, it makes me think of working out.

1 out of 10 rating, I give Paul's book a 10. But because of the Peter bashing and making me have to defend Peter, I reduce it to a 9. It's still the best of the four.

## JUST TO ADD

I think Lydia's book *Sealed with a Kiss* is not only a great read but has the best pictures of any Kiss book to date. I'll never forget the day when it was delivered to my door. I was so excited, I ripped the package open right there on my doorstep. I just want to say thank you, Lydia, for writing a great book with such great pictures.

Why Gene and Paul can't get their heads out of their asses and release a book with past unseen obscure pictures of the band is beyond me. It's something the fans would actually enjoy. Oh, I forgot, they *did* release something the fans really wanted, a giant Kiss book that cost four grand, with really cool photos inside and every copy autographed by each member. I can't wait to order my copy. I should put it on my credit card today! Yes, Sheldon, that's sarcasm.

I would also like to add that my favorite Kiss book has always been C.K. Lendt's *Kiss and Sell: The Making of a Supergroup*. I've read it more than ten times. It always relaxed me to read it while traveling. Now if we can only get Bruce, Eric, Tommy, and Vinnie to write honest tell-all books about their time in the band. Maybe one day...

# Chapter 54

# ROCK AND ROLL HALL OF SHAME

When I heard Kiss was going to be inducted into the Rock and Roll Hall of Fame, I can't say that I really cared. I never took the RARHOF seriously to begin with. Kiss fans and non-Kiss fans knew it was way overdue. I felt that the only reason they were inducted was because of pressure and politics, not because the Hall actually cared about the band or their influence and impact on rock and roll and pop culture in general. The Hall could only ignore the elephant in the room for so long.

We all know there are a lot of credible acts who deserve to be in there but aren't. And there are a lot of acts who are in there that make you scratch your head or ask "Who are they? What song did they sing?" I mean, you've got one hit wonders and people who only put out one or two albums in the Hall. I have no problem with different types of music or artists in the Hall, rock, country, pop, or rap, if it's deserved or you had some type of impact or real contribution to music. Some people forget how far rock goes back and how and where it generated from. And when others think of rock, they only think of guys with long hair and guitars from the late '60s through the mid '80s. So they get upset, protest, and yell at their computer monitors when they see what they consider to be a different form of music or group being inducted. But if we wanted to get technical, the origin of rock is more than loud guitars and long hair. In fact, it was the opposite. The point I'm making is I didn't then and I don't now need that kind of an organization or any other, for that matter, to validate my band or tell me that Kiss is the hottest band in the world!

## WHO SHOULD HAVE BEEN INDUCTED?

The RARHOF, Kiss, and Kiss fans did not agree on which members should have been inducted. Should it only have been the original band, or should some of the other members have been inducted too? For forty years, Kiss has been what it's been for a reason. But how is an organization with no real emotional connection to the band gonna decide which members were important and relevant enough to be inducted? For me, the fact that they only inducted the original members was just their way of trying to get it done and over with and sweep the whole inducting Kiss thing under the rug as fast as they could. In other words, "Let's quickly induct the original members so we can get this Kiss thing out of the way and move on to more important business." That was the vibe to me. Now, does that mean that I feel that all of the members should have been inducted? No. But in my opinion, Eric Carr for sure and probably Bruce should have been. But even though initially they were in the band longer than the original members and gave more heart, love, and appreciation than the original members didn't matter because they weren't in *Kiss Meets the Phantom*, they weren't on the *Alive!* album, they don't have an action figure or their faces on a baseball card. In other words, they weren't a member during the popular era for the band. And to some people, Kiss fans and non, that's who Kiss is and always will be. But not to me.

## WHY CAN'T THE ORIGINAL KISS JUST PERFORM FOR THE FANS ON THIS ONE NIGHT

I don't understand why some fans acted offended or acted like Gene and Paul owed it to the fans to perform with Ace and Peter on that one night. I totally understand why they didn't want to get up onstage with Ace or Peter, even for one night on that ceremonial occasion. Especially Paul. Paul has not forgotten all of the bullshit those two put him and the band through. All those years of dealing with their demons, insecurities, drama, immaturity, and arrogance. Let me ask this question, how come these same fans don't hold Ace and Peter accountable for their bullshit or say, "If you two weren't pulling the shit you were while in Kiss, maybe Gene and Paul would have wanted to perform with you again on that night of celebration"? No, these fans always want to act like Gene and Paul are the problem, not Ace and Peter. Then you've got Ace and Peter doing interviews and playing dumb, like they just don't understand why Paul doesn't want to perform with them again, like they're just these honorable guys who want to do what's right for Kiss and the fans, and they talk like Gene and Paul are the ones being unreasonable. Why didn't Ace or Peter want to do the honorable thing when they were in the band? Does any fan really believe that Ace or Peter came back to Kiss because they wanted to be there or because it's what the fans wanted? They came back because they had to. Poor pathetic Peter had a gun in his mouth, pretending again that he was going to commit suicide, but then he realized he didn't have an audience to stop him or baby him. And Ace's story speaks for itself. Bottom line, when given a second chance, Ace continued to be a drunken drug addict and Peter continued to cry and pout about not having anyone to cover his hotel windows, wanting more money, and complaining that there was never anybody around to change his diaper. So why would particular fans think Paul would want to put himself or the band back into that same situation and perform with those two idiot losers again, even for one night? For me, as a fan, Kiss didn't disappoint me by not performing with two unappreciative members that night in an environment that really didn't want them there in the first place.

## I THINK THE ORIGINAL BAND PERFORMING WOULD HAVE BEEN AN EMBARRASSMENT

Another reason I didn't want the original band performing on that night was because I feared it would have sounded awful, and in the eyes of the RARHOF powers that be, it would have proven them right. Let's say if Kiss would have performed the obvious songs that night, "Rock and Roll All Nite" and "Shout It Out Loud." Yeah, I think if Ace and Peter only had to do those two songs and not a long show, they could have pulled it off. But at the same time, I'm not a hundred percent convinced they could have, especially Peter. It might have sounded decent, but not great. So I would rather they played with Tommy and Eric. I guess in a perfect world, it would have been great if they had Tommy, Bruce, Ace, Eric, and Peter all onstage playing together. But that's just fantasy.

Again, this is just my opinion and perspective about the RARHOF situation, which is worth about a nickel. I wasn't there, don't know who was on the voting board, or what was going through the minds of each member of Kiss. It's all speculation.

# Chapter 55

# *THE WOMAN ON THE SIDEWALK*

In the summer of 2012, I found out that Kiss and Mötley Crüe would be playing at the Mandalay Bay in Las Vegas that August. Currently living in Las Vegas, I was looking forward to going to this concert.

At that time, I had never been to the Mandalay Bay and was misinformed when I was told that it seats up to thirty thousand people. Having heard that, I figured I had more than enough time to buy my ticket for the show, so I put the subject aside until it was closer to the date.

By the time August rolled around, there had been enough hype and talk about the concert that I decided I shouldn't put it off anymore and should purchase my ticket to secure a seat. When I arrived at the Mandalay Bay box office, I got some horrific news, the Kiss concert was sold out! Instantly, I had a lump in my throat and it sank to my stomach. The clerk informed me that the arena didn't seat thirty thousand, but only twelve thousand people for sporting events, and for concerts, it only held nine thousand. After kicking myself in the ass for the next few days for missing an easy opportunity, I came to the conclusion that my only options were to buy a ticket off Craigslist or try to buy one from a scalper on the day of the show.

Trying to buy a ticket online didn't work, and most of the sellers' asking prices were through the roof. Some sellers never called me back, even when I told them that I would meet them at a certain time and location to buy a ticket from them. I suppose they found other buyers who would meet their asking price. I gave up on the online sellers and realized I would have to place all of my hopes on the ticket scalpers hours before show time.

The morning of the concert, I woke up alert, focused, and ready. My only function that day was to buy my Kiss ticket—nothing else. Like the Terminator, I was programmed for my objective and nothing was going to sway me otherwise. Or so I thought.

Hours before the show, I was showered, dressed, and ready for battle. I grabbed the items I was taking with me and walked out the door. I decided to walk the half hour distance to the show to avoid traffic and having to find a place to park. I made it about a block before I heard God speak to me, saying, "Go back home!" I thought *Why is God telling me to go back home?* I ignored the order, and because I was in such a hurry, I chalked it up to my imagination. I put my mind back to focus mode and walked two more blocks, when I would hear God's voice again. "Go back home!" This time, it was more demanding. *Why is God telling me to go back to my apartment?* I wondered. What was the big emergency? Did I leave the stove on? Did I forget something? It really annoyed me, but I decided to just listen and go back home. I was cussing with every footstep. This was interrupting my plan to get a Kiss ticket, and I was losing time.

I made it back to my apartment and looked around to make sure that everything was in place and the stove was off. I double checked to make sure I had all of the items I needed, including my driver's license in case the Mandalay Bay wanted to see my ID. Still, nothing seemed out of place or out of the ordinary. I asked, "God, what did you send me back here for?" I assumed I was just trippin' because of my nerves about having to still get a concert ticket for the show. Feeling like I had wasted my time coming back home and that God wasn't really speaking to me, I headed for the door. Before I could grab the handle, I looked to my left and saw a small booklet on the chair. It was a pocket sized Christian book on the healing powers of God and scripture. Sometimes, I would mail order CD sermons of certain preachers and I would get small gifts from these churches, like the small book or a free bookmark. The truth is, I don't even remember putting it on the chair, but there it was. I didn't know why, but I just stared at the book on the chair, and that's when I knew that this small book was the reason I was sent back home. What purpose it was going to serve I didn't know or try to figure it out. I had a Kiss concert to get to, and I had to get back in focus. Putting the small book in my pocket, I quickly went out the door and walked even faster to make up for lost time. Whatever it took, I wasn't missing that concert.

Walking through the Las Vegas streets, I was surrounded by fanatics wearing Kiss makeup and costumes from different eras who were also on the way to the show. A couple who had just gotten married wearing Kiss makeup were throwing cigars out of the sunroof of their limo. Other fans were standing on street corners with their guitars, playing Kiss songs to get the already excited fans' blood rushing even more. As for me, I was totally jealous of every single one of these nut jobs because I knew as weird and fanatical as they were, they had Kiss tickets in their pockets and I didn't.

I was only a block away from the Mandalay Bay. Now my heart was racing even more. I began looking around the area for scalpers or anybody holding a sign that said Kiss tickets for sale. Walking down the sidewalk, I noticed I was approaching a hippie looking woman sitting on the ground cross-legged. She didn't exactly look homeless, but at the same time, she looked like she was struggling in life, with her unkempt clothing and hair. When I walked toward her, she looked at me with an expression that said "No matter what happens in life, everything is going to be OK." She said, "How are you this evening?" What was weird was in that simple question, she actually sounded sincere, not at all like a simple attempt for small talk or that she wanted anything from me. This stranger with this great smile really wanted to know how I was doing. The problem was I had a mission to buy a Kiss ticket and wasn't interested in feeble small talk. Without looking her in the eye, I cockishly responded, "Great," and kept walking past her.

I was approaching a crosswalk at a busy intersection when, as luck would have it, I spotted a man across the street holding a sign that said Kiss tickets for sale. At this point, I didn't care what his asking price was, I just had to have a ticket. I kept my eye on him to make sure he didn't walk away and no one else got to him before I did. Finally, the walk signal came on, but still keeping my eye on him, something weird happened. I couldn't walk. I mean my body actually couldn't go forward. My feet felt like I was wearing thousand-pound boots made out of cement; they wouldn't move. I started to feel nauseous, and the more I struggled to go forward, the more nauseous I felt and the heavier my body became. My feet stayed planted to the ground. Then I heard God say to me, "Go back and speak to that woman!" In my unauthorized submissive state, I actually tried to argue with God that I couldn't and I had to get to the man across the street with the Kiss tickets for sale. God didn't respond to my reasoning. I also saw that this was a battle He was going to win. Still, I gave it one last effort and tried to go forward, but again, my body wouldn't move. I decided to give up and realized what I had to do. Not only that, but the faster I got back and spoke to the woman, the faster I could get back to my business.

Frustrated, I walked back to the strange woman who was sitting on the ground, still smiling. I began speaking to her. "Hey, I'm sorry if I was rude when I walked past you. I was just in a hurry and wasn't really thinking. But again, I'm sorry if I came off as an ass." At first, she just looked at me and smiled really peacefully. Her smile said, "Whether you talk to me or not, we're still friends and children of God." Never have I felt so humbled and ashamed at the same time by just someone smiling at me, but there I was. "Don't even worry about it," she said. "I could see you were in a hurry." I really didn't know what to say to her or why God had sent me back to her. Was it because I was rude and needed to apologize to her? Well, I already did that, but was that it? Was it a test? I said the only thing I could think of, "So, are you OK?" What she said next blew me away. "Yeah, I'm OK because I believe I'm OK. I have a life-threatening illness in my body, but I'm not worried because every day, I ask God for healing. I know He hears me. I've never been to church or even read the Bible, but I know who God is and He knows me. I know in my heart God loves me." With those few words she spoke, I was extremely impressed by her faith. She had a life-threatening illness, and she was still standing her ground and believing in God with a big smile on her face. Even I didn't have that kind of faith. My biggest concern at that moment was buying a concert ticket! Boy, I felt two feet tall. It was at that moment I realized why God had sent me back home to pick up that small book on the healing powers of Him and scripture; He wanted me to give it to her. In my mind, I said, "I know, Father, I know." I told her I had something for her and pulled out the small book. When she saw that it was a book on healing, her eyes began to water, and she said to me, "See, God sends me signs like this all the time, I told you God knows me. I know He loves me!" We talked a little while longer, I gave her a hug, and we parted ways.

After talking to her, I was no longer in a hurry. I slowly walked away and thought about the faith I had just witnessed. I got my concert ticket, and that night, even though I was staring at my childhood heroes onstage, I couldn't stop thinking about the woman on the sidewalk.

## IT'S ONLY FOR NOW

That's my story. I've been a Kiss fan since '78, and it looks like I will be until the day I die. Who knows, maybe I too will be buried in a Kiss coffin. I want to personally thank you for taking the time to purchase and reading this book. I've had all of these thoughts in my head for over thirty-eight years, and I feel relieved to be able to express them and clean out my Kiss attic. I love being able to share my stories and experiences with other Kiss fans around the world. We've all got'em. As I put a period on this book, I wonder what new and exciting things will happen in the Kiss world in the future. Only time will tell.

But now, I would like to thank Gene, Paul, Peter, Ace, Carr, Vinnie, Bruce, Singer, and Tommy for everything you've contributed to the band. What each of you has given to the name "Kiss" can never be taken away.

Printed in the United States
By Bookmasters